What Became of the Sundance Kids

By Link Kaiser

First Printing 1995 in the United States of America
Copyright © 1995 by Link Kaiser

What Became of the Sundance Kids

By Link Kaiser

Dedicated to

Fannie Perrigoue Kaiser, mother of these Sundance Kids, taught them honesty, hard work, education and love was the way to a better life.

Chapter One

Duane, my little brother, lay on the ground bleeding and the horse we had been riding went racing off. Still stunned from the fall, I examined the gaping cut in the back of Duane's head and I thought I could see his brains showing through the opening made by the axe he had been carrying. I couldn't believe my seven-year-old brother lay on the ground dead and it was all my fault. It was all my fault because I was nine, old enough to know better than to be riding a half-broke mare without a saddle or a bridle. I was too scared to even cry. I tried to scream for help but couldn't utter a sound. No one could have heard me anyhow because our ranch house was out of sight and over a mile away.

It had to be a bad dream. I wanted to wake up and find it hadn't really happened.

The day had started as a normal August morning, it was my turn to bring in the horses and Duane went with me. An older brother told me to bring an axe back with the horses since we would be near where he had left it.

Duane and I meandered along through a dusty pasture looking for the work horses. We could hear meadowlarks singing and smell the scent of pine in the morning breeze. We found the horses near a hayfield where bees were busy among the alfalfa blossoms. We were in luck I thought when I saw, Babe, a young mare we could ride. We decided if we could catch her we would ride and not have to walk. I knew the only way to catch Babe would be to pick some choice alfalfa and offer it to her. She would let you feed her this way, unless you had a bridle. If she saw you had a bridle or a rope, she wouldn't let you get near her. I had seen Buck, my brother who was two years older than me, fool her by hiding a small rope behind his back. When she was eating the grass he slipped the rope around her neck. He improvised a bridle by tying the rope around her lower jaw. A piece of rawhide used this way was the kind of bridles Indians used on their horses. Since Duane and I didn't have anything with us to scare Babe, our plan worked.

While Babe was eating our offering, I put an arm around her neck and helped Duane climb on her back. We coaxed her to a fence where I was able to get on in front of Duane. Even though we didn't have anything to use for a bridle, I could steer her by patting her on the side of her neck. By holding my hands over her eyes so she couldn't see, I could slow her down and stop her by saying whoa.

We rode her to a wire gate that led into the hayfield where we would find the axe. I was able to open the gate without dismounting. Buck would have made me shut the gate but Buck wasn't there. When we got to where the axe was we were in luck again, it was leaning against a fence post. I was able to make Babe stop by holding my hands over her eyes and say whoa. Duane reached the axe without getting off Babe. He carried the axe because, without a bridle, I needed both hands free to control Babe.

Everything went fine until we returned to the open gate. I knew I would catch hell for leaving the gate open when I saw the other horses inside the hayfield. We had to drive them out and shut the gate.

Unless you've tried to drive hungry horses from a hayfield where the alfalfa is over a foot high to an almost bare pasture, you have no idea of my problem. When the horse you are riding has neither a saddle nor a bridle and a little brother is clinging on behind you, the job is no easier. The only way I could get the horses to leave the choice alfalfa was to let out a cowboy yell and make them run. I forgot about the axe Duane was carrying for the moment. When the horses started to run it wasn't toward the open gate, so I had to race in front of them to turn them. When Babe broke into a full gallop she did what all quarter horses are bred and trained to do best. She could outrun any horse on the ranch and she could turn as quick as the best of them.

Duane was holding on to me so tight I couldn't reach her eyes with my hands to make her slow down. When Babe made a sharp cut to turn the horses we were after, I could feel we were slipping and knew we would both fall off. It was then I thought of the sharp axe Duane was carrying and knew he should drop it. I yelled for him to let go. He must have thought I meant let go of me, but he didn't let go of the axe or me. The next thing I knew, we both were on the ground and Duane had fallen on the axe.

I wished I knew more about how to pray. I had only gone to Sunday school or church a few times, but I remembered my mother saying, God could do anything if you asked him and it

6

was something he thought you were entitled to. Especially if it was for someone else. I got down on my knees and looked at the cut in the back of Duane's head some more. I didn't know what to do. I was afraid to touch him. I had never seen a dead person.

When I was finally able to talk I repeated over and over, "My God. My God."

How God, or anyone could tell if I was praying or swearing, I will never know. I felt very cold and then very warm, and so all alone. I was petrified with fright. There was no one to turn to for help. I couldn't just leave Duane and go for help. How could anyone help him now?

I thought about the time when Duane was about two years old. We were playing by the baby chickens. He squeezed his hand through a small opening in the baby chick brooder to reach the chicks. When he pulled the chick out through the small opening so he could play with it, he had to shut his hand so tight he killed the chick. He killed several before our mother saw what he was doing. She gave me heck for not stopping him. I didn't stop him because I thought he would get in trouble, not me.

Another time while we were playing together, I crawled over the fence and got into the chicken pen where our mother was saving the eggs for hatching. I told Duane to stay out of the pen because the rooster was mean. I had a stick to keep the rooster from chasing me. When I saw Duane was coming in anyhow I left him there and ran to the house and played at my mother's feet while she washed clothes. From where I sat I could see the rooster chasing Duane around and around in the pen. When our mother heard him yelling she asked me where Duane was and I told her I didn't know. In order to get away from the rooster, Duane broke the catch on the gate and let all the chickens loose. That was one time our mother didn't blame me for what Duane had done.

I thought of other times when I had not been so nice to Duane and I wished he wasn't laying on the ground dead. I was imagining all sorts of things, like hearing voices. I was reminded if Duane went to live with God now he would go to heaven. If he lived to be a man he might do something bad and he would go to hell forever. Which would I rather have happen to him?

"Please," I begged. "Make him live. He can live and still go to

7

heaven. I promise it. I'll see that he is always good."

I wanted to cry, but I was afraid to because I felt as someone was watching me. If that someone saw me cry he might not let Duane live.

The next thing I remember was hearing Duane crying and yelling, "I'm bleeding. I'm bleeding."

Duane was alive. I helped him to his feet. Maybe he only had the wind knocked out of him. The cut was still in the back of his head and the bleeding didn't look as bad as when I first saw it. I just knew my prayers had been answered. I felt so glad, I smiled. I wanted to scream with joy.

When Duane saw me smiling he yelled at me. "I'm bleeding to death and God damn-it, you think it's funny."

"Are you okay?" I asked.

I knew he had lost a lot of blood.

I'm going home," he told me. "You can bring the God damn horses in by yourself."

"Okay," I said.

I didn't want him to swear anymore. I wondered if people go to hell for swearing. I knew Duane wasn't out of danger yet.

"You take the axe home and I'll bring the horses."

I knew I was in trouble if I didn't bring the axe and the horses as I had been told.

"Don't bawl," I told Duane, "or you'll make the bleeding get worse."

"I'm going to die anyway and I can bawl if I want to."

He started toward the house dragging the axe, shuffling his bare feet along the loose dust in the trail. Neither of us were wearing shoes. I wasn't sure if I should let him go by himself or go with him. I knew I had to get the horses out of the hayfield or I would get a beating when I got back to the house.

There was blood spattered down the back of Duane's blue denim shirt that our mother had made. There was blood on the patched bib overalls he was wearing. They were the ones I had new when school started last year and I had outgrown. The overalls I was wearing had holes in the knees, they were the ones Buck had outgrown and our mother hadn't found time to patch them yet.

I watched Duane until he went out of sight behind some pine

8

trees near a round haystack. It would be mostly downhill the rest of the way until he got near the house.

Even if Duane made it back to the house before he bled to death, I knew I would be blamed for him getting hurt. I knew if I left the horses in the hayfield I would be in trouble. I needed some time to think. I was afraid to go home. I didn't want to face the rest of my brothers and sisters.

My mother would be unhappy with me but she seemed to always understand even when the rest of the family blamed me for something.

"Bobby," she would say, "you must stop and think what is going to happen before you do something."

My mother called me Bobby, but my dad named me Lincoln when I was born. Maybe he thought that would make me great, but he never stayed around long enough to find out.

Let me tell you before you say, "Abe Lincoln was a friend of yours," I'm no Abe Lincoln.

Chapter Two

My mother told me it was 10 degrees below that January night in 1918. Winds of 45 miles per hour were trying to force snow between the weathered logs of our 16-foot by 22-foot Wyoming cabin. Inside with her and Dad were my three brothers and two sisters. Brother Milt, the oldest, wouldn't be 10 years old until the next June.

Our mother was in need of a doctor who was supposed to be on his way from Sundance that was our closest town, some 12 miles away. I guess our dad knew the doctor had lost his way in the storm so he had to go out in the night to look for him. The flame of his kerosene lantern was extinguished by the howling wind as soon as Dad stepped out the door. He was forced to feel his way through the darkness with only the help of his horse.

You could say my mother needed a doctor because of me but it really wasn't my fault. Milt had the responsibility of keeping a crackling fire going in the heating stove until our dad got back with the doctor. Because the stove door had to be opened from time to time to add more wood, the aroma of pine smoke filled the interior of our stuffy little cabin.

Our mother suffered with pain in a small bedroom that was partitioned off in one corner from the rest of the living quarters. She asked Milt to bring her a pillow. My other brothers and sisters: Howard, seven; Eunuch, five; Helen, three and Buck, two; weren't permitted to see what a mess I had made of our mother's bed. I guess it wasn't very considerate of me not to wait until Dad got back with the doctor before I made my grand entrance.

The morning sun filtered through the blowing snow before Dad showed up with Doctor Clarenbach and Leslie Hooper. Mr. Hooper ran the livery stable in Sundance and he was bringing the doctor to our place in his horse-drawn sled when they got lost in the blizzard. My mother told me she had me propped up on a pillow and I was still attached by my umbilical cord when Dad got back with the doctor. Old doc might have thought he cut me loose from my mother but somehow I always felt attached.

Would you believe I have never liked waiting for people ever since that cold January when I was born? Like in the movies they boiled some water and Dad also brewed a pot of coffee so

Mr. Hooper and Doctor Clarenbach could have breakfast while they waited for the storm to let up before starting back to Sundance.

You might wonder how six kids and our parents could all live in a log cabin that was only 16 feet by 22 feet. I guess maybe I forgot to mention one other room that was about eight feet square. We called it the middle room. It connected the cabin to a cellar that was dug into the hillside. The cellar could weather the cold Wyoming winters and was big enough to hold our winter's supply of spuds, home canned goods, etc. Our house, as we called it was built by our dad on a side hill like a cow-ranch range shack. The view was great to the south. We could see over halfway toward a little town called Upton, some 20 or so miles away.

When our dad first homesteaded, the house was plenty big. Then Milt was born in 1908, and every two years like clockwork another baby was born. That cold January night in 1918 I was the sixth kid to be born in that log cabin. In 1920 Duane came and made our house a little more crowded. Then Grace joined us in 1923. All but Grace were born on even years, two years apart. Born on the odd year, she still likes to be different. That could be why even to this day when she comes to a family gathering she is sometimes late, not a year maybe, but nevertheless late.

Sure we had other buildings on the homestead. There was a chicken house and a barn. We milked old Blanch and Mollie in one end of the barn and there was room in the other end for our work horses, Tony and Shorty. Two other small buildings were an important part of the ranch. You would agree they were small, about four feet by four feet. The one in front of the house was the smoke house. The smoke house was where we smoked the parts of a pig we used for bacon and hams. The other little house was in the back so we called it the back house.

One time Buck stopped me from using the smoke house for a back house even though it didn't have any hams or bacon in it at the time. He always told me he wouldn't let me do dumb things to keep me out of trouble. Most of the time if he didn't tell on me, I wouldn't have got into trouble.

With eight kids you could say it was a little cozy in our house at times, but in the summertime we had a tent set up behind the house with two beds. My two older brothers, Milt and Howard, slept in one bed and Buck, Duane and I slept in the other. Buck was two years older than me and Duane was two years younger. I was the one in the middle, and that was the way we three slept in a bed.

When you are the one in the middle you should always know your place. I never was very smart about learning my place. As I remember it, if I elbowed Duane to give me more room, he would squawk and Buck would hit me for being mean to my little brother. If I elbowed Buck, he might bust me one in the nose. No one ever seemed to tell Buck not to hit his little brother unless I got blood on the pillow. He said I bled on the pillow on purpose so he would get in trouble, but I wasn't smart enough to think of that until he said it first. Anyhow, we three were real close, night and day.

Without any nearby neighbor kids to play with, us three boys had lots of fun together. Our closest neighbor was George Beal and his family. We could see their house about a mile from ours. They had two boys, one my age and the other a year younger, but we weren't permitted to even speak to them. They went to a different one-room school to the south and our dad forbid us to go to their place. It was as if they didn't exist.

The homestead act was amended so Dad could increase our homestead from 160 to 320 acres, Dad beat George Beal to a 40-acre parcel of land he wanted that had a good spring for watering cattle. Walter Bramel was in charge of the government land office in Sundance and he was married to our dad's sister. Uncle Walter made sure Dad knew when it first became lawful for homesteaders to file on the additional land before it was announced to the general public. By the time Mr. Beal found out, Dad had already filed on the 40 acres Mr. Beal wanted. Even though our ranches joined, our dad and Mr. Beal couldn't agree on each other's share of the cost of building a fence. Each built his own fence a few feet from the other's, forming a lane we kids called, "The Devil's Lane."

When one of our pigs strayed into Beal's haystack, someone shot her in the face with a shotgun and blinded her. Dad brought her home and put her in a pen because she was blind and could no longer be turned loose. Dad went to the sheriff, the sheriff told him if he had left her where she was shot he could have helped, but now there was no way of proving where she was when she got shot or who did it.

When I was small I rarely saw our dad. Our homestead wasn't big enough for a family of 10 to make a living. Most of the ranchers had several homesteads and eked out a living by raising cattle or sheep and growing grain. Dad was away from home most of the time working in mines. Sometimes he worked in coal mines in Sheridan, or hard rock mines in Montana or the gold mine in Lead, South Dakota. I looked forward to the times he would be home for a few weeks.

I was about four when Dad left to work in the gold mine in Lead. The next day our mother sent Milt, who was 14, to town to get groceries. When he came home without anything for us to eat our mother cried. Milt told her something about Mr. Frank, who ran a general store in Sundance, not giving us any more credit. Before Dad got his first paycheck, he said he mailed home two sacks of flour from the company store at the mine. It never arrived so someone must have stolen it out of the mail.

When our mother was trying to figure out what to feed us kids, a neighbor rancher and his wife showed up for some rhubarb and you could tell they intended to stay for dinner. We had a long row of rhubarb that was considered the best in the area. Our mother would always invite our friends over for rhubarb and they usually stayed for dinner. It was a common practice among homesteaders to stay for a meal when visitors were at a neighbor's house at meal time.

We were out of bread and had no flour for baking biscuits. There was a sack of oats we had been saving to use as seed for planting. We had a small food grinder that we turned by hand and sometimes it was used to make whole wheat flour or corn meal. Our mother ground some of the oats, then she sifted out the hulls with a flour sifter and made some oatmeal muffins. She killed one of our laying hens and cooked some of the potatoes we were going to use for planting. She never let the neighbors know we were out of groceries. When they left, they thanked her for the rhubarb and she assured them we had more than we could use. I knew we did too, because we were out of sugar and you can't eat rhubarb without sugar.

One winter Milt and Howard went to school in Lead where Dad was working in the gold mine. Our regular school was about

13

three miles from our ranch and it ran all summer, from March until Christmas. I never knew why they didn't stay home, maybe it was because they were needed in the summer to put up the hay. Maybe Milt wouldn't go to school without our dad there to make him. I know they learned things they didn't learn in a one-room country school. Howard learned how to fight other kids and they both learned how to smoke. Our mother didn't know, at first anyhow, that they used tobacco.

The next year they stayed home to go to our summer school. One time Milt was happy because the creek he had to cross to get to school was so full of water from a heavy rain that he couldn't get across. That was the last time Milt ever attempted to go to school. When our mother tried to get him to go the next day, he said no and slammed his hand down so hard on the stove he broke a lid on the stove. Our mother cried. I guess she realized he was too big for her to force him to do something he didn't want to do. She couldn't even get him to go back to school long enough to take the eighth grade exams that were required in Wyoming before you could go to high school.

I'd seen our mother cry before. She didn't make a loud noise like us kids. She cried but we bawled. Like the time I was supposed to be asleep when Dad was home. They were talking in very low voices. I don't think I was supposed to hear when Dad told her there were just too many kids.

"Some of the younger kids should be put in a home for adoption," Dad said. "The ones that are too small to work, maybe we could provide for the four older ones?"

At the time I didn't know what adoption meant. I knew it meant something about Buck, Duane and I would no longer be part of the family. Grace wasn't born yet. Without any nearby neighbors our family was all we had. I knew my mother didn't want to do it. Dad insisted. When she cried I could no longer pretend I was asleep and I bawled so loud they heard me. Our dad stopped talking.

My mother came to my bed. "No matter what," she said. "We are not going to let anybody else have you kids."

She held me until I quit bawling. I made a promise to myself that night, no matter what, I would someday repay her some way if she was able to keep all of us kids together. She held me until I went back to sleep.

The next day I asked my mother what adoption meant.

"You must have had a bad dream last night because you woke up crying," she said.

I knew it was not a dream.

I asked her if she had many brothers and sisters.

She told me she had three brothers and four sisters, counting her, their family had eight kids the same as ours. They used to live in Wyoming, until they moved to Washington state.

"Why did you leave Wyoming?" I asked.

"Because my dad was having such a hard time making enough to live on in Wyoming."

"Is Washington different?"

"My dad, your granddad, ran a sawmill in Wyoming and we raised a garden and milked a few cows. In Washington the trees are bigger and there are a lot more of them. It rains more and that made our vegetable garden a lot better. The grass is a lot taller for the cows. We raised our own fruit, like apples, pears and plums. It doesn't get as hot in the summers or as cold in the winters. Some winters it hardly snows at all."

"Did you all stay together when you went to Washington or were some of your brothers and sisters adopted out?"

She held me close and I could hear her sniff like she wanted to blow her nose.

"Why don't we move to Washington?"

"I wish we could. I only wish we could."

When I saw she was crying I stopped asking questions.

She wiped her eyes with her apron. "Look what you made me do," she said. "You run along now and play. Don't fight with Buck and keep Duane out of trouble."

15

Chapter Three

When I was six years old I awoke one morning with a belly-ache. As I lay in bed I heard my mother stirring sourdough pancakes in a big crockery jar. When the spoon rubbed on the inside it made a grinding sound. Our old red rooster was shouting from his perch on a stump near the chicken house, telling the hens it was going to be another hot summer day, or maybe he was complaining because the screen door was shut and he couldn't get into the house.

That morning our mother started breakfast as usual, before the rest of the family was out of bed. I thought if I hurried I could ask her for some peppermint before Duane or Buck got up because if they heard me they would want some too. Whenever we had a stomach ache our mother would put a teaspoon of peppermint extract and some sugar in a cup of warm water for us to drink.

"What are you doing up?" Ma asked me as she tucked some loose hair into the ball where it was rolled up on the back of her head. She wiped her hands on her apron and puts some more wood in the stove that heated the large pancake griddle.

"I got a bellyache and I want some peppermint," I told her.

"I can't understand," she said. "I cooked a whole kettle of potatoes last night."

I waited and watched as she spooned pancake batter onto the griddle forming seven white puddles.

"My stomach hurts," I told her. "I want some peppermint."

She ignored my whimpering and flipped the pancakes, using a table knife for a turner . "Look what you made me do," she said, when one pancake came down partly on the stove and partly on the edge of the griddle. She used the knife to scrape it off the stove and put it back onto the griddle.

"I want some peppermint," I pleaded.

"You sit at the table," she commanded putting an enamel plate before me stacked with hot pancakes.

"But I got a bellyache."

"You eat," she insisted as she poured some Karo corn syrup over the stack of cakes and handed me a knife and fork she took from the large coffee can that contained our tableware. Some of the syrup spilled off my plate onto the oilcloth table cover.

"Look what you made me do, stop your whining and eat."

I force down the first few bites and soon the pain in my stomach is gone. I didn't get any peppermint that time.

"After Buck has his breakfast, I want you to go with him to the ice hole and get some ice for ice cream," she said. "I'll kill a couple of fryers for our Sunday dinner."

This would be the first time I was allowed to go to the ice hole. It was a couple of miles from our house on a neighbor's ranch. The ice hole was a slit in the ground, or a crevice between rocks. You could go down a few feet to where the ice is located. The ice is always there even during hot Wyoming summer days.

"You better put on some shoes because you may run across a rattle snake," my mother said.

"My shoes don't fit no more. They are too tight and besides they have holes in the toes."

"Oh never mind the shoes but watch for snakes. Look at you, the knees are worn through in your overalls. There won't be anything left of them for Duane by the time you get done with them."

"But I didn't wear out the knees. This is the way they were by the time they were too small for Buck."

"Oh never mind. I suppose Buck put the twists in your suspenders too."

I unfastened the suspenders on my bib overalls and removed the twists as my mother watched. I backed away so she wouldn't notice I needed patches on the seat of my pants too.

"Be careful and watch out for rattle snakes," my mother repeated as I left for the barn to wait for Buck to help harness the horse.

Buck is eight and can drive a horse pulling the stone boat. A stone boat is a homemade sled. Ours was about six feet long and three feet wide, built of pine poles about six inches thick tapered on the front ends to form the runners with boards nailed crosswise forming a platform to ride on. I guess they are called stone boats because homesteaders used them to haul stones off their new plowed fields. We sometimes used it to haul water from the well on wash day.

Buck had been to the ice hole before and knew the way. Helen helped us put the harness on old Shorty, hitch him to the stone boat and we were on our way. Buck rode on old Shorty's back while I rode on the stone boat and held onto the gunny sacks we took along to fill with ice. The ice hole is located on higher elevation where the land levels off forming a flat hill between us and our neighbors.

When we got up the hill above our house it was more or less flat for a couple of miles, then dropped off again overlooking Beaver Creek to the west and north. The hill is much steeper directly above our house by the Fourth of July tree, in fact you couldn't really say that trail was a road. It is to steep for a wagon. The Fourth of July tree was a big pine where we sometimes had picnics on the fourth, sometimes with some neighbors. It had spread branches for shade and a good limb to hang a swing.

Our mother told Buck to take the wagon road up sand-gate hill, which was a little farther but not quite as steep. I guess she thought it was safer.

My brothers Buck, Duane nor I never wore shoes around home in the summertime and since we hardly ever went to town we were barefoot all summer. Our bib overalls came from the Montgomery Ward catalog and our shirts were made by our mother with a Sears and Roebuck sewing machine. The usual patches, on the knees and seat of our pants, had to be sewn on by hand when our mother had time.

I shouldn't complain because I had to wear Buck's hand-me-downs because I would get a new pair of overalls and a new shirt next year when I would be seven and start school. We always got new shoes after summer was over before it snowed and they had to last until the next spring when we could go barefoot again. I couldn't start first grade this past spring because the school house was about three miles from our house and we only had a horse named Skeeter, and a burrow named Jack to ride. With Howard, Eunice, Helen and Buck, I would have made three on one animal. Buck had to wait until he was seven too, because Milt was still going to school when Buck was six.

Old Shorty was breathing hard by the time we reached the top of sand-gate hill, so Buck let him rest awhile and catch his breath. The gate was open. It was made of wire not sand. I guess we called it sand-gate because the wagon tracks cut deep into the soft sand where the road went through the gate. After being on top of the divide we came to a fork in the road near the trees where Skeeter scraped Howard off, the time old Skeeter ran away. Buck pulled on the right rein to steer old Shorty to the road that led north toward the ice hole.

The time old Skeeter ran away, Howard and Fred Littlefield had been cultivating potatoes. Fred Littlefield was a neighbor we hired sometimes when Dad was away working in a mine.

They had finished for the day and Mr. Littlefield sent Howard home with the horse by way of sand-gate hill while he walked. When a horse is pulling a cultivator the singletree (the horizontal crossbar to which the tugs of the harness are fastened) is high enough so it won't touch the horse's heels. With no load to pull there is slack in the tugs that lets the singletree droop and hits the horse on his heels. We were always warned to unfasten one tug so this won't happen. Howard who was 12 at the time, had started home without unfastening one of the tugs. Skeeter ran when the singletree hit his heels. The faster he ran the harder it hit, he was soon running wild and out of control.

When Skeeter returned to the barn his heels were bleeding and Howard was missing. Mr. Littlefield looked for him along the road but couldn't find him. When it started to get dark they still couldn't find Howard so our mother phoned neighbors for help.

I was too young to remember everything, but I never knew, before that night, we had so many friends. Some came from as far away as Black's Flat, which was halfway to Sundance. They all had lanterns.

When they arrived, they were greeted by Buck, who had crawled to the top of the chicken house and was yelling at the top of his voice, "Goodie, goodie, Howard's dead. Goodie, goodie Howard's dead."

I don't know what the neighbors thought or how long Buck yelled. I know Buck thought with Howard dead he wouldn't get any more birthday lickings.

In our family then, we never got presents or a birthday party— we got a birthday licking from the other brothers and sisters. We got one swat for each year we were old. I was lucky because Buck always got two more swats than I did. When Howard didn't do the swatting himself he would hold you and let someone else

19

beat you. They would use a belt or a paddle. When it was my turn, I never hit Buck very hard because my birthday was only three weeks later. That way he never hit me very hard either.

I remember it was real spooky seeing all the men searching for Howard that night in the dark. Their lanterns looked like a lot of lightning bugs.

While everyone was out looking for Howard, Eunice stayed in the house to watch Duane and me. Duane was two and I was four. After she fell asleep, Duane and I had fun playing with the kerosene lamp. We would take turns turning the wick up, which made the lamp smoke, then turning it low so it would almost go out. We were doing this when our mother returned from looking for Howard. She got real mad at Eunice for being asleep when she was supposed to be watching us, and that made Eunice mad at me for getting her in trouble. She told me Duane was a baby but I was a brat and old enough to know better.

It was well past midnight before someone found Howard. They guessed the runaway horse had run under the limbs of some trees that brushed him off and knocked him unconscious. He may have laid there on the ground until he came to, then he wandered around semiconsciously in the dark until someone found him.

I guess Buck was unhappy because they found Howard. Eunice was mad at me for getting her in trouble by letting Duane play with the lamp and she was mad at Buck for wishing Howard was dead. I think she must have liked Howard better than Buck or I did. I was mad at Duane because I never liked to be blamed for what he did. Eunice was usually mad at Buck, Duane and me most of the time anyhow. She would call us the three brats. After everything was over, Howard wasn't dead and he could still give us our birthday lickings.

With the place where Howard fell off old Skeeter behind us, Buck and I continued on our way to the ice hole. I would reach out and pick wild flowers that grew beside the road. We had our own names for the different kinds. There were shooting stars, buttercups, honeysuckles, bluebells, larkspurs and many others. They all smelled nice but different. The clover that grew beside the Long Bean Patch had about the best smell of all.

We crossed the Long Bean Patch where at one time we must have grown beans, but this summer it is planted with potatoes.

As the name implies, it was only a few feet wide but very long, following the contours of a little swale getting the benefit of what little rain that might fall in a growing season. Beyond the Long Bean Patch we had to go through a gate. Since Buck is on old Shorty and I am riding on the stone-boat, Buck had me open the gate. It is a wire gate with a loop of wire that had to be pushed up over the gate stay. The other end of the wire was fastened to the gate post. I was able to get the gate opened and Buck drove Shorty through.

"Why do we need to shut the gate?" I asked. "We'll be coming right back."

"To keep horses and cows from getting out."

"I don't see any horses or cows around here now," I told him.

"You got a lot to learn. You always leave gates as you find 'em. If they are open it's okay, but if they are closed you gotta shut 'em."

"Okay," I told him, but as much as I tried I didn't have the strength to hold the stay pushed in and pull the loop of wire over the top. I struggled with it for a while and Buck finally got off the horse.

"Okay baby," he said. "Let me do it."

He would call me a baby when I couldn't do something the older kids could do.

He tried to shut the gate, but he found it wasn't as easy as he thought.

"Now who is the baby?" I said.

"Okay then," he said, "you pull the wire over the stay while I push."

Together we got the gate shut. Next I had to hold his foot so he could pull himself back on Old Shorty and we were on our way again.

As old Shorty pulled the stone-boat along it would bounce off rocks from time to time. When that happened I had to hold on and stop picking flowers beside the road. It was more of a trail than a road. We stopped once to look in a robin's nest on the low branch of a pine tree, but Buck wouldn't let me touch the little robins. When I made noise trying to sound like a mother robin, the little birds all opened their beaks wanting to be fed. Buck wouldn't let me feed them the grasshopper I had caught for them.

"It might make 'em sick," Buck said.

He let me keep a bug I was going to feed the baby robins. We called it a locust. When I held it so it could move its wings it made a buzzing sound like a car. We didn't have a car but I had seen them in Sundance at the county fair. In fact I had ridden in one once. The car belonged to Tom Hawkins and he drove us back to town from the rodeo grounds to our tent pitched in a friend's yard.

When we got to the ice hole, Buck got off old Shorty and tied him to a pine tree so he wouldn't go home without us. The ice was down in a slot in the ground, between some rocks, on the north side of the Kaiser Divide overlooking Beaver Creek. It was on the edge of the Hewes ranch. They sometimes referred to us as the over the hill Kaisers. Their ranch was over the hill from ours. Their ranch was one of the best in Crook County, since most of it was in the valley. They were about as good a neighbor as you would ever expect to find anywhere. Sometimes they would pay our dad; or older brother Milt for helping them put up hay.

Buck and I entered the ice hole through a slit between the rocks that went down into the ground. It was spooky crawling down what remained of a pine tree with limbs sticking out forming a kind of a ladder. I don't think our mother had ever been down there or knew how spooky it was. It was like a cave, only we climbed down through the ceiling until we got to the ice. It was cold down there, even though it must have been over 90 degrees outside. We found plenty of ice for making ice cream. Buck took an axe and cut the ice into small enough chunks to get in the gunny sacks. We carried them up the tree ladder and out through the slit in the ground. It was hard for me to understand how ice could be found so near the surface on such a hot day.

After we had what Buck said was enough ice, we rested and gazed out across the valley below. Less than a mile away on the Hewes ranch they were making hay. I had never seen a hay stacker used before then. When we put up hay on our ranch we always pitched it in a wagon and then upon the stack by hand. They collected the hay shocks with a big rake pushed by horses. When they had collected about a half wagon load it was pushed up to a

22

stacker. A horse pulling a long rope raised the hay up into the air and dumped it on the stack. A man on the stack spread it out before the next load came up. It was like magic the way they stacked hay compared to how we did it at home, all pitched by hand.

"It's time we started back with the ice," Buck reminded me.

"Can't we watch some more?"

"If it was left up to you, you'd lay here and daydream until the ice all melted.

"I'm not daydreaming, I'm thinking."

"If you're not, then tell me what you're thinking about."

"Lots of things, like I remember you never gave me that two bits you promised when your skunk almost got away."

"Yeah I almost forgot."

"Well I haven't forgot, how that skunk was in your trap and you tried to kill it with a rock and when you hit the trap instead of the skunk, the trap broke and the skunk got loose. It would have got away too if I hadn't hit it with a big rock and broke its back."

"Okay. Okay. You don't need to tell me the whole story. I remember. The only reason you did what you did was because you were too dumb to know what that skunk could have done to you. It was just dumb luck you broke its back so it couldn't raise its tail and squirt you."

"The reason I did it was because you were letting the skunk get away and I knew its fur was worth enough to buy a new pair of shoes."

"Since when do you need a reason for doing anything dumb? Okay, I'll give you the 25 cents when we get back to the house, but don't you ever tell anyone how we killed that skunk. Now hold my foot so I can get on old Shorty. Let's go while we still got enough ice to make ice cream."

Sometimes we made ice cream by gathering hail stones after a storm. One time when we saw a storm approaching, everyone rushed around getting the baby chickens into their coop and the clothes off the line. The excitement was fun. I liked the flashing of lighting and the sound of thunder as the storm got closer. I liked to help but I knew Duane and Grace were too small to help. When our mother saw me she told me to get in the house.

"Why?" I asked. I was helping Buck catch the baby chicks.

"You might get hit by lightning. Hurry get in the house."

I noticed she didn't say anything to Buck, Eunice or Helen or anyone else. I knew she didn't like me better than Buck. Why would she be worried about me being struck by lightening and not Buck? I could think of only one way I was different from the others. I was the only one that had white hair, not blond, but white. That is, it would have been white if it was ever clean.

"Does white hair attract lightening?" I asked my mother.

The other kids laughed as though I had asked a dumb question. They always liked to tease me about my white hair attracting lighting.

When I was with Buck I didn't have to worry about getting into trouble. I let him do the worrying. I think he did enough worrying for the both of us.

I reminded Buck, "You know, I never told any one how we killed that skunk, like Duane would have if he had been with us. Why is it when I'm with Duane I always get in trouble and when I'm with you we hardly ever do? Is it because you're Ma's pet?"

"It's because I don't let Duane tag along and I don't let you do so many dumb things."

Chapter Four

The January of 1925 wasn't much different from any other in Wyoming, cold with blowing snow, except this year I became seven years old. After the usual birthday lickings were over I looked forward to March when I would start school. Our school year was from late March until Christmas. We attended the one-room Hewes School that was about three miles from our homestead. School was delayed a few days because of the breakup. The breakup was when the ice and snow all melted in a few days, causing Beaver Creek to overflow its banks. We had to wait until the water went down and we could get across to the schoolhouse.

Buck and I rode Skeeter most of the time. If there was ever a horse that had seen better days it was old Skeeter. His front hooves were turned up resembling two blocks of petrified wood and he had difficulty moving faster than a slow trot. We were told, this was because Milt once ran him real hard and let him drink all the cold water he wanted before he cooled down. Anyhow he was safe for Buck and me to ride. When he tried to run he wobbled and was so rough to ride without a saddle we would get sore butts, so we let him walk most of the time.

Eunice and Helen rode Jack, our burrow. It was hard to get him to go much faster than Skeeter, except the time Howard put a muskrat trap on his tail. That time he bucked Helen off. Sometimes when our mother didn't use Tony and Shorty on the wagon, Howard rode Shorty. When our mother needed Shorty, the four older kids had to take turns walking. When I walked I got tired and was too slow so they let me ride most of the time.

We set traps along Beaver Creek for muskrats and looked after them each night on our way home from school, until the weather got warm and the fur was no longer good. This was the way we kids earned our spending money. We had to use most of our spending money for clothes. I had one trap that I bought with the dollar my granddad in Washington state had sent me. He sent each of us kids a dollar that Christmas. Buck helped me skin my muskrats and stretch their pelts to dry. I caught enough to buy a new pair of shoes, with some money left over to spend when we would be going to the county fair in Sundance the next fall.

Howard had said I should give him the money I was saving to spend at the fair, to pay for the rabbit of his I had killed. I was afraid he would find where I was hiding it so I carried it in my pocket until I lost it all before fair time.

Howard had these tame rabbits that were nice and soft and great to play with. Some were white, some black and white and some tan. Helen and I liked to catch and feed them. We would gather clover or alfalfa or whatever they liked to eat and watched them wiggle their noses as they chewed down the stem of whatever we fed them. Howard got real mad if he knew we even touched his rabbits. Helen knew it was safe to play with them if Howard wasn't around.

One time I was helping Helen catch a rabbit and it ran around the house with us both after it. When Helen got close, it tried to dodge her and she stepped on the rabbit's head. It lay on the ground kicking. I picked it up to see how bad it was hurt. She told me to drop it and get away from there before Howard found out. She told Howard the rabbit died because I dropped it.

Howard whipped me so hard our mother told him he could hurt me, as I was only four at the time and he was 12. Whenever he thought about me killing his rabbit he would hold me so I couldn't get away and tickle me until I wet my pants. Then he called me a baby for wetting my pants. I sometimes had dreams of him tickling me and I would wake up after I had wet the bed. This made Buck and Duane mad at me because we slept in the same bad.

My first grade teacher was Mrs. Ruggles. I think she liked me most of the time, but not the time when I had been playing with my mud cars at recess. The gumbo around the fog pond was wet enough to mold like clay. The older kids didn't like me to play one-oh-cat (it's like baseball when you don't have enough for two teams) with them because they said I only got in the way. I had lots of fun making all sorts of things out of mud, like cars, horses, cows houses, etc. When Mrs. Ruggles rang the bell because recess was over I didn't have time to go to the back house or wash or anything. When she saw my muddy hands on top of my desk she said, "Wash those dirty hands."

I could tell by the look in her eyes she was real mad. She didn't take time to get a ruler, and when I saw her hand coming down real hard to hit me on my hands, I pulled them out of the way at the last instant. Her hand hit my desk with such force she spattered mud on herself and the other kids and almost broke her hand. I lost no time in washing my hands. I wanted to tell her I was sorry when the other kids snickered, because she was the best teacher anyone could ask for, but I was afraid to say anything.

Sometimes on Fridays, she would bring all the kids treats. It was the first time I ever had a whole candy bar I didn't have to share with Buck or Duane.

The time we were playing musical chairs, I beat this bigger kid, Julius Hewes, to the last chair. He came into the chair from the other side with such force he pushed me to the floor and bumped my head on the corner of a desk. I know he didn't intend to hurt me and Mrs. Ruggles picked me up and held me in her arms until it quit hurting. When something like this happened at home, someone would call me a baby and tell me to stop bawling. I think my mother liked me some of the time, but there were too many kids for her to take the time to show me this kind of affection.

It was lots of fun when the big kids at school would let me play with them, like the time we were playing store in the barn. Howard was the storekeeper. He would use whatever was handy, like rocks or old cans, and even stuff he found on the floor of the barn and pretended they were things you buy in a store. When you came into his store you might ask for a bucket of lard or a package of gum and he would hand you an old tomato can or whatever, and you would pay him whatever he asked with pretend money. Julius came into Howard's store and asked for some Juicy Fruit gum. Howard, with a big smile took a stick and got some juicy stuff off the barn floor. Julius changed his choice of gum to Spearmint.

Howard handed him the dirty end of the stick and said, "Here spearmint on this."

When we woke up on the morning of Eunice's 13th birthday in May, she was gone. She must have left sometime during the night. A little tent was also missing and the lard pail she usually carried her school lunch in was missing. We figured she left so she wouldn't get a birthday licking. Our mother was worried but

27

Howard thought it was funny. That morning on the way to school we caught up with Eunice. She was walking as we rode up behind her. Howard made us other kids, Helen, Buck and I agree not to talk to her all day and not let her ride with us on Skeeter or Jack. This made Eunice very unhappy and we all thought it was funny because she slept in a tent all night and all to keep from getting a birthday licking. I thought it was funny that is until we got home that night. Our mother was very upset and she told Howard in no uncertain terms there would be no more birthday lickings. I wished she had thought of that a long time before then.

After Howard took the state eighth grade exams and passed, he no longer had to go to school and we didn't have to take turns walking to school anymore.

Milt bought a Model T Ford that summer. He earned the down payment by trapping and helping Mr. Hewes put up hay. He seemed to like to buy things by paying a little down and the rest later when he had the money. He got real mad when Sears wouldn't sell him a new harness for the team of horses he bought until our mother signed something. He also bought the horses and a new mowing machine on credit. He had to pay cash though, when he sent to Sears for tobacco. Our mother didn't know they smoked. Milt or Howard would wait for their tobacco at our mailbox on the Sundance-Upton road. The mailbox was about two miles from our house.

When Dad came home that summer from working in a mine, it had been so long since I last saw him I almost forgot what he looked like. Before he had left he had bought a Baby Ben alarm clock. A Baby Ben was a small version of a regular alarm clock that was called a Big Ben.

Dad asked our mother, "How's the baby been?"

She thought he meant the clock.

"Howard broke the face out of it," she said.

Dad got the weirdest look on his face and started to laugh. He was asking about Grace our baby sister. Our mother had been worrying about Dad being mad because Howard had broken the clock.

Milt let Dad drive his Model T although he had never driven a car. When he drove up to a gate in front of our house, Dad hollered whoa. When the Ford didn't stop I heard him yell, "Whoa you son of a bitch, whoa," just before he ran through the gate. He got mad when we kids who were watching all laughed at him. Dad didn't like Milt's car, his horses, new mowing machine or the new harnesses either. Milt was 17 at the time and told Dad he could pay for them when he sold the hay on the place he had rented. The rented hay land was our uncle Will's homestead. Uncle Will was our mother's brother who had left and moved to Washington state.

When our dad or mother went to Sundance for groceries they usually came home with a bag of mixed candy. One time they brought some oranges for our school lunch. The next day it was a long wait for lunch time because I had never remembered tasting oranges before and I knew I had half of an orange in my lunch. Most of the time our school lunch was bread and butter. Sometimes there was a piece of salt pork between the bread. Sometimes we had hard sugar cookies our mother baked, but this was the first time we had oranges.

We were always warned to watch out for rattle snakes, especially when we were barefooted, which was most of the time in summer. One day when our teacher was standing near the open schoolhouse door, she gasped and grabbed a hatchet that was used for splitting kindling for the heating stove. I could hear her chopping something just outside the door. When she came back in she told us that we could not go outside for recess that afternoon and when we left to go home to be very careful because she had tried to kill a rattle snake. She said she had cut it in two and the head end, where the poison is, had crawled under the school house through a crack in the rock foundation.

That afternoon when school was let out the rattle snake was waiting by the door, caught in the crack in the foundation with its head end ready to bite. Julius Hewes finished killing the snake with the broom. He hit it so hard he broke the broom handle. When I think about the hatchet Mrs. Ruggles used, it had a handle only a little over a foot long, I know she must have put her students' safety ahead of her own.

Our dad went to a horse sale in Upton, a town about 15 or 20 miles south of our homestead and bought a mare we named Babe. She was gray and not very big. She was only three years old and us younger kids couldn't ride her. Dad told us she should be broke

29

well enough by next year so Duane could start school when he would be six. Dad said she was a quarter horse.

Duane said, "She was smaller than Tony, (one of our work horses) but she was bigger than the quarter of a horse."

The year Duane started school Helen rode Babe most of the time. She said Dad had bought Babe for her. I couldn't understand why he would buy one kid a horse when he had eight kids.

When our mother had to go to town for groceries and Dad wasn't home, she left Eunice in charge of the smaller kids. Eunice liked to play school, she would be the teacher and made us smaller kids pretend we were her students. Helen gave her more trouble than anyone. Sometimes Eunice used the broom to make Helen do the dishes or make the beds or whatever Helen was supposed to do. One time she hit Helen so hard she broke the new broom handle. Our mother was very unhappy with Eunice because the next time she went to town she had to buy another broom.

When our mother was in town one time I cut the end off a finger. I never told our mother, like Eunice made me promise, so she wouldn't get in trouble. It was my fault anyhow. I was three or four at the time and should have known better than to stick my finger in the exhaust port of an old engine. Someone turned a wheel and it cut the end off the index finger on my left hand. Eunice was afraid of what our mother would do if she found out so she got the piece that was cut off and put it back on and wrapped it to hold it in place. I remember how it hurt, but our mother didn't think anything of one more cut finger. She never knew the end had been cut off until she changed the bandage, by then it was growing back.

Our mother always wore her best dress and hat when she went to town. She had this one hat she wore as long as I could remember. Sometimes she would change the flowers, the ribbons or the other pretty things on the hat to make it look different. One time Helen asked her if she could have the hat after our mother died. After that she somehow got money for a new hat. I don't think Helen ever got the old one.

When our mother was away, sometimes Helen liked to dress me in dresses and curl my white hair and put ribbons in it. I was teased a lot by my brothers and sisters because my hair was white and they all had brown or black hair. It wasn't white most of the time anyhow, because if I got it dirty they couldn't call me whitey or Swede. Once Helen fixed a ring so it was above my head, she called it a halo. Eunice told her one thing I wasn't, was one of God's little angels and she made Helen take it off. Eunice said if Helen wanted something to do she should fix Buck, Duane and me with horns and a spear for a tail because we were three little devils. Angels we were not. What we called fun, Eunice called raising hell.

Sure we would fight each other sometimes, especially if Duane called me whitey and I would bust him one in the nose. Buck and I would fight too. Buck would hit me if I gave Duane a bloody nose. I knew Buck was bigger than me and would always win but I would get so mad I would fight him anyhow. Sometimes I would give Buck a bloody nose before Eunice or our mother made us stop fighting. Even though we fought each other, we would stick together if we were picked on by Eunice or other members of the family.

When Eunice first found out our mother was going to have another baby, before Grace was born, she told our mother, "If the new baby is a boy, I'm going to run away from home."

The summer after Grace was born, Dad built a bunk house for us boys to sleep in.

Sometimes Buck and I would sneak off and go fishing without Duane. I guess Buck knew if we took Duane he would tell. One time we were leaving on Jack for Beaver Creek when Milt saw us and called for us to come back. Since he wasn't my dad I thought we should go fishing anyhow and pretend we couldn't hear him.

"We don't need to tell him where we're going," Buck said, "but we should go back and see what he wants."

Buck was right as usual. Milt had borrowed a camera from a friend and only wanted to take a picture of us four younger kids, Buck, Duane, Grace and me on Jack. After we had our picture taken, we had no trouble getting rid of Grace but Duane wanted to go along. Buck promised him he wouldn't have to pull weeds for the pigs that night if he would go back to the house and not bawl. We took turns pulling weeds or alfalfa for the pigs and it was Duane's turn. Duane never liked this job but Buck would remind him from time to time he should help feed the pigs if he

Left; Grace, Duane, Link and Buck on Jack the day Buck and Link slip away and go fishing.

expected to eat any.

After we got rid of Duane, Buck and I went fishing in Beaver Creek. We rode Jack because the fishing hole was a little too far to walk, about three miles from our house. I wanted to go swimming too but Buck wouldn't let me. The only reason he gave me was, because I couldn't swim and the water was over my head. The fish bit better than usual and we soon had a good string of chubs and headed back home. Chubs are a little like catfish only smaller. I looked forward to showing our fish and having a good fish dinner that night, then Buck told me we had to throw all the fish away.

"Why?" I asked.

"Have you forgot we didn't have permission to go fishin'."

"But this is the best string of fish we have ever caught, better than when we went with Howard and we didn't ask Ma that time if we could go fishing."

"But that was different because we went with Howard."

"He didn't ask."

"He don't have to."

"You mean I have to throw away the biggest fish I ever caught and not get to show it to anyone?"

"Unless we want to get in trouble that's what we have to do."

"I still don't think we should throw them away."

"You don't think. That's why you always catch hell when you're not with me."

Buck took the string of fish and threw them as far as he could into some bushes to the side of the road.

Another time Buck's thinking didn't do him any good.

When our mother baked bread, which was usually several times a week, sometimes she baked a pan of cinnamon rolls. After they cooled she put them in what we called the cellar.

Our house was built on the hillside like a cow ranch line-shack with the cellar dug into the side of the hill and covered with dirt so it wouldn't freeze in winter. The only entrance to the cellar was a door off the middle room that was between the house and the cellar. Our mother would put things in the cellar she didn't want us hungry kids to snitch. If we tried she could see us when we came out. The time Buck was outsmarted he tossed a cinnamon roll out the vent in the top of the cellar. When he came outside to claim his snack, Howard was already eating it. Because Howard was six years older, all Buck could do was watch Howard eat the roll and get laughed at.

One day when I was in the first grade, I pretended I was sick so I wouldn't have to go to school. It was snowing and I didn't have a warm coat. Our mother had bought a box of Washington delicious apples for Christmas. The kids that went to school all got half an apple in their school lunch. I didn't know when I decided to be sick we were going to have half of an apple for lunch. Duane and I were told to be very quiet because Grace, who was two, was taking her nap. I knew the apples were in the cellar and it would be hard to get one without getting caught. I had to take the chance and let Duane in on my plan. Since we had to be quiet, why not play in the cellar near the box of apples. Duane and I both took a whole apple and ate it before we left the cellar. I had trouble talking Duane into eating all of his.

A short time later our mother said. "You boys have been so quiet I hardly knew you were in the house. You have been so good to let Grace sleep, you deserve a treat."

She sat us down at the table and gave us each half an apple. Duane couldn't eat all of his so I had to eat his when our mother wasn't looking, because I was afraid he would tell why he couldn't eat it all. As hard as I tried I couldn't finish mine.

"You really are sick," Ma said when she saw I was having trouble eating the last of the apple. "That's why you have been so quiet."

I may not have been sick but I sure felt rotten. My mother never knew just how rotten I felt.

The summer I was in the second grade my teacher was Mrs. Hilton. I didn't have to do much in school because our teacher was busy mostly with Julius Hewes. That year he did three grades so he would be ready for high school by September. Eunice finished the seventh and eighth grades, so the teacher spent some extra time with her too. When I didn't have anything to do, Rosalie, Julius' older sister, would come to school and read to me and tell me stories. I liked that a lot better than regular school work anyway.

Milt and Howard both smoked since both had lived with Dad in Lead, while going to school there. They had money from trapping to pay for their tobacco ordered from Sears. Howard and Milt raised tobacco, just to see it grow, they told our mother. It grew real good. When some of the plants were six feet tall they were hung up in the bunk house to dry and smoked with dry cabbage leaves. Milt and Howard found it was too strong without the cabbage leaves. Somehow Julius Hewes found out about our homegrown tobacco. He kept pestering Buck to bring him some so he could smoke it. Buck kept putting him off, but finally gave in just to get him to stop pestering all the time. When Milt and Howard smoked our homegrown tobacco, they used a pipe they made out of a corn cob, but like I said, they always weakened it with dry cabbage leaves.

Julius was about 12 years old and wanted to act as if he was a high school kid so he said he wanted to smoke it full strength. After he had finished his lunch he rolled himself an after-dinner cigar, as he called it. He showed us younger kids how to inhale and enjoy a good cigar. The school bell rang while he was still enjoying his smoke. We hadn't been back in school very long when I noticed Julius had turned white like a ghost. He let out a groan as though he was dying and then threw up all over his desk. The teacher got scared and she acted as she thought he was dying. We had no phone in our school house so Eunice had to ride a couple of miles to the Hewes ranch and tell his parents Julius was sick so they could take him to a doctor. His mother told the teacher he had eaten too much candy the night before. None of us dared tell her why he got sick.

After Julius had passed his eighth grade state exams and was ready for high school, we were told The Hewes School would be closed. I was only halfway through the second grade. We would either have to go to the Canfield school that was about the same distance south of our ranch or move to Sundance for school. Going to the Canfield school would mean we had to cross Beal's ranch and we would be going to school with the Beal kids. Our dad would never permit this so our mother decided we would move to Sundance and go to the town school.

Our mother explained we would rent a house and have a chance to meet a lot of new friends, even have an opportunity to go to church and Sunday school.

I could tell she was glad to get away from the ranch, but I thought what she really wanted was to live in Washington state where she could see her mother, brothers, sisters and friends again.

I remembered when Howard and Milt had gone to town school in Lead, they both learned to smoke and Howard had to learn how to fight. I thought I might have to fight other kids but if we stuck together, Buck, Duane and me, should be able to take care of ourselves.

Chapter Five

When our family moved from the ranch so we could go to school in Sundance it was like entering a new world. I had only been to town a few times, mostly when we would all go to the county fair. This happened once a year. I had never played with many kids near my own age, other than Buck and Duane, and expected the town kids would want to fight me like they fought Howard when he went to school in Lead. We started school in Sundance right after Christmas, when I was in the second half of the second grade. I was nine years old that January while most of the second graders were seven. I was bigger than all the boys in my grade and most of the ones in the third grade.

Duane was in the first grade and we both had Mrs. Faulkes for our teacher. She taught the first, second and third grades. Buck was in the fourth grade, in another room. His teacher was Mrs. Hawkins and she taught the fourth, fifth and sixth grades. Helen was in the seventh grade in Mrs. Hilton's room. Howard and Eunice were freshmen in high school. Milt was the only one to stay on the ranch. He refused to go to school anymore. Dad was away working in a mine some place and sent home $75 every other month.

The only one of us that had to fight, at first anyhow, was Howard. Dick Smith, a kid whose dad ran the pool hall, told me about the fight when he found out Howard was my brother. Three kids picked a fight with Howard. They called him a hick from the country. I guess they didn't know he had gone to school in Lead. Dick told me how Howard beat up all three of them, knocking one through the front window of his dad's pool hall breaking the glass. Leslie Hooper, the man who brought the doctor when I was born, was the town marshal and he put all four in jail until he decided what to do with them.

While they waited in jail they became friends more or less and had figured out how to take the hinges off the jail door. The marshal came back before they had a chance to carry out their plan. Someone told the marshal that the other kids started the fight and they got more than they bargained for. Mr. Hooper made the other kids pay for the window. Sundance was a small town and everyone knew about the fight. I may have been a hick from the country but no one ever told me I was. For some reason no one ever picked a fight with Duane, Buck or me, not when we three were together anyhow. I liked living in town because we had so many kids to play with and most of them were friendly.

Our family lived in four rooms of a big, square, eight room house located only a few blocks from the school. We rented it from a family named Moore who lived in the rest of the house. We had three bedrooms and a fourth room for cooking and eating. The house was like a palace compared to our homestead log cabin. There was an outside back house and we only had to carry the water from the other family's kitchen, not a long haul from a well like out on the ranch. They let us use the barn for old Blanch, our milk cow, so we had plenty of milk.

The school was a beautiful two-and one-half-story stone building, big enough for the high school, a library and three rooms for all the grade school students. We didn't have a stove in our room for heat like our country school. A coal fired furnace was in a room that was used only for the furnace. I thought it was like magic the way the steam was piped to radiators in each room for heat. There were electric lights in each room, the first I had ever seen. Light bulbs were on the end of four wires that hung from the ceiling. The electricity was made by a gasoline-driven generator located next to the furnace room. Most Sundance homes didn't have electricity and there were no street lights when we first moved to town. Almost everyone in town used kerosene or gasoline lamps for light, while a few had their own electric generators.

The schoolhouse was only four years old when we moved to town according to its corner stone, dated 1923. There were no outside back houses and I had never seen an inside one before. I didn't know you could go inside until one time I just had to go. I wasn't even sure if I had gone in the right place, but no one could see me with the door closed and I had to take the chance. I was scared, thinking maybe I had gone in the wrong place so I told Buck what I had done. He laughed at me because he knew that was what it was for all the time, but nobody ever told me.

I soon met many kids my age to play with and didn't have to play only with Buck and Duane if I didn't want to. Most of the time we three played together and with the other kids. When the

37

weather got warm in the spring, we learned a new game they called football.

Buck and I found a skunk den up on the hill north of Sundance. Buck set a trap and caught a skunk and he wanted to use the money to buy a football, but our mother said he had to buy a new pair of shoes first. He earned some more money splitting wood for Otis Reynolds and we used that money to send to Sears for a new football. There was a vacant lot next to our house where Buck, Duane and I could play. Elvin Ewing and another kid named Dinny Hampton would come over and the five of us would play football during most of our spare time. We decided to have our own team and play against other kids. We didn't care how many they had on their team, the five of us would take on the bunch of them. We had watched the high school team practice and we learned how to block, tackle and all the other stuff. We had plays too, such as the reverse that always seemed to work. One of us would start an end sweep and give the ball to a teammate going the other way. Sometimes all the other kids would follow the first guy like a mob and never see the ball was passed off until we scored a touchdown. Sometimes a kid would bawl when we blocked or tackled him too hard and that kid wouldn't play against us anymore.

I remember a kid named Buzz, whose dad had been the sheriff. Buzz wanted to play on our team because he wanted to have a turn in winning sometime, he said.

We gave him a tryout and decided against letting him play with us because he hurt too easily. None of us had helmets or pads of any kind. We would play at noon or recess with the five of us against all who wanted to play on the other team. I soon got the impression that most town kids, as we called them, were like big babies.

I don't remember if Buck or I ever had to fight that first year in town school. Duane was a lot smaller for his age than we were and once when we weren't around, a kid named, Frank Graham, fought Duane because Duane won all his marbles. They were playing for keeps and he wanted them back. Frank's older brother, Lyle, broke up the fight.

Duane asked Howard, who was watching the fight, "Why didn't you help me?"

38

"Why should I?" Howard asked "You were doing a good job of taking care of him yourself. Lyle broke up the fight before you killed his little brother. You noticed he didn't say anything about you giving back the marbles."

That first year in town schoolwork wasn't easy for me as most of the other second graders were better readers. Mrs. Faulkes was a good teacher and she made me work a lot harder than I did when I had Mrs. Hilton, who spent most of her time getting Julius Hewes through three grades in one year. I had caught up with the other kids by the time school was out for summer vacation.

Before we moved back to the ranch for the summer, I became sick with what my mother called measles. We didn't know for sure because she never took me to a doctor. Doctors cost too much. Going to school in town had been fun but it was good to get back out on the ranch even though it meant doing my share of the work.

Dad came home that summer driving his own Model T Ford. When he asked about Grace they told him I had given her my measles. Dad had small pox years ago and he knew the difference between measles and small pox. He said Grace had small pox.

Grace was the youngest of us eight kids, five years younger than me. She never had to do any chores and I always seemed to get in trouble whenever I played with her. I got into trouble when I let her play with my mud cars and she got all dirty. I got into trouble for not letting her play with some pine cones I called my horses. It didn't seem to make any difference who she complained to, I would catch it for not being nice to our baby sister. When I got sick I let Grace play near me. I mostly watched her play with her dolls because the other kids were told not to get near me or they would catch what I had. Her dolls were made of paper and she pretended they were talking, only she did all the talking. When Grace got sick with my small pox I tried real hard to be nice to her by helping her cut out paper dolls. I got the Sears catalog and we cut out a lot of people for her dolls.

I knew I wasn't supposed to use the new catalog so I borrowed the one from the back house. I could tell that wasn't a good idea when I heard Dad swearing as he came from the back house.

"Who the hell took the catalog out of the back house?"

"Bobby did it," Grace said, in her sweetest voice.

I was nicknamed Bobby, since I was a baby when Buck couldn't say baby.

"That damn white-headed kid again," Dad said. "First I find out he brought small pox home from school to give to this poor baby, then he takes the paper out of the back house."

Even though my nickname was Bobby, I didn't like to be called that, it sounded too much like baby, but it was better than being called whitehead.

One time Dad called Duane a black-eyed wop. Duane had dark eyes and dark hair like our mother. Dad had brown hair and blue eyes. I didn't think whitehead was as bad as being called a black-eyed wop. I had heard about wops from Howard. That was what he called the kids he fought when he went to school in Lead. Dad talked about the wops in the mine where he worked.

I usually got into trouble when I tried being nice to Grace, but one time she kept me from getting a licking. Someone broke the handle off a fingernail file and our mother was determined to find out who did it. She made Eunice, Helen, Buck, Duane and me all stand in a row and ask each one of us, "Did you break this fingernail file?"

I thought Helen broke it because she used it most. I knew I didn't because I never cleaned my fingernails. I was the last to be asked and I was scared because all the rest had said no. I was afraid to answer because I knew I would get two lickings, one for breaking the file and another for lying.

"I knew it was you all the time," our mother said, as she gripped the strap she used on us kids. It was the end of a leather harness tug cut so she had a handle to hang onto and the other end had six straps that hung loose.

Grace wasn't in the line up but she was watching. Because our mother was real mad I knew I was in for a hard licking, that is until Grace spoke up.

"I bend it and I bend it and it broke," Grace said.

When they realized it was Grace who broke the fingernail file everyone thought it was funny, everyone but me. It was hard for me to understand why I would have got a licking if I had done it, but because Grace did it, she was cute.

Even though Dad was sure Grace had small pox he didn't

take her to a doctor because we would have all been quarantined. If that happened, no one could come to our house nor could any of us go any place. When Dad went to town he bought Grace special things to eat like cantaloupe, bananas and canned fruit. Things I had never ever tasted.

I don't think Grace ever understood why I felt the way I did or why, when no one was looking, a nine-year-old brother would tear the heads off his four-year-old sister's paper dolls.

When we put up the hay we all had to help but Howard did most of the hard work. The hard part was hauling and pitching it upon a stack by hand. When Milt sold the hay from the place he rented from our Uncle Will last year, he bought a second-hand Overland car. The car was all Milt's and not even part Howard's.

One job Duane, Buck and I did together was hitching Shorty to the stone boat and picking corn for a pig we were fattening. When Duane would complain about having to work, which was often, Buck would remind him if he wanted to eat any of the pig he should expect to help pick the corn. Buck always had to put the harness on Shorty because if I tried, he would lower his ears, this meant he was mad and ready to kick me if I came any closer. Buck said he had me bluffed. I didn't think he was bluffing. For some reason Shorty didn't like me, maybe it was because I would get Tip, our dog, to bite him when it was my turn to get the horses.

When it was time to start cutting the hay that summer Milt offered to let Dad use his horses and new mower, but Dad said he didn't like Milt's damn outfit. He hitched Babe, our new quarter horse, up with Shorty. Tony, the horse that we had always worked with Shorty, had died the winter before. Babe had never been in a harness before and the noise of the mower scared her. Instead of pulling like a work horse she more or less jumped. Milt said she was too small to pull a mower.

Milt's hayfield was next to where Dad was trying to mow. Milt with his bigger team and new mower had no trouble, while Dad had to give up because the alfalfa was damp and his horses pulled so slow the mower's wheels slid and wouldn't cut.

Dad went back to work in a mine in Montana before the haying was done. Our mother cried after he left. I didn't know what she meant at the time when she said something about seeing Dad for the last time.

41

Chapter Six

I'll never forget that warm August morning when it was my turn to bring in the horses. Duane went with me, and Milt had told me to bring an axe back to the house when we returned with the horses.

Babe, the horse we were riding ran away and we both fell off. Duane got a gash in the back of his head where he landed on the axe. With blood running down his back he stumbled for home. I watched until he went out of sight behind some pine trees. I had to return with the horses.

Not knowing if he would make it back to the house before he bled to death made it the longest horse drive I or anyone else ever made. With everything racing through my mind it couldn't have been any farther from Texas to Montana.

I was able to get the horses to leave the hayfield and head them toward home. I shut the gate and followed.

Walking back to face the rest of the family, not knowing if Duane was dead or alive was a frightening experience.

Returning with the horses didn't seem that important anymore. I even thought about running away so no one would ever find me, but I had to know if Duane made it home okay.

When the horses finally got in sight of the house they headed for the water trough by the well.

Despite moving the pump handle up and down as fast as possible, I had difficulty replenishing the water as fast as the thirsty horses could siphon it. Because of my size, it was necessary for me to jump and leave the ground in order to get a full stream of water on each downward stroke. I knew the squeaks and bangs of the pump could be heard in our house about a hundred yards up the hill from the well. I kept an eye on the house as I pumped, anxious to know how Duane was, but afraid to go to the house and find out.

Duane and Milt finally came out of the house, Duane was wearing my good coat, one Buck had outgrown. I watched out of the corner of one eye as they got into Milt's car and started the engine. I knew Milt must be taking Duane to a doctor.

As they drove away, Buck came out of the house and headed toward me at the well and I cringed waiting to get my first reprimand.

"What the hell happened?" Buck asked.

"Didn't Duane tell you?"

"He showed up all splattered with blood, dragging the axe and when I got near enough so I could hear, he started bawling. When I asked him what he was bawling for he said it was because he wasn't going to get to eat any of the pig."

"Didn't he tell you Babe ran away and we fell off?"

I finally got it out of him, but at first all he would say was he was going to die and he wouldn't get to eat any pig, after he had to help pick corn and pull weeds.

"He isn't going to die is he?"

"Milt is taking him to Upton to get the cut sewed up, but, you are sure going to catch hell. You could have killed him you know."

"Why Upton?"

"That's where the closest doctor is. Doctor Clarenbach is not in Sundance, he's away for some reason. Duane said you were riding Babe without a bridle."

"That's the only way I could catch her."

"All I can say is I'm glad I'm not you when Milt gets back."

The whole family treated me as if I was some kind of a criminal for a while, which I knew I was, but I was so glad Duane was going to be okay I didn't care.

I knew what my mother was going to say. "Bobby, you are going to have to learn to think before you do something like riding a half broke colt without a bridle while carrying an axe. We can only thank God that Duane wasn't killed."

I knew she was right about thanking God. I was afraid to tell her or anyone about how I had promised not to let Duane go to hell if God would let him live. I knew they would all laugh at me.

The doctor in Upton used three clamps to close the gash in the back of Duane's head. The doctor said his skull had been cut and his brain was exposed but not damaged. He charged five dollars that some said I should pay because it was my fault. I would have gladly paid it if I had the money and I didn't need to be reminded that it was my fault. They were supposed to take Duane back to the doctor in two weeks to have the clamps removed, but our mother decided to remove them herself to save the money.

In September we moved back to the big square house in Sundance. This time we rented the whole house from the owner. The Moores had moved to Sheridan. We sub-rented enough rooms to pay our rent. Two rooms upstairs were rented to Bryants. They had four kids, Opal and her three younger brothers, Marvin, Louis and Everett who attended school in Sundance while their parents lived on a ranch. Everett had white hair like me and was called Swede. Another room downstairs was rented to Alta Wood. She was a friend of my sister Eunice and her mother was a friend of our mother.

We brought our chickens and cow in from the ranch and our dad still sent home 75 dollars every other month. Milt brought in hay and wood from the ranch and he stayed out there alone and took care of the other stock.

We always raised a big garden and our mother canned garden-grown vegetables as well as wild fruit. Choke cherries were used for jelly or syrup. Wild plums and buffalo berries were very sour tasting. We had lots of service berries, which were good for both pies and sauce.

When we first moved into Sundance to go to school it was hard to make our own spending money. We found a skunk den on the hill above town where Buck caught several skunks and I got a job doing the chores for an old lady named Mrs. Zane. She was over 80 years old and got a small pension because she was the widow of a Civil War veteran. Every night I filled her coal bucket, cut kindling, chopped wood and carried it in. She couldn't walk to a store so I would take her shopping list and buy groceries or sometimes she would phone in an order and all I had to do was pick them up and take them to her. I would go directly to Mrs. Zane's home from school every night before going home. She paid me a quarter for two nights work and a whole quarter on Saturday. I made a dollar a week altogether. It was enough so I could buy most of my own clothes. Buck also got paid for cutting wood for a lawyer named Otis Reynolds. Duane didn't think it was fair because he had to carry in most of the wood at home and didn't get paid anything. I guess it was hard for him to see the difference but he didn't pay for his own clothes, while Buck and I did.

Even though it was our own money we seldom were permitted to spend any for foolish things like picture shows or candy. One time our mother let me use a penny for candy and she gave Duane a penny to spend too. We went to Frank's general store where they had good penny candy. Mrs. Frank complained about having to bend over to reach for the candy we wanted in the bottom case. When Duane handed her his penny, she dropped it and it went rolling under a display case. She got down on her hands and knees and retrieved it like a dog after a rabbit.

Duane said, "Did you notice how quick her back got well?"

Howard had raised a good crop of potatoes that he tried to sell to stores in town but most of his crop had to be thrown out in the spring because it seemed everyone wanted to trade potatoes for groceries. He sold only a few and got paid 50 cents for a 100-pound sack.

Buck, Duane and I helped Bob Schloredt with his chores and he would pay our way to a picture show. I guess he knew if he gave us money we would have to use it for food or clothes. Bob's folks both worked in a grocery store they owned, so many times we would help Bob cook dinner and eat at his place. Several people in Sundance had cows and they rented pasture from Bob's folks. He would take their cows out to pasture each morning and bring them back at night. We would help him, sometimes on foot and sometimes with his horse. Bob was two years older than Buck and we had a lot of fun together. He showed us how to tackle and block hard in playing football, but since he was in junior high school he couldn't play on the same school playground as us younger kids. One time when a minstrel show came to town just about every kid in town was going. When Bob found out we didn't have any money, he paid our way so all three of us could go and said we could do chores for it later.

Buck, Duane and me, liked to fish in Sundance Creek. Many times when we weren't doing chores for someone, we would catch enough fish for dinner. They were mostly chubs or suckers and sometimes trout. One Saturday when I had to cut wood for Mrs. Zane, Buck and Duane went fishing without me. When they were coming home they were stopped by Joe Dudrey, a big kid, even bigger than Bob Schloredt. Joe asked Buck and Duane to empty their pockets to see if they had any money. When they refused he pulled out a knife and threatened to cut Duane. Buck told Duane to give Joe a nickel, the only money they had on them. Buck could have told Otis Reynolds about the incident, the lawyer he cut wood for, but he had a better idea. He told Bob Schloredt. Bob beat Joe up so bad they had to take him to a doctor. Joe recovered okay in a few days, but he never did get well enough to take nickels away from little kids again, at least not Duane.

When school was out in the spring our mother decided not to move back to the ranch for the summer. Milt was in partnership with Lloyd Lull and had rented several parcels of land adjoining our homestead. They had a Fordson tractor and were farming. They plowed some of the level pasture land and planted it with grain. Lloyd and his wife were living in the house on Uncle Will's homestead. It was one of the places they were renting.

Helen claims Babe is her horse.

46

Helen was worried about how Babe was being treated since she claimed Babe was her horse. She asked me to walk out to our ranch with her and we would bring Babe back to town. While we were out there we could check on Jack, our donkey. It was about 12 miles to our homestead and another two or three to Babe's location at Uncle Will's place.

We took a shortcut hoping to cross Beaver Creek, but found the water was too high so we ended up walking just as far as if we had stayed on the county road. We finally found a place to cross the creek near Tom Hawkins' place. When we went by their house to get back on the road we found Tom Hawkins didn't live there any more. A family moved in that had six boys with the oldest a little older than Helen on down to a couple younger than me. They all stood in the door of their house smiling and gawking at us as we passed. This was the first time I saw the Platner kids who became good friends of the Kaiser kids later.

By the time Helen and I got to our homestead I was starved and tired. There was no one living there and no food in the house. Milt was staying with Lloyd and his wife. All we could find to eat were some turnips that had been left in the garden and somehow made it through the winter. I ate one that was very tough and after eating it I was still hungry.

It was late afternoon when we got to where Milt, Lloyd and his wife were living and they were making ice cream for their Sunday dinner. Lloyd had been riding Babe to work each day where he drove a tractor in the field. He tied her up all day without anything to eat or drink. It was no wonder she was so thin you could count all her ribs. When Helen told Lloyd we were taking Babe back, he wasn't too friendly. They didn't ask us to eat with them at first. I told Milt we hadn't eaten since breakfast and I was about starved. When Mrs. Lull found out we were staying for dinner, she got sick all at once. She had to lie down and wouldn't eat with us. Milt said she always got sick when people dropped by around dinner time.

It was dark before Helen and I got back to town riding Babe.

We didn't have a pasture so we staked Babe out on a long picket rope so she could eat wherever we could find good grass on vacant lots and vacant land east of Sundance. She slowly gained weight and was finally her old spunky self again. Kids in town begged for rides, so Helen made some of them pay so she could buy oats for Babe.

That summer when we stayed in town, we had a big garden as we always had on the homestead and I worked for Mrs. Zane doing her chores each day. Between playing football, working and horseback riding, I didn't miss the ranch that much.

The fall of 1928, Milt talked Howard into quitting high school and staying with him on the ranch. He convinced Howard they could farm without Lloyd as a partner. Milt had made enough that summer to buy a second-hand Fordson tractor, a plow and a disk. They would rent the surrounding homesteads that no one was living on and grow grain.

I was in the fourth grade and Buck was in the sixth, we were both in Mrs. Hawkins' room. During the school year, Dad quit sending home money and he told our mother he had no intentions of sending any more. Besides Dad not sending our mother any more money, he still owed Frank's store about a thousand dollars. After Frank wouldn't give him more credit we bought our groceries from Schloredt. Dad still owed one of Granddad's friends a thousand dollars plus interest. Dad had borrowed the money using the homestead as collateral. Dad had spent the money to buy a new wagon, a team of horses and some stock in a creamery in Sundance. Dad got the job picking up cream from the farmers one summer until the creamery had to close for lack of business. Our mother said Dad was always going to pay off the mortgage on the homestead when he got part of his inheritance.

Granddad had been dead for three years but Dad didn't inherit anything. Dad's youngest sister, Myrtle, was then living with Grandmother in Washington state. It looked as though she would get everything. I didn't know exactly how much Granddad had when he died, but he sold his farm in Missouri for around 50 thousand dollars that was a lot of money in those days. Granddad was what you would call a private banker and loaned people money, but Dad never borrowed from him.

Our dad had not been on friendly terms with his parents for some time. When he was in his teens, one fall after being gone all summer working on a large cow ranch, he came home and put his saddle horse in the stall normally used for Granddad's work

48

horses. Granddad always kept a team in the barn in the winter to haul hay for the cattle. There was only room for one team. Once you start keeping a horse in the barn in cold weather you should keep it in all winter or the cold would be too much of a shock. When Granddad turned Dad's horse outside with the rest of the stock, before the weather got cold, Dad got so upset he left home and was never on friendly terms with his parents again.

Granddad died in Washington state in 1925 and soon afterward Aunt Myrtie, Dad's sister and her husband Alton, bought a new car. They wrote and told us that the four of them, including Grandma and our Cousin Roger, were taking a motor trip to Washington D.C. They were going to stop at our place on their way through Sundance.

They had a new car and could afford a trip like that while we were struggling to have enough to eat. Dad told them to stay the hell off our ranch. I don't know if he was mad because he thought they were living high on Granddad's money or because he was too proud for his own mother to see our living conditions. I do know he wasn't so proud that he changed those conditions before he quit sending money to our mother and us eight kids.

We sub-rented part of the big square house as before to pay our rent, this year to Mable Staton and her brother Willis. Most of the ranchers who sent their kids to high school rented a place where they could cook their own meals. Some stayed with families in town and paid for their room and board. There were no school buses.

Helen made pretty good money baby-sitting for Otis Reynolds. She gave our mother $15 to make the final payment on a sewing machine. That was how Helen paid for Babe.

Without Dad sending home any more money we would have to move back and live on the ranch where Milt and Howard were farming.

Our mother got sick and didn't get out of bed for a long time that spring. She called it rheumatism and all the doctor would do was give her some salve to rub on. He said something about she had to want to get well. I couldn't figure out how he thought someone would want to stay in bed all day if they weren't sick.

The Bryant family stopped at our house when our mother was sick in bed. Their kids had stayed in rooms they rented from us the year before. They were poorer than us. They didn't even have their own ranch anymore. Mr. Bryant had a job working on a ranch where their house and cow were furnished. Before that he mostly cut wood and sold it for a living. Even though our mother couldn't get out of bed they asked her to go with them and stay for a while. Mr. Bryant said the change would make her get well. She stayed with them only a week or so but when she came home she didn't have to stay in bed with rheumatism any more.

I was able to save some money from doing chores for Mrs. Zane. My mother agreed to let me buy a camera if I saved enough money by the time school was out.

One night after school when I went to Mrs. Zane's house as usual, to carry in her wood and get what she needed at the grocery store, she couldn't talk. The doctor said she had had a stroke. There didn't seem to be anything I or anyone could do for her and because I was a kid they wouldn't let me see her again before she died. I had been doing chores for her for nearly two years and it was the first time I had been so close to a person who died. I was scared to go to her funeral by myself, so my mother went with me. It was the first funeral I ever attended and one I will always remember.

I knew we would be going back to the ranch and attending the same school with the Beal kids next year. Since Dad wouldn't be coming home anymore, Milt would be running things. He said our dad's fight wasn't his fight and we could make friends with the Beals.

Milt became 21 in 1929 when I was 11. Our mother let Milt run things like the way she had let Howard give us all birthday lickings. She didn't say if she liked the way Milt took charge.

We cut a big pile of wood so we could buy seed and tractor fuel for farming. Money from the wood sales had to be used to pay for groceries we charged after Dad quit sending money. Milt borrowed from the bank and mortgaged the cows in order to have money to put in the crops.

Milt promised if we all worked, we would all share what we made when we sold the crops. One field of flax was to be Howard's, another smaller field was Buck's and even a couple of patches were for Duane and me. We had to work six days a week

50

with only Sundays off after the chores were done. I don't remember what Milt promised Helen or Eunice. I know Helen helped milk the four cows that first summer we were back from Sundance. We sold a five-gallon can of cream once a week for about five dollars, that paid for most of the groceries.

One job Milt wanted done was to fence all the land he was now renting to keep the stray stock out of our grain fields. Buck, Duane and I had the job of digging post holes. Buck said I had to dig at least five post holes before I could quit for dinner and another five before supper. Buck always did as much as or more than he made me do, but sometimes he would help Duane dig his five post holes but not me. We dug post holes most of the summer, unless we were putting up hay or until it was time to shock grain.

After the grain was cut and tied in bundles with the binder the bundles had to be placed in shocks by hand. The shocks were left in the field to dry with the grain end up, until it was time to thrash.

Milt bought a new binder on credit for cutting the grain. The flax was left loose in the shock for thrashing, but wheat, barley and oats had to be tied in bundles and shocked. Buck, Duane and I followed the binder and shocked the grain as fast as the binder could cut it. This was hot sweaty work when the Fordson tractor ran as it should, but when they had trouble making it run we got to rest. We got to rest quite a bit because the coils would come loose or the tractor would slip out of timing or something else. I remember Milt doing a lot of swearing.

Even though Milt was good at getting old engines to run, he lost his patience with this old Fordson. He had been talking to Ben Justice about renting some land for farming the next year. The rent would be one-third of the crop. The land was on Black's Flat about six miles from our homestead. Scotchy Roberts, who sold farm equipment in Sundance, told Milt he would sell him a new John Deere tractor on time if he had a written rent agreement with Ben Justice. Ben had about 150 acres of good level farmland, which should produce more than enough to pay off the tractor in one season. Milt said flax would yield about 10 bushels per acre and was selling for around four dollars per bushel. Even after giving Ben Justice one third for rent that would leave 4,000 dollars. The tractor only cost 1,000 dollars.

We hardly had enough money from selling cream to buy groceries yet Milt bought the new John Deere tractor on credit. We didn't get to rest any more that fall when we were shocking grain, waiting for the old Fordson to run.

School would be starting before we got all our grain thrashed. I knew I would miss my friends in Sundance as we would be going to the Canfield school for the first time with the Beal kids. I had only seen George Beal, their dad, once and that time he swore at Buck and me about our dad when we were fixing a section of fence at the end of Devil's Lane. Devil's lane was the space between our ranches. George Beal and our dad each built their own fences when they couldn't agree on sharing the cost of building only one. Mr. Beal told Buck and me not to touch his fence. We built our fence within a foot of his. The range horses couldn't get by, so we didn't need to touch his fence. This made him mad.

Mr. Beal said, "I don't blame you boys a bit but I do blame your damn dad."

Another time Buck was with our dad when they caught George Beal's brother taking wood from our Uncle Will's place. He had to cross our place to get to the wood. Dad had a handgun on his belt and he dared Mr. Beal to draw. Mr. Beal didn't have a gun and Dad told him to get the hell out and not to set foot on our place again. At least it was implied if he did, he could expect to get shot.

Milt knew we had to cross Beal's place to get to school. The oldest Beal kid, Joe, was my age and Milt told me in no uncertain terms I was not to fight him even if he started the fight. I knew his dad was bigger than our dad so I figured he would be bigger than me. Joe had a brother named Harold who was a little older than Duane.

I told Buck, "I'm not sure I can go along with the conditions Milt has set down for us. Grace will be starting the first grade. What if one of the Beal kids tries to get fresh with her?"

Buck said, "Let's try it Milt's way first and see what happens. The three of us have always been able to get along without Milt telling us what we had to do."

Chapter Seven

Late in the summer of 1929, we weren't through thrashing when it was almost time for school to start. This would be our first year at this country school that was located about three miles from our house. Our school bus would be a horse and a burro, Babe and old Jack. I didn't like to ride Jack, he was too slow. Grace was six and starting the first grade so she and Buck would ride Babe.

That summer the Platner boys would ride over on Sunday afternoons and we would go swimming in Beaver Creek on Uncle Will's homestead. Usually Orian, Otis, Joe and sometimes Frank would go with Howard, Buck, Duane and me. When I complained about not having a real horse to ride to school, Otis suggested we get one of the horses running loose on the open range.

When Fred Henderson who had been raising horses went broke, the bank took over his ranch. There was no place for his horses to go but the open range. The open range consisted of land where homesteaders had starved out. Henderson's and many others' horses just ran loose and no one seemed to claim them.

Otis Platner told me if I saw a horse I liked he would break it to ride for me. The next time he came over to go swimming I had a horse in the corral for him to try to ride. We put a saddle on her and he rode her until she quit bucking. Then it was my turn. I preferred riding her without a saddle because that was the way Duane and I would ride her to school. She bucked a little at first without throwing me off, then she calmed down. Duane got on her behind me and we rode to the swimming hole that same day. We named her Liz because that was the brand on her left hip.

On our way to the swimming hole Otis challenged Howard for a race. Howard was riding Babe. Buck was on the same horse with Otis. Howard knew there was no way Otis's horse could beat Babe in a race even if Buck wasn't riding behind Otis. With Duane behind me I held Liz back and watched the race. Howard was way ahead when I saw Otis's horse go down. Buck went sailing off and landed in a ditch. The horse didn't try to get up at first and when Otis picked himself up the first thing he did was check on his horse who had its head doubled back under it. I asked if Buck was hurt and Otis said he wanted to see if his horse had a broken neck first.

Buck kidded Otis, "You think more of the horse than you do of me."

"The Boss would raise hell if I broke that horse's neck." They always called their dad the boss. Neither Buck nor the horse was hurt.

We never did know who turned Liz out to fend for herself. Even though she liked to buck a little, usually when I first got on, Duane and I had a horse to ride to school instead of old Jack.

Buck decided instead of waiting until school started we should ride over and find out exactly where the school house was located. We knew it was somewhere on the other side of Beal's ranch. We thought the three of us (Buck, Duane and me) could take care of ourselves in case we saw the Beal kids. The school board knew we would be attending. George Beal was on the school board and he agreed it was okay for us to cross his place to get to the school.

As we rode up to the first gate that opened into Beal's ranch there were two kids on a horse as if waiting for us.

"Let me do the talking," Buck said, before we were in hearing range.

As we got closer one of them got off their horse and opened the gate for us.

"Hi," he said. "My name is Joseph F. Beal and this is my brother Harold. You must be the Sundance kids."

"We went to school in Sundance last year," Buck said and told them our names.

I thought, so these are the Beal kids I had been so worried about.

Joe, the oldest, wasn't as big as Duane and we always considered him a runt. Harold looked even smaller. The way they were so polite I figured they were afraid of us and wouldn't be starting any fights. I could see they didn't want to give us any trouble.

"We thought we'd ride over and find the school house before school started," Buck said.

"Can we go with you?" Joe asked. "We'll show you the way."

"That would be great if you would," Buck agreed.

As we rode along, I soon came to the conclusion Joe and Harold were two friendly kids and to think our dad would never let us play with them all this time. This happened despite they were our closest neighbor living only a mile from our house.

The school house was one room about 14 feet by 20 feet, the same as the school where I had started the first grade. It was located in a sheltered ravine with a pump at the well to supply drinking water for us and our horses. Like most Wyoming country schools there were two outside back houses, one for the boys and one for the girls. There was no barn for our horses but several trees where we could tie them in the shade and plenty of level area near the school house for playgrounds.

The Beal kids told us there would be 11 kids in school altogether: Gene and Helen Guilford, both would be in the fifth grade; Leona, and Kenneth Canfield in the sixth grade; Rachel Canfield in the fifth grade; Joe Beal would be in the seventh grade and his brother Harold, the sixth grade. Buck would be in the seventh grade, Duane in the fourth grade, Grace first grade and I in the fifth grade. I was glad that out of 11 kids in school, four would be in the same grade with me. Our teacher would be Mrs. Jessie.

I was anxious for school to start now that I saw the school house, Duane and I had a real horse to ride not a donkey and we had new friends in the Beal kids. I didn't even care if they called us the Sundance kids because at least our new school friends wouldn't try to refer to us as hicks from the country.

We raised a fair crop of flax and wheat that was ready to thrash. Milt bought a nearly new Chev truck on credit. He made a deal with Carl Platner, the Platner kid's dad, to use Milt's new tractor with Platner's thrashing machine on the thrash run. Howard ran a bundle wagon. A bundle wagon was used to haul the bundled grain from the field to the thrasher. Milt's job was to stay with the tractor to see that it ran okay.

Running a bundle wagon is about as hard work as anything you can do. First you pitch the heavy bundles of grain from the field onto the wagon, then unload them one at a time into the thrashing machine. You have to keep your turn with the other four to six wagons so there is no waiting for your load of bundles.

Once Milt got the tractor running in the morning and they started thrashing, he more or less just watched everyone else work until quitting time. Buck helped pitch the bundles onto the wagons in the field. His job was called spike pitching.

55

CANFIELD SCHOOL 1929—Front row left; Helen Guilford, Grace Kaiser, Duane Kaiser, Harold Beal, and Joe Beal. Second row left; Eugine Guilford, Kenneth Canfield, Link Kaiser and Buck Kaiser. Back row left; Leona Canfield, Mrs. Jessie (teacher) and Rachel Canfield.

When Buck was helping thrash, Duane and I had to do the chores at home. Eunice had a job that summer working in the post office and stayed in town. Helen helped milk cows until high school started, then she moved back to town where she and Eunice rented rooms and they both attended high school. Grace sometimes helped bring water from the well and helped our mother in the house. The chores consisted of feeding the pigs, feeding and milking the cows, hauling water from the well up the hill to the house and cutting and bringing in the wood for both cooking and heating. Cutting wood included bringing in the logs to be cut. Milt or Howard never helped do any of these chores, as long as we stayed on the ranch. They considered chores to be kids' work. Bingo, our big dog, helped Grace pull the sled with a five-gallon cream can of water when we had enough snow. I guess Bingo had to earn his keep like the rest of us.

By the time we started thrashing our own grain, Milt forgot all about how he promised each one of us a patch or a field of flax for working all summer. He said if he had to buy the groceries so we could eat, the money that came in was all his. He often reminded us we had to earn our keep. Howard didn't get the money from his field of flax either and he worked harder than Milt.

Milt seemed to owe everyone money, including Scotchy Roberts for the tractor and other farm machinery, rent on a couple of places, and payments were past due on the truck. Wheat and flax didn't bring the prices it had brought the previous year and the yield was a lot less than what Milt expected. The taxes had to be paid on the homestead and nothing had been paid on the mortgage for the money Dad had borrowed.

When we had gone to school in Sundance, Buck and I could work and earn money for our clothes. When we went to the Hewes school we trapped muskrats on Beaver Creek. At this school Beaver Creek was to far away. We set what traps we had for weasels, skunks, bobcats, coyotes and badgers. Muskrat traps were okay for weasels and skunks, but not big enough for the other fur bearing animals. We had enough money left from what we earned in Sundance for new clothes when school started but if we wanted a warm coat we would have to take one away from a coyote or a couple of skunks first.

Milt didn't give Buck, Duane or me a cent for working all summer. Buck stayed home during thrashing until the county superintendent of schools talked to our mother about Buck missing so much school.

Going to this school after spending two and half years in Sundance was quite an adjustment. There weren't enough kids to play football. Even when we played one-o-cat, which was baseball when you don't have enough for two teams, we had to let the girls play to have enough players. Our teacher let us put a basketball hoop on the back of the school house so we played that a lot. We had to show the other kids how to play because they had never even seen a game played. Most of the kids were friendly. Sometimes Leona Canfield, who was my age, would argue about the rules even though she had never seen a basketball before. The Canfields went to Upton to do their shopping since it was as close for them as Sundance was for us. I didn't mind it when they called Buck, Duane and me the Sundance Kids. We sometimes had friendly arguments about if Sundance or Upton was the best town, sometimes the arguments weren't so friendly. Leona liked to brag about their Buick that was only two years old. One time she asked me if they sold shoestrings in Sundance. My shoestring had worn out so I replaced it with a piece of soft copper wire. I think she knew I didn't have the nickel it took to buy a new pair. I was mad enough to punch her in the nose but I couldn't because she was a girl.

When the weather got cold it was sure a lot worse to ride three miles than walk three blocks as we did in Sundance. Duane and I rode Liz without a saddle because it was warmer. She turned out to be a good horse to ride to school. She would only buck when I first got on her after school, when she had been tied to a tree all day. I would get on first without Duane and buck her out before I'd let Duane get on behind me. Our teacher would yell at me as if she was afraid I was going to get hurt or something. I couldn't see what her concern was at the time, after all I was almost 12 years old and had ridden horses to school when I was only seven. Liz was okay after she got warmed up. It's very hard to stay on a bucking horse if someone is on behind. I still remembered the time Duane pulled us both off and he got cut by the axe.

The other kids brought oats for their horses. Milt wouldn't let us have any of the ground barley for our horses. Buck and I would sneak it out, sometimes half a sack at a time so we could take it to school when Milt wasn't watching. Our horses usually had grain one way or another, without Milt's knowledge.

We made our spending money by trapping fur-bearing animals. Buck caught a coyote using a dead horse for bait. He got 16 dollars for the coyote pelt, it was more than the horse was worth when it was alive. Buck was able to buy a new warm sheepskin coat and I got his old one.

Just before the New York stock market took its famous plunge in 1929, the Sundance Bank demanded Milt pay the 600 dollar note that was due. Milt didn't have the money so the bank took all our cattle. The bank allowed Milt only enough to pay off the note and wouldn't let us keep even one cow for our own milk. A week later the cattle were worth much less than what Milt had owed the bank. We ended up with hay and no cattle to feed it to.

When Milt couldn't make the payments on the truck the dealer in Upton asked him to bring it in so he could store it in a garage for the winter. They told Milt he could have it back in the spring, when he could continue with the payments. They sold the truck the first chance they got and Milt lost what he had already paid.

Milt sold the hay that winter to Nefsys on the SY ranch. Their ranch included the west side of Crook County and parts of Weston and Campbell Counties, their total spread was about 100,000 acres altogether with leased land. Some said they had 3,000 head of cattle grazing their range. Milt sold them our hay. They brought some of their herd bulls over to our place instead of hauling the hay over to their ranch on Kara Creek. We agreed to feed their bulls until the hay was all gone.

They measured the hay stacks and the tonnage was to be determined by the total square footage. They had agreed to pay 10 dollars a ton. Tom Nefsy insisted on using a way of figuring the square footage as if the stacks sloped in from the bottom and came to peak at the top. In other words he called the stacks a triangle. They were much closer to a rectangle shape. By using his method they would pay for a lot less hay than was actually there. It meant Milt got a lot less than 10 dollars a ton for the hay. Tom Nefsy sat at our table with a cup of coffee that my mother poured for him as he went through his figures. After he finished his figuring he insisted on using his method or no deal. As he sipped his coffee, he watched our mother fix our school lunches that consisted of eight scrambled egg sandwiches for the four of us and a pint jar of stewed prunes. Our mother carefully divided two scrambled eggs to make the eight sandwiches. This was our usual school lunch. Sometimes we had stewed dried peaches or wild fruit instead of prunes. I guess Mr. Nefsy was more concerned about the cost of feeding 3,000 head of cattle than whether or not we had enough to eat.

Milt was in no position to hold out for what he knew was a fair price for the hay. He had to accept Tom Nefsy's terms. This was the only money we would have for a long time. Dad didn't send money home anymore.

When Nefsy's stock had eaten all the hay they paid for, they were supposed to come and take the herd back to their ranch. By the time the hay was all gone, the snow was also gone and they left their bulls until they had eaten all of our good winter pasture. Our horses had a hard time finding anything to eat until the grass grew again in the spring.

Mrs. Hewes would come over and see my mother from time to time and bring some magazines and the back issues of The Sunday Denver Post. I looked forward to the funny papers. It didn't matter if they were a month old if we hadn't seen them they were new to us. In the spring our mother always saw to it that Mrs. Hewes took home a good supply of our rhubarb. Ours was the red kind and all our neighbors liked it.

I noticed an ad in one of the magazines. The Kodak company was giving a camera free to any one born in 1918. It would be on the basis of first come, first served at all their dealers until they ran out. You had to be accompanied by a parent or guardian. The drug store in Sundance sold Kodaks and I knew I had to be there the first day to get one. My mother said she couldn't go with me that day so I asked if I could ride a horse to town by myself. Eunice, who was going to high school, could be my guardian.

"You would have to be there before she starts school in the morning and then maybe they wouldn't let you call her your guardian," my mother said.

"It's worth a try," I said. If I leave home by six I can be there when they open the store at eight and Eunice can still get to school on time."

"How about you missing school?"

"If my teacher says it's okay can I go?"

"Well I don't know. I guess so if your teacher agrees."

My teacher did agree so Eunice and I were waiting when Mr. Faulkes opened his drug store.

"Where are your parents, err I mean where is your mother?" Mr. Faulkes asked.

Sundance was a small town of about 400 people and everyone knew my dad had left.

"Eunice is my guardian," I told him.

"Aren't you living on the ranch?"

"Yes."

"What time did you leave the ranch?"

"It was six o'clock. I rode a horse to town."

"I think you deserve a Kodak if any kid ever did."

I got the Kodak. It was somewhat like the one I had planned to buy before Mrs. Zane died. Mr. Faulkes even gave me a free roll of film.

That spring Scotchy extended Milt enough credit to get the crops in. Milt still owed him money for the tractor and binder. In order to farm the land Milt had leased on shares from Ben Justice he needed a plow and disk for the new tractor plus a seader for planting. Scotchy delivered them with nothing down. We no longer had any cows to milk so we couldn't sell cream and Milt had lost his truck because he didn't make the payments.

Milt promised us so much a month instead of our own patch of flax. I don't remember how much it was because we never saw any of it anyhow.

Our mother got a letter from Grandma Perrigoue, her mother in Washington state, who said she was going to come out to Wyoming for a visit. I knew it was too much to ask for but I hoped she wanted us all to move to Washington so we wouldn't have to go through another Wyoming winter like the one of 1929 and 1930.

Chapter Eight

In addition to farming the homestead, we had to plant crops on area around the homestead as well as on Black's Flat. By putting a light on the new John Deere tractor, some of the work was done at night. The tractor pulled a plow that turned three furrows at one time making it possible to plow about an acre an hour. With the old walking plow pulled by two horses, an acre a day had been considered a good day's work.

It took about 10 days to convert the 150 acres of level pasture land on Black's Flat into plowed fields and then the new plowed ground was cut up with a disk for planting flax. A harrow was attached behind the planter, or grain drill we called it, so the fields were smooth after being planted. That completed the operation until harvest time.

Buck, Duane and me, "The Sundance Kids," were busy working around home after school and weekends while Milt and Howard farmed the land Milt had rented on shares from Ben Justice on Black's Flat.

I rode Babe all one weekend rounding up the Nefsy bulls so they could be returned to the SY ranch on Kara Creek. I found a few head on Strawberry Hill, a few up the draws east of the house, a few here and a few there. They were scattered all over our pastures. Once, when I got too close behind a bull, he turned and tried to gore my horse. She reared up to get out of his way but he still grazed her with one horn tearing out some of her hair. It was only by luck I didn't fall off or that Babe didn't get gored by that bull.

Even though Milt had the new tractor, Buck and I had to plow the garden and the potato patches with a plow pulled by Pat and Mike, our two work horses. One of us drove the horses while the other held the plow in the furrow. After we got the ground ready, our mother, as usual, helped plant many of the vegetables.

We were all pretty excited getting ready for Grandma's visit. It had been 20 years since our mother had last seen her. Eunice helped build a new back-house using a dinner plate for a pattern for one hole. The other hole had to be bigger.

When we were living in Sundance, and Milt was on the ranch by himself, he used the bunkhouse for a chicken house. Before

Grandma got there we had to move a couple of beds out of the house and set them up in the empty hay loft in the barn. Us five boys would sleep there while Grandma was staying with us. The loft floor was made of 1" by 12" pine boards except one place where our dad had taken a board to make a bench. We needed the bench so Buck, Duane and I could sit down at the table in the house. I liked that a lot better than sitting on an apple box or standing up. Dad had replaced the spot where he borrowed the board with pine poles. That kept hay from falling down on top of the horses and cows. The straw ticks we slept on were mattress sized pillows filled with new wheat straw. After thrashing last fall we didn't have to use hay anymore. Hay sometimes has sticks and it isn't nearly as soft and nice as straw. Grandma would sleep on the bed in the house that had a mattress.

The day Grandma's train arrived in Upton no one was there to meet her so she gave Mr. Dudrey five dollars to bring her and her trunk to our place. I remember I had been planting beans that day and Milt and Howard had borrowed a truck to get a load of tractor fuel from a refinery in Osage. The tractors used a low grade of gas that was between kerosene and gasoline. Milt and Howard were almost home with six 50-gallon barrels of fuel when they tipped over the borrowed truck. No one was hurt and I guess the truck wasn't damaged much but it happened when it was dark and they had to leave it there until daylight the next day.

The last time Grandma was at our place she stayed with our mother when Howard was born. Grandma reminded Milt of the last time she had seen him he was two years old and she had to watch him to keep him from tipping over the chickens' water. Milt laughed and told her he tipped over a lot bigger things now.

Grandma hadn't said exactly how long she was going to stay but we all figured it would be most of the summer. The very next day after she got there, instead of unpacking her trunk she asked about getting someone to take her to Upton so she could take a train back to where she lived in Washington.

She said something about not wanting to be in the way. Our mother pleaded with her to stay.

That afternoon it hailed and rained so hard everyone had to come in the house. We had time to get a mother hen and her baby chicks in their coop before the storm hit. When the rain stopped I found the chicken coop filled with water and the baby chicks were floating around, except the ones that were on the mother hens back. When I yelled, Grandma came to see what was wrong. We gathered all the little chicks in her apron and took them in the house. There were about 75 or 80. I know it was all those that hatched in the incubator a few days before. Everybody helped and we revived many of the nearly drowned chicks by blowing in their mouths. If Grandma hadn't shown us what to do we would have lost a lot more.

When the hail storm hit, Buck was out looking for the horses and he had to wait under a tree until the storm passed. He came in right after we brought all the baby chicks back to life that had almost drown. Buck was all excited because one of the horses was very sick. He couldn't get it to come back to the corral. He told Grandma how it acted and she said it sounded as if the horse was sick from blow flies. Horses will die sometimes if they aren't wormed. She fixed up some stuff with tar and turpentine she said would cure the sick horse of worms, but it must have been too late because the horse died.

That first day Grandma was there so many things had gone wrong. We all felt bad, thinking she was leaving, that is until Grandma started unpacking her trunk. She decided to stay a little longer. One of the things she wanted to do she said was find the graves of her four children who had died in Spearfish before my mother was born. Milt told her he would have time to take her to the cemetery in Spearfish in a few days. He had to go down there anyhow on business.

Milt bought two horses from a guy with the understanding that if he didn't want them after he tried them out he could return them and not pay anything. One turned up lame and the other we named Spook became Milt's favorite saddle horse. Milt paid half of the price they agreed on for both horses and he took the lame horse back. A neighbor asked Milt if he could borrow Spook to roundup some cattle. Milt didn't know it was just a trick way of getting Spook to the guy Milt bought him from. The horse was taken to a ranch 40 miles away near Spearfish, South Dakota. When Milt went to see the guy to get Spook back he demanded the money for both horses. He wouldn't give Milt the money or Spook. Because the horse was then in another state, the guy couldn't be charged with horse stealing without getting the governors of both states to cooperate. Milt lost his horse. I heard the same guy was later charged with stealing cars.

Grandma stayed with a cousin in Spearfish a few days before coming back to our place. She found the graves of her four children who had died with diphtheria in 1883.

Our mother hadn't found time to put patches on our overalls because of the time she spent preparing for Grandma's visit. I remember Grandma did a good job patching mine. She even put patches on the patches.

Grandma told us about our other grandma, our dad's mother, who lived in Washington.

Helen told our visiting grandma, she was the good grandma and Dad's mother was the bad grandma.

Grandma Perrigoue corrected Helen in no uncertain terms.

"She is a good lady," Grandma said "and there is no reason you shouldn't all like her. Your father's quarrel should not be your quarrel."

She told me about a cousin named Roger who lived in Washington. She said I should write to him. Roger was the son of our aunt that got control of our granddad's estate.

"Because your father doesn't get along with his sister is no reason you and Roger can't be friends," Grandma said.

I thought a lot about what she said. She thought it was good that we were now friends of George Beal and his two boys, Joe and Harold.

School was out for the summer. We would go down to Beal's place and play and they would come up to ours. If they were at our place at mealtime they would eat with us.

After I ate at their house, Eunice would always ask me what I had to eat. I thought she was too nosy so I would tell her fried chicken, ice cream, chocolate cake, potato salad and all the good things I could think of. It took her a long time to get wise to me. To this day I don't think she will believe me when I tell her what I have had for dinner.

Mr. Beal invited Buck, Duane and me to go fishing down on Sand Creek with his boys. Our mother wouldn't let me go at first because my pants had too many patches on them. I knew Huckleberry Finn wore overalls like mine but maybe not with quite as many patches. Grandma found an old pair of short pants called knickers that Milt or Howard used to wear when they were my size. Grandma sewed them up so I got to go fishing. I felt silly wearing those pants because kids never wore knickers anymore. But I had to if I wanted to go fishing with the Beals that day. We all caught fish, a lot bigger fish than we ever did in Beaver Creek. Later my mother was going to make me wear those knickers to town, but just before we left I tore them so bad I couldn't go. I knew if any of the kids I knew in town saw me in those pants there would be a fight, it was better that I stay home.

When it was time to put up the hay everyone had to help. Milt rebuilt an old hay-stacker he bought from a friend so we didn't have to pitch the hay upon the stack by hand. Milt drove a team on the buckrake that pushed the hay on the stacker teeth. Duane and I kept the hay from sticking to the buckrake when Milt backed away. We would pitch the loose hay back on the stacker before it was raised up to the haystack. Buck drove a horse that pulled the rope that raised the load of hay. Howard was on the stack spreading the hay around when he wasn't working for Hewes. When Howard didn't help, I drove the horse and Buck worked on the stack.

Grandma was 75 years old that summer. She, our mother and Grace would walk up to the field and watch us stack hay. When Grandma found an especially good bunch of alfalfa, she would hand it to me and tell me to put it in center of the stack so it wouldn't get snowed on. The cows will like that next winter, she would say. I guess she forgot we didn't have any cows since the bank took them all.

When we were through haying the first cutting, Howard drove the tractor with Milt on the binder cutting the flax, wheat, barley and oats. On the second cutting, Buck drove the team on the mower and rake. Duane and I helped Buck make hay until Milt had me drive the tractor on the binder because Howard had to work for Hewes so we would have money for groceries. Sitting down driving the tractor was a lot easier than pitching hay all day. I remember how tired I got in the heat and dust that summer. It was as if my butt was glued to that tractor seat all the daylight hours. The tractor seat was metal with holes and grooves that were supposed to help keep it cool. After being stuck to it for over 12 hours my rear end felt like a burnt waffle. I could still feel the vibrations of the tractor and grain binder long after we quit at sundown.

One night when I was almost too tired to eat, and that was about as tired as I could get, I stayed in the house and listened to Milt and Grandma talk before I dragged myself up to my bed in the hay loft. Grandma told Milt she had a dairy farm in Washington state that he could rent and she would help him get started. The summers weren't as hot and the winters weren't as cold as Wyoming. Everything was green and not dried out. We kids could milk the cows and there was a good school nearby. I thought it sounded like what our mother wanted for a long time. Milt didn't say yes and he didn't say no. I was sure he couldn't turn her down. I went to my bed in the barn that night hoping we had spent our last cold winter in Wyoming. I dropped off to sleep content that we would soon be moving to Washington.

After the grain was all cut with the binder it was time to start thrashing. Buck and I drove a bundle wagon. He was 14 and I was 12 that summer. When Milt traded help with the other farmers he got credit for one man for the two of us. No one complained about us not keeping up or doing our share of the work. It usually worked out so that we did more than the work of one man. The spike pitchers who helped load the wagons in the field would help the other guys load because they saw two of us.

The best part about thrashing was that each place where we thrashed the women folk tried to outdo each other with their cooking. When we thrashed at the Pritzkau's place they complained to Milt that Buck and I did the work of a man, but we ate as much as two men. After working all day pitching bundles I think I ate as much as two men myself. It would have taken more than one complaint to get me to eat less.

While Buck and I ran the bundle wagon, Milt's tractor powered the thrasher (the machine that separated the grain from the straw). He would fuel up the tractor and get it going at about daylight. The tractor had to be fueled up again at noon when we shut down to eat and feed our horses. The rest of the time Milt only had to watch the tractor run. We usually thrashed until it was too dark to see. One day, Willard Canfield, one of the neighbors who drove a team on a grain wagon, must have thought I

Link, 12 years old, helps Buck haul bundles when it's time to thrash the grain.

looked tired so he told me to rest while he pitched our load of bundles into the thrashing-machine. When you run a grain wagon you drive the wagon under a spout of the thrashing-machine and wait until your wagon is full. Your work is mostly shoveling the grain from the wagon into the granary, so Mr. Canfield was still doing his work while he was letting me rest. That night Milt gave me hell for letting Mr. Canfield unload our wagon.

I told Milt, "I hadn't asked for help. He must have thought I looked tired."

"Then don't look tired."

I didn't argue with Milt but when you're 12 years old and you pitch heavy bundles day after day from daylight until dark it is pretty hard to fake it. It didn't do any good to give Milt any lip.

I looked forward to the start of school and the county fair in Sundance. That fall we went to two fairs, one in Sundance and the one in Upton. They had a merry-go-round at the fair in Sundance and a guy named Fred who collected your tickets, was sweet on Helen. Buck won a little cedar chest playing bingo and he gave it to Grandma for her birthday.

We went to the Upton fair because Grandma had to get on a train there that took her back to Seattle. I had never been to Upton before, in fact the only town I had been in besides Sundance was Beulah when we went fishing with the Beals. Beulah was a couple of gas stations, a grocery store, a cafe, a dance hall, a flour mill that ran part of the time and a few houses. Upton was about the size of Sundance and it had a railroad. I had never seen a train before I went to the Upton fair that fall.

I hated to see Grandma leave for her home in Seattle. Milt had told her we would not rent her farm and move to Washington. I couldn't figure out why at the time. I know he promised to pay Scotchy Roberts for all the farming equipment he had bought on time. I guess it would have been a dirty trick to tell Scotchy he could have all his equipment back instead of paying for it.

When the grain was sold there wasn't near enough money to pay the people Milt owed. He tried to keep his promises to pay other people before he paid us kids. We never got a cent of what he promised us for working all summer. Milt saved one bin of barley for our pigs and seed for next spring. Buck and I managed to hide a few sacks of barley where Milt wouldn't find them, for the horses we rode to school. When Milt didn't pay the rent for the Seabuck place, a place he had rented next to the homestead, the landlord came with his truck and took the rest of the barley.

These were days of the Great Depression and even landlords had to look out for their own interest the best way they could. I guess people in cities had a worse time than we did. Our economic depression started two years earlier when Dad stopped sending money home. Before that we only had hard times. When you are already used to going without, having a little less is easier to adjust to. We raised our own potatoes and a couple of pigs had to be butchered, now that there was no grain to feed them. Our mother had canned quite a bit of wild fruit and berries. Milt made a deal with Fred Schloredt, who ran a grocery store, to winter his cattle with our hay. Part of the deal was we could milk some of the cows for our own use as long as we didn't sell cream. If we wanted any new clothes we would just have to find good places to set our traps for fur-bearing animals.

Chapter Nine

After Grandma left for Washington it was time to start another year at the Canfield school. I don't think I liked school as much as I was glad to be rid of the jobs of driving the tractor pulling the binder or pitching bundles on the thrash run. Buck, Duane, Grace and I had the chores to do after school and on weekends. Each night Buck divided the chores in three parts, we called bargains. He always gave Duane first choice, me next and Buck did what was left.

"Does Duane get his pick again before me?" I asked.

"Do you want to make the bargains and get last choice or have me make 'em and I'll take last choice?" Buck asked me. "I think that is only fair since he's smaller. And of course Grace will help ma in the house."

"It ain't fair," Duane said. "I can't split the wood because I ain't big enough, so you always make my job one that takes longer. I always have to find the cows."

"It's okay if you make the bargains," I told Buck, "but don't listen to Duane."

"One bargain will be to get the cows in and carry the water to the house," Buck explained. "Another will be to cut and split the wood, carry it in the house and feed and water the pigs. Or you could feed and milk the cows, feed the calves hay and carry them their water. Duane gets first choice, Link you get second and I'll take what's left."

"It ain't fair," Duane said. "I don't know how to milk. That means I have to go find the cows and I don't know where they are. Why can't Grace help me carry water? She helped Link last winter."

Buck said, "But there was snow then so Bingo could pull a sled. Link filled the five-gallon water can. Grace only started Bingo up the hill and yelled, "get to the house!"

"Besides, it was fun for Grace," I said. "She just hung on to the back of the sled and kept the can from tipping over. I tell you what Duane, I'll go find the cows for you if you'll saw and carry in the wood for me."

"You probably already know where the cows are."

"We can't stand here and argue all night. Ma's about out of

water and wood. Link, if you know where the cows are tell Duane."

"I don't know for sure, but they might be in the trees above Andy's barn where I killed that skunk with a rock, the time it broke out of the trap. If Duane wants to bring in the cows and carry the water then I'll feed the pigs and pack in the wood, if I can use that dry log behind the house we cut and drug in last Saturday."

"I never said I wanted to get the cows and carry the water."

"Well do you?"

"Yes. If I have to, but the cows better be where Link said they are."

Sure I complained at the time, but I'm sure Buck was as fair as he knew how.

In the mornings Buck and I would go find the horses that we rode to school. Our mother never got involved as long as she had water, wood and had no reason to believe the other chores weren't being done. She never knew we stole grain to feed our school horses and Milt and Howard didn't suspect either.

Eunice and Helen were going to school in Sundance. Helen was in high school and Eunice was doing post graduate work. She was preparing to become a teacher. One additional year after high school was all that was required to teach grade schools in Wyoming.

Howard kept busy cutting wood but we couldn't burn any of Howard's wood in our own stoves, even though we helped him sometimes on weekends. His wood was for sale.

Milt had a car and he was always going some place. Carl Platner, The Boss, said all Milt did was ride around on rubber tires while the rest of us stayed home and did all the work. I think, if the truth was known, The Boss did even less work than Milt and he was jealous because he didn't have rubber tires to ride around on. There were six Platner boys that did the work on their ranch.

Milt was good at working on gas engines, especially John Deere tractors. That winter when he overhauled George Water's tractor his pay was a quarter of a beef.

We had a different teacher this year but the big news at school was Guilford's new car. It wasn't really a new one but the second-hand Chev was their first. They were the last of all our neighbors to use a buggy pulled by horses.

I was permitted to shoot our 22-caliber rifle and I usually carried it with me when it was my turn to look after our trap-line. It was a big thrill whenever I succeeded in bringing home a cottontail rabbit, a grouse or a pheasant. When that happened we had meat for dinner. I never shot our shotgun very much mostly because the shells cost almost a nickel apiece while 22 shells were 35 cents for a box of 50. If I missed a rabbit or something I was afraid to tell anybody that I wasted a shell.

Milt had sold all our hay to Fred Schloredt and we had his cattle at our place to feed. Our school horses had to dig through the snow for their food. Buck and I had to get up by daylight to be sure we could find the horses and not be late for school. I can still remember hearing Buck say, "Hurry up or we'll be late. Hurry up or we'll be late for school." He worried a lot about being late for school and had to prod me almost every morning. I guess because he worried I felt I didn't have to. When the temperature was near zero and the ground was covered with snow, we were on foot until we found Babe and Liz. They would be pawing away the snow so they could find dried grass. It wasn't so plentiful after Nefsy's cattle had eaten it so short the spring before. We kept the bridles in the house to keep the bits warm, but by the time we found the horses we usually had to blow on the bits before we could put them in the horses' mouths. Otherwise the frozen bit would stick to their tongues. Before the winter was over we had fed our school horses all of the barley Buck and I had hidden from Milt.

When Spring came, the snow melted and we didn't have to wade through snow, we walked to school. Our horses were in such poor condition Buck was afraid they might get sick or die. I knew Buck was right when he said we needed the exercise and the horses didn't. Liz was in such bad shape she wasn't any fun to ride. She wouldn't even try to buck me off anymore.

It was about three miles to school and we made it a game to see who could get home first, running most of the way. Grace was only seven, in the second grade and couldn't keep up so one of us had to wait for her. When Buck waited for Grace it became a race between Duane and me. Our lunches of a pint jar of stewed prunes and two scrambled eggs spread between eight slices of bread for the four of us was long gone by the time we got home between 4:30 and 5. There was no snacking and the chores had to be done before supper unless, that is, you were the first one home and got to the cold oatmeal left over from breakfast.

On April Fools' day our family would play tricks on each other. Most of the time it was fun and when the victim found it was a trick you would say April fool and everyone would have a good laugh. If the trick had been played on you, you wouldn't get mad. Instead of getting mad you tried to get even.

One April Fools' day after running almost three miles, I beat everyone home from school. When I got into the house I didn't pay any attention to Milt watching me as I got the dish of cold oatmeal. It looked like a little more than usual, one good-sized serving. I put sugar and milk on it before I noticed it smelled different. I started to put a big spoonful into my mouth and noticed just in time that Milt had filled the dish with cow manure and covered the top with oatmeal. It wasn't until I discovered the manure that Milt yelled April fool and laughed like a jackass.

The man that held the mortgage on our homestead hadn't received a cent, I guess, since our dad first borrowed 1,000 dollars. He told our mother if she would sign the homestead over to him so he wouldn't have to go through the legal expense of foreclosing, we could still live there. He only wanted enough rent money to pay the taxes. That sounded like a good deal because we had to pay the taxes when it had been ours anyhow. The rent hadn't been paid the past year as agreed because 50 dollars for the taxes was still a lot of money. Howard agreed to use the money he earned from selling wood. The wood had to be cut by hand because we sold the power drag saw last year when the taxes were due. Milt made Howard some kind of promise to repay him when they sold the crops the next fall.

Milt promised that someday we would buy the homestead back. In the meantime, since we would be living there we would build a bigger house and it would be closer to the well. Milt promised if Duane and I would cut the logs and peel them we could have our own bedroom. He said that would be a good job for us next summer.

If we had a new and bigger house, if it rained a lot so the

73

crops yield was good, if flax was again worth four dollars a bushel and wheat a dollar a bushel, maybe, just maybe, Milt was right in not taking Grandma up on her deal to rent her dairy farm in Washington. It sounded like too many ifs but we had to believe something.

One day John Mullenbrink and Fred Schloredt visited our ranch. It seemed Mr. Schloredt, who had bought our hay, wanted to see how well we were feeding his cattle. They went with Milt to get a load of hay, a job Buck and I always did. I think Milt was trying to make it look as if he fed the cattle all the time. Schloredt was satisfied we were taking good care of his stock. Milt laughed after they left at how John asked a lot of questions, such as how big was the homestead, how much hay did we raise, how many cattle would it feed, etc. Milt thought it was none of his business so he bragged about what a good ranch it was. He told John that a couple of the good hay fields we rented were part of the homestead.

Milt didn't laugh anymore when he found out why John was asking all the questions. A few days later he learned John had bought the homestead. We had to move. Milt by then had paid the money for the taxes as was agreed. Milt was told that money was for last year's rent and the place now belonged to John Mullenbrink.

It didn't make any difference that he had been promised we could stay there if we paid the 50 dollars. Nothing was in writing and we had to leave as soon as school was out at the end of May. We had been farming rented land all around the home place. The only place we were renting that had any housing was Uncle Will's place. The house was even smaller than the 16-feet by 22-feet house we had been living in. There was a good spring for water and the barn was bigger and better. It was located on the west side of our other rented land and you had to go down a steep hill from our other fields to get to the house. Part of it was on Beaver Creek where we had gone swimming with the Platners. It would be about a mile farther to school. We had no choice. We had to move when school was out.

The land we had been farming surrounded three forty-acre tracks of government land in such a way no one could get to them without going across our place. We had been using this land without paying any rent or taxes. That had changed now with Mullenbrink on the homestead. Milt talked Howard into filing on these three forties for his homestead before Mullenbrink got the idea of claiming a couple of the good fields we had been farming. For some reason Howard, not Milt, applied for a government seed loan. The money was needed to buy tractor fuel and seed to plant the crops. I think Milt owed Scotchy so much money he may not have been eligible for a loan.

Moving from the house where all eight Kaiser kids were born was a very emotional thing for me. When we moved to Sundance to go to school, that was different, we knew we could come back whenever we wanted to. This move was like uprooting a tree that had sent down eight roots of different sizes. It was a sign of failure. I couldn't talk about it at school. When the main tap root, our dad, had left, the tree was in trouble. Even though we didn't have very many possessions to move, it was tough to leave the place that created memories of growing up. Those memories we could never move. It didn't help me any to know our whole country was in a depression and people in the cities were a lot worse off than we were. Banks were failing everywhere. Why hadn't Milt accepted Grandma's offer and let us move to Washington state? Maybe Dad was right? Maybe we four younger kids should have been put in a home and offered up for adoption? With Buck guiding us like our mother and father, we four younger kids were like a different family anyhow.

We always relied a lot on chickens in the summer because without any kind of refrigeration it wasn't possible to butcher our own fresh meat. In order to have fried chicken throughout the summer it was necessary to have baby chicks hatch at different times. Several hens were given hatching eggs in the barn on the ranch we would be moving to when school was out. It was my job to ride over to our new place each night after school and feed and water the setting hens.

This gave me an opportunity to look over the place a lot before we moved. I thought a lot and maybe brooded a little about having to move. There were some things that made it exciting including some advantages and some disadvantages.

We would be closer to Beaver Creek for swimming and we could trap muskrats again. This was where Buck and I used to sneak off without Duane and go fishing, like the time when we had to throw the fish away so no one would know where we had been. We could fish now and keep all our fish. The water supply was a spring that was closer to the house than the well on the homestead. We wouldn't have to haul water up a steep hill. The water was not as hard with minerals and tasted better. The land near the house should be better for raising a garden and maybe we could grow watermelons. We boys could sleep in the garage that was already built and we could build a bunk house before winter. The log cabin was located among pine trees with the smell of pine in the spring air. There would be shade in the hot summer and the wood supply was better and closer to the house. We could still go to the same school although it would be about four miles instead of three.

It took several wagon loads to get all our stuff moved from the homestead to our new home. Duane and I went back to the homestead to get the last load. The main thing we were supposed to get was the water trough at the well. Our dad had made it by hollowing out the center of a log. John Mullenbrink had moved in before we had a chance to get all of our stuff moved out. When Duane and I went to the well to load the trough it was full of water.

I tipped it over and we were loading it when John approached and said, "What the hell Do you think you're doing?"

"Taking our trough," I told him.

"What the hell do you need it for? You don't have a well any-more."

My thoughts were, yea thanks to you, you old son of a bitch.

What I said was, "Our dad made it and we can use it for a pig trough."

"You going to take the God dam pump too?"

"Not this load," I told him.

Milt wanted to know what I said to make John so mad.

"We have to get along with him," Milt told me.

I didn't answer Milt but I thought, maybe you do but I don't.

We had to cross the old homestead, John's place, getting to land we were farming and going to our school.

After we got settled into our new home the first job Buck and I had was to cut pine trees for a log bunkhouse. We sometimes called this ranch the May place because Uncle Will had sold it to his brother-in-law, Lee May.

Uncle Will owned it again because May had left in such a hurry he didn't even take his furniture out of the house. We were living over the hill on the homestead at the time when the sheriff and a deputy came to our house and asked directions on how to get to where Lee May lived. You couldn't drive there from our homestead in the cars they had in those days because their car would never have been able to get back up the steep hill above Mays' house. The sheriff and his deputy left their car at our ranch and walked the two miles or so in from the backside. I call it the backside because the usual road Lee May used to get to Sundance was along Beaver Creek. The sheriff and his deputy were gone all day before they came back to get their car. They never said what their business was, at least I didn't know. This was during prohibition and Helen told me some wild story about how May was making whiskey and the sheriff was looking for the still. Helen also told me about the Easter Bunny, the Tooth Fairy, Santa Claus and she told Howard I killed his rabbit, even though she stepped on it.

One day we were exploring in the big canyon above the house and we found an old stove. I think Howard knew what he was looking for when he looked in some thick brush and found a big copper container. It was as big as a barrel and the top looked like a huge teakettle. There was a lot of copper tubing like the fuel line on the tractor except this was bigger. There was a bunch of oak boxes with lids nailed on top with holes that could be plugged with corks. The insides of the oak boxes were charred as if they had been in a fire. I never knew whether May left because he knew the sheriff was looking for him or maybe he found him and told him to leave.

We cut the top out of the copper kettle and used it to soak barley for the hogs.

Something else was different when we moved into the May place. Buck had finished the eighth grade and would be going to high school and staying in Sundance the next year. I would no longer have him telling me to hurry up or I'd be late for school. It would be my responsibility more or less to look out for Duane and Grace. I would no longer have Buck helping with the chores or helping Duane and I sneak grain for our school horses. It had been Buck that decided we wouldn't smoke tobacco when we went to school in Sundance even though Milt and Howard smoked when they went to school in Lead. It was Buck who said we wouldn't fight the Beal kids and we became good friends. It was Buck who wouldn't let me make Liz buck all the time or teach her to jump a pole fence. He said we might both get hurt. It was Buck who wouldn't let me put a frozen bit in a horse's mouth. He said it would pull the skin off their tongue. He had taught me how to set steel traps for wild animals so we could sell their furs to buy most of our own clothes. He showed me how to aim the 22 rifle so I could hit what I was shooting, or at least part of the time. As long as I could remember he did my worrying for me. He said it was my thinking. Sure we fought when we were younger, even when I knew he would win the fight. If I could make his nose bleed before someone stopped the fight I felt as I had won. It was like me getting a hamburger while he got a steak. He had been my guide and conscience. I guess nobody likes what their conscience tells them to do, not all the time. I knew life would be different with Buck going to high school in Sundance and I would see him only on weekends.

Chapter Ten

The first summer we lived on the May place, I drove the tractor pulling the binder until dark every day for over a month straight. We never got a very early start in the morning because Milt liked to sleep late. I helped Buck and Duane do the morning chores until Milt was ready to go. Milt traded work with Mr. Platner, called "The Boss" by his kids. We did binding for The Boss in exchange for work his boys did for Milt. Anyhow, my 13-year-old butt was glued to that tractor seat from early July until we started thrashing about the middle of August.

A great portion of the land we rented was not farmland because it was too steep, covered with trees, rocky or all of the above. Part of the area that couldn't be plowed was pasture-land but we had no stock of our own. The cows we took care of for Schloredt had to be near where we lived so we could milk some of them. Milt made a deal with John Mullenbrink, who lived on our old homestead. They rented pasture to a sheep man and John got the job of herding the sheep because Milt needed all of us to work for him.

Buck and I wanted Duane to attend to the pigs and that would be all the chores he would have to do. I think we were tired of him griping all the time about us making him do as much as we did. He was a lot smaller than either Buck or me. He finally agreed to take care of the pigs if we wouldn't call him the pig tender.

When Milt and I were binding we had to stop often to oil or grease the moving parts of the binder. It was hot and dry while we worked in a cloud of dust most of the time. My face and the binder and tractor were always covered with dirt. It was impossible to keep the dirt out of the bearings or off the moving chains. Under those conditions, drive chains and bearings had to be replaced. If it couldn't be fixed with bailing wire, Milt would always wait until we broke down before he replaced anything.

One time a bearing gave out and the binder would no longer tie the bundles. It was necessary to take several parts off to get to the worn out part. After working at it for several minutes without the proper tools, Milt lost his temper and took a hammer and smashed the wheels and cogs that were in his way to get to the part that had to be replaced.

When Milt got mad I did my best to stay out of his way. I suppose it could have been funny to someone watching but not to me. I was scared of him and he warned me not to tell anyone how the binder got smashed up. Whenever we broke down and it couldn't be fixed with bailing wire, Milt would go to town for new parts and I would help Buck and Duane either shock grain, put up hay or whatever they were doing until Milt got the binder fixed.

The summer of 1931 was a very poor farming season. We didn't get enough rain for a good yield and the grain prices were way down.

Eunice got a teaching job that fall at a school that was located way over on the other side of Sundance. She made close to a hundred dollars a month. Our mother always insisted school for us kids was more important than anything else. Eunice proved that you can make a lot more money with an education. She paid the rent in Sundance for Helen and Buck so they could go to high school. The year before, Helen had been writing to her dad and sweet-talked him into sending her a little money, but it wasn't enough to pay the bills. Eunice had to pay off the grocery bill after she started teaching.

Helen was in her senior year in high school and still writing to Fred Schock.

Milt didn't come close to making the payments on the farm equipment. There was no money for Howard to pay on the seed loan he had borrowed last spring from the government to put in the crops.

When Scotchy Roberts pressed Milt for money Milt agreed to work for him. Milt stayed in Sundance with Helen and Buck, and drove a truck for Scotchy hauling freight.

When I needed a new pair of shoes Eunice gave me enough money to buy them. I had intended to pay her back but I wasn't having much luck trapping muskrats on Beaver Creek.

Howard had a lot more traps than Duane or me, besides he took the best places to set his traps. The same grade pelts we had been paid a dollar and a half for last winter were now bringing only 25 cents. Howard had built a log house on the place he homesteaded, but never lived in it. I don't think he was able to find any water in the well he dug.

With Milt not there to stop us because he was living in Sundance that winter, Duane and I saw to it that we had hay and grain to feed the horses we rode to school. Almost every weekend Duane and I would cut down an old dry pine tree for firewood and haul a load of hay for our livestock. Before we started down the steep hill from the haystack to the barn we would tie the log behind our load of hay. The log served as a brake to get the load of hay down the steep hill. The hill was so steep when we didn't have a log for a brake we would use the log chain to tie one hind wheel of the wagon so it couldn't turn. If we had the sled, we wrapped the chain around a sled runner so it would dig in and not slide. One time Duane was alone when the chain came unfastened from the hind wheel. The horses couldn't hold the wagon back and just before the wagon loaded with hay went crashing into some trees, the loose chain caught a spoke in the wagon wheel. It was just plain luck both he and the horses weren't killed. We had many close calls that we would laugh about afterwards.

Milt traded some of our hay for an old Maxwell car and he told Howard to deliver the hay. When Howard told him he didn't need the car or he paid too much for it or some other reason, Milt got real mad. He told Howard if he didn't deliver the hay Milt wouldn't pay for any more groceries. We were used to hearing Milt tell Buck, Duane and me we had to earn our keep, but I never heard him talk that way to Howard.

When John Mullenbrink was herding sheep he lost quite a few. We found some stragglers the coyotes had killed. One day while coming home from school, after our first heavy snow, we found a sheep that had almost starved to death. She was so light I was able to get her on my horse so I took her into the barn where Duane and I milked the cows. We kept her inside with the calves while nursing her back to health. We didn't tell Milt for fear he would make us give her to Mullenbrink. It was no problem keeping Milt or Howard from knowing about our sheep because they never helped milk or feed the cows. When our sheep was strong enough, we turned her out and she always stayed with our school horses when they were around. When Milt did find out we had a sheep he had us feed her grain for a while before he butchered her.

The whole country felt the depression more than ever that fall. Joe Beal had to quit high school because they couldn't afford to pay for him to stay in Sundance. When Beals shipped their sheep to Omaha they got a bill for the freight. One farmer took a truck load of oats to Upton to sell and when they offered him six cents a bushel he became so mad he drove away with the back of the truck box open and the oats spilled out on the road on the way home. A friend of George Beal's was broke and had no job so George let him cut wood for his board and tobacco. I remembered when Leona Canfield made fun of me for having copper wire for shoe strings a couple of years before. I somewhat enjoyed it when I saw her dad with his shoes laced up with binder twine. It was the fuzzy kind of string we used in the grain binder to tie bundles of grain together.

Helen found out the Red Cross was distributing flour for free. She signed up for two sacks and had Howard pick it up the next time he was in Sundance. When Milt found out he was very upset. He said, he wasn't going to let any of his family accept charity. So that was the last of the free flour for us that winter. Our mother didn't have any money for everyday clothes so she cut the sleeves off Milt's or Howard's old shirts and wore them for blouses. She made her skirts from flour sacks. She saved her other clothes to wear if she went any place.

The school where Eunice was teaching made her take a cut in pay because people couldn't pay their taxes. Our school district had its credit stopped at the bank so our teacher was paid in warrants. She could cash the warrants for face or full value when the district had money again. The bank and stores would cash them but only pay a part of the face value. If they held them until the district had the money they would get the full amount. The bank in Sundance was one of the few in all the towns around that area that didn't go broke.

Since we weren't allowed to sell the milk from the Schloredt cows we were being paid to take care of, we made cheese. Duane and I were milking four or five cows in the morning before going to school and again after we got home at night. Our mother made about a three-pound mold of cheese every other day. I don't remember how much we had by spring but I know it lasted a long time. We had cheese sandwiches in our school lunches instead of scrambled eggs all the time.

We had a different teacher each year at the Canfield school, probably because we didn't pay them as much as other schools.

Miss Canoy, our teacher this year, seemed to let us kids get out of control. No one knew much about her background. She liked to tease the boys a lot and thought it was fun to embarrass us. One time when Harold Beal had to go to the out-house she put some water in his seat and spilled some on the floor between his seat and the door. When he came back she pretended she was mad and told him next time to ask to go before it was too late. Everyone but Harold thought it was funny.

My voice was changing and I couldn't help it when it would go from a high squeal to a low bass. She told me it was because I was getting too big in my britches and then laughed as if she had said something funny. She threatened to pull us boys off the seat if we stayed too long in the outhouse. This was her idea of fun, but it wasn't to the boy who was her victim at the time.

If Buck had been there I'm sure he would have handled it differently. There were five of us boys in school and we discussed among ourselves what to do to defend ourselves against this embarrassing harassment. We formed a club and held meetings and thought up different ways to get even with our teacher. We wouldn't let the girls attend our meetings so this led to the girls being on the teacher's side.

We caught a weasel, sold the pelt and used the money to buy an official basketball hoop that we put on the back of the schoolhouse. We boys would play basketball with a football we had and wouldn't let the girls play with us.

One day, Kenneth Canfield chased our teacher with a dead bird. She screamed and scrambled upon her desk to get away from him. He made her promise not to punish him or tell his parents before he would take the dead bird away and let her down. She had always acted sweet toward him before that and I think she realized her advances were not understood. He was only trying to get her to leave him alone.

I thought it was strange that when Kenneth tormented her, she made me stay after school. She wouldn't tell me what her problem was until all the rest of the kids had left for home. When she started to cry I couldn't figure out what I had done wrong.

83

"I'm 19 years old," she began between sobs, "and I thought since you are the oldest boy in school you will understand."

"Understand what?" I asked her.

"I don't want to have to go back to that reform school," she said before she broke out crying.

I was scared. I didn't know what I was supposed to be old enough to understand. I had reached the wise old age of 14 only a short time ago and I had no idea what she expected of me. After she calmed down and was able to talk I asked her what she wanted me to do.

"No you don't understand. How could you?" She cried some more before she was able to continue. "As you know I have lost control of this school. Before they hired me to teach here I was in the reform school in Sheridan. That's a jail for girls that have been bad. When they find out I can't control this school they'll make me go back to jail."

She looked at me through real tears, the saddest eyes I had ever seen, a look that made me ashamed of all the tricks we boys had played on her. Then she cried some more.

"I think I should tell you everything about me. I need your help."

"My help?" I asked.

"Yes. You know you are the leader of this school now and not me. These kids will do what you tell them to do. If you say let's play baseball, they play baseball. If you say let's play basketball that is what they'll do."

I had never thought about this before, but since Buck was going to high school I guess I somewhat took charge of Duane and Grace and maybe, as she said, the other school kids too.

"You said you should tell me everything about you so I could help?"

She used a handkerchief to wipe away the tears. "I'll start from the beginning, before I had a problem. I'm from a large family. My dad was a drunk and left my mother with more kids than she could provide for. She said my sister and me, who were the oldest, were boy crazy and she could no longer handle us. She had us committed to the state orphanage in Cheyenne. When I was 15, a girlfriend and I ran away from the home with a couple of boys that were a few years older than us. The boys stole a car and we registered in a hotel in Denver as husbands and wives. That's where we were when the authorities caught up with us."

I was old enough to understand what a girl 15 and a boy 17 pretending to be husband and wife might do in a hotel room in Denver. I wanted to help her but I was afraid of how she might offer to pay me for my help.

"Do you see now why you are the only one that can help and keep me from going back to jail."

"What do you want me to do?" I asked. I had to be sure of what she expected of me.

"Don't tell anyone what I've told you and help me get control of this school again. I'll do whatever you want. Please. I don't want to go back to jail."

I thought of what she said. I knew I could get the kids to stop all the pranks. I realized we had been mean to her.

"I'll do it. I promise." I didn't want her to start crying again.

Her strange smile made me feel uncomfortable.

"I'm so glad," she said. "How can I ever pay you?"

I was thinking of what she had told me. She was only asking me to do what any decent kid should do for his teacher. I felt guilty and ashamed for how we had all acted.

"Think," she said. "There must be something you want. It'll make me feel better if you let me do something for you." She used her handkerchief to wipe up the moisture from the tears where they ran down the front of her dress.

"I can't ask you to do this for me without me returning you some favor."

I knew I had to tell her something. "There is one thing," I was afraid to continue when my voice changed from a high squeak to a low growl.

"Don't be afraid," she said, as she moved close to me, putting her arms around my waist and pressing her warm breasts against my chest that gave me a sensation I had never experienced before.

I squirmed to get loose, but she held me tighter.

"You just name it. Anything."

"There is one thing," I hesitated.

"Yes, go on," she encouraged me.

"If we had a new outdoor official basketball," I blurted out.

She gave me a weird look.

"Have I asked for something that costs too much?"

"Is that what you want the most right now?"

"If we had a basketball it would be easier to get all the kids to stop playing mean tricks on you. We would let the girls play basketball with us again."

Her face was a few inches from mine. She gazed into my eyes and smiled a teasing smile.

"If that isn't asking for too much?" I added quickly. I thought she moved her lips as though she was expecting me to kiss her. I had trouble prying her arms away where she was holding me.

After removing her arms from around my waist she stepped back and gave my hand a motherly pat. She stared at me as though it was the first time she had ever seen me.

"I guess you are a lot better kid than I imagined," she said. "A new official basketball it will be. You go home now and help your brother with the chores."

I have thought a lot about what happened and what could have happened that day I was kept after school. I believe that was the best proposition any 14-year-old kid ever made for the good of both himself and his teacher. Playing basketball became a very important part of my life later.

She taught the rest of the school year. We kids played basketball most all recesses with no more tricks by her or us. Miss Canoy became Mrs. Zane before the school year ended and they were expecting a baby in a few months. I was happy for her because as a wife she no longer had to report to her probation officer or the reform school.

Chapter Eleven

Grandma Kaiser, our dad's mother, who lived in Washington state, died in 1932. Helen graduated from high school that spring. We got word that our dad's sister, my aunt Myrtie, her husband Alton and our cousin Roger, were driving from Washington to Wyoming to see us that summer. Helen had been writing to them and expressed her desire to be a beautician. Aunt Myrtie told Helen she could ride back with them, stay at their place while taking her training so that someday she could open her own beauty salon. The last time they had been to Wyoming was after Granddad had died and they took a trip to Washington, D.C. in their new car. Our dad was home at that time and he told his own mother and sister to stay the hell off his place. It was as Grandma Perrigoue had said, our dad's fight was not our fight and we welcomed our relatives from Washington.

I have to admit, after all I had heard about Aunt Myrtie I felt a little apprehensive about meeting Roger. How could they afford new cars, long motor trips and Roger attending high school in California? It was obvious they were spending money that was from the Kaiser estate, while we were having trouble paying for our groceries. I had never met a first cousin before. Most of our relatives lived in Washington because both my dad's parents and my mother's parents had moved from Wyoming to Washington.

Since Roger was four years older than me, he seemed to look at me as though I was a mere kid. That is normal I guess for an 18-year-old toward a 14-year-old. He was at our house only one day and we all tried to make him feel welcome. The one thing he wanted to see was a porcupine, so Duane found one, roped it and drug it down to the house so Roger could see it. When we talked about the ice hole, where we got our ice all summer when we lived on the homestead, Roger wanted to see it. It was quite a steep hike from where we lived to the ice hole. Roger had trouble keeping up. He said it was because he wasn't used to the high altitude in Wyoming, which was nearly 4,000 feet above sea level compared to almost sea level in Washington. He told us many of the nice things about living in Washington and we should come and see him sometime. I thought when they left with Helen how lucky she was to actually go there. She would get to meet the rest

THE SUNDANCE KIDS—Left; Buck, Link and Duane, the day Duane ropes a porcupine so Cousin Roger can see it.

of our cousins, aunts, uncles and see Grandma Perrigoue again.

We thought 1931 had been a bad year for farming, but it was a boom year compared with the growing season of 1932. The grain we had planted in Black's Flat dried out so much from lack of rain and the hot sun that it was quite apparent it would not mature as grain. In order to salvage what we could, it had to be cut for hay. Buck and I did most of the mowing. Milt traded our help with the Boss. Part of the time we mowed for him when his hay was ready, then one of the Platner boys mowed for us. Sometimes we had three mowers going in the field at one time. Howard worked for Hewes in order to buy groceries and pay a little on the government loan owed from the previous year.

When Helen wrote from Washington she said things weren't working out the way Aunt Myrtie had promised. She liked Washington as a place to live and enjoyed seeing all our relatives, but living with Aunt Myrtie was something else. Roger was okay, but all Aunt Myrtie seemed to want was Helen for a maid. In

Left; Helen 18, Grace 9 and Eunice 20.

September, Roger and his mother were going to live in Long Beach, California where Roger would be going to high school. Helen was supposed to stay in Arlington and keep house for Alton, Myrtie's husband. Nothing was said about when Helen would attend beautician training as had been promised. In the next letter, Helen told us she had borrowed money from Grandma Perrigoue for her train ticket home and she wanted someone to meet her train in Upton.

Milt got a letter from our dad saying he was stranded down in Arizona, broke and he wanted Milt to send him enough money to get him back to Thermopolis, Wyoming. Milt borrowed whatever Dad said he needed (I think it was 50 dollars) from Eunice, telling her it was needed to buy tractor fuel. I don't think Eunice would have loaned the money to Milt if she had known it was for our dad.

We played basketball during recesses and spare time at school. Buck scheduled a basketball game for our school to play the Sundance junior high school team. It was agreed even though Buck was a sophomore in high school he could play on our team and so could Kenneth Canfield who was a freshman in Upton. We were doing very well even though only about four players on our team were any good at all (Buck, Duane, Kenneth and myself). The referee could see Buck and I were most of our team and we were beating the Sundance team until he fouled Buck out of the game in order to even things up. From then it was like playing with three players. They won but we had a lot of fun in giving them a good run for it.

While attending high school, Buck lived in Sundance in a rented one-room shack that was barely big enough for his bed and a stove so he could cook his own meals. Eunice paid his rent and gave him one dollar a week to buy his groceries.

Scotchy Roberts had started a wood and coal business and Buck got a job splitting and piling wood. I went to town a couple of weekends to help and Buck paid me 25 cents a cord to pile wood while he split it. The job didn't pay much but it kept Buck in groceries. When the wood was all cut and piled he had to quit high school because he couldn't buy groceries on one dollar a week. He hated to tell Eunice he couldn't eat on what she allowed him because we agreed she was doing more than her share already. Milt was no financial help at all. Buck reasoned he could skip the second semester of his sophomore year and make it up by taking five subjects instead of the usual four the remainder of the time he was in high school. I reminded him he would miss his chance to play basketball for Sundance that year. Buck told me he wouldn't make the first team anyway because Rex Bird was a better player than he. I was also concerned if Buck didn't go next year I probably wouldn't get to go either. Buck assured me he was going to finish high school and go on to the University of Wyoming one way or the other. I wished I had been able to help, but trapping wasn't very good. Besides, the prices for furs were a lot less than they had ever been. I knew Buck was right about not eating on one dollar a week.

After last year's crop failure on the Black's Flat, land Milt had rented on shares, he was in no hurry to renew the lease. I don't think Ben Justice would have renewed it either, after Milt and Ben almost came to blows. I don't know exactly what the argument was about, but I do know there would have been a fight if Milt wasn't so chicken and Howard hadn't stepped in and told them they were both acting like a couple of nuts.

Instead of worrying about renewing the lease with Ben Justice, Milt was busy working out a deal to rent the Thompson ranch. It joined the ranch we lived on and it was a lot bigger. It included several miles on Beaver Creek, altogether it was close to 5,000 acres. Milt had to find someone to go in with him because much of the Thompson ranch was pasture and we had no stock of our own. If we rented it we wouldn't need the Ben Justice land on Black's flat.

There was no one living on the Thompson place at that time so Duane and I extended our trap line up the creek as far as our traps would go. When the creek was frozen over we could no longer trap for muskrats. By using a dead jackrabbit for bait, the creek bed made a good place to catch weasels.

That fall I had gathered up my muskrat traps so they wouldn't get frozen in the ice all winter. When I thought the ice was thick enough to walk on I set traps for weasels. I had to cross the creek several times on the ice in order to place them in good locations. I knew the ice wasn't thick enough yet to hold up the weight of a horse, so I was on foot. When I stepped off a beaver dam where the water must have been moving fast I broke through the ice and was in water up to my arm pits. Talk about being cold! I was able to grab hold of the creek bank and pull myself out but by the time I got home my pants were frozen stiff.

The next spring, when it was nearly time to change back to trapping muskrats, I rode our horse Babe to pick up my weasel traps. The snow and ice were melting and where it had been frozen over it was all covered with water. I was in a hurry and had crossed over on the ice several times until I crossed where I didn't know the ice had all melted. Before I knew what was happening, I found my horse and myself both in water up to her back. I jumped off and got to the bank holding onto the bridle reins. I tried to lead her out but she just humped over and wouldn't budge. I knew she couldn't last long in that cold water. I had to do something and fast. I found a willow branch and laid it down hard across her rump. It took several swats before I could get her to even try to climb the creek bank. I was sure she was going to die before I could get her out of that cold water. I could visualize what everyone would think of me, for killing our best school horse, such a dumb thing to do. It would be like the time I almost killed Duane when he fell on the axe. This was about the second dumbest thing I had ever done, up to that time. I was lucky enough to get Babe out before she was overcome by the cold water. I didn't have to go home and tell anyone.

Milt was successful in renting the Thompson place. We had the use of the farm and hay land, and Mr. Sheldeorf rented the pasture. We moved in by the time school was out for the summer. This was the best house we had ever lived in without sharing with someone else. There were three bedrooms upstairs and two more downstairs. It had a big kitchen with eating space as well as a pantry. The front room had double doors that opened into a sitting room. We didn't have enough furniture to come close to filling this big ranch house.

Eunice bought our mother a new mattress for her bed but Milt took the new one for his bed and let our mother have the one he had been using. When Eunice found out she was very unhappy.

Our teacher said our school and the Douglas school wanted to have a dance as our last-day-of-school party. Last year we had a picnic with this other nearby school. They wanted to use our big house for the dance and Milt agreed to let them. It was common practice at country dances to pass the hat to pay for the music. Nothing was said about who would pay for the music and when they started to pass the hat, Milt stopped them. He said if he furnished the house, the teachers of the two schools should pay for the music.

Wyoming schools required all sixth, seventh and eighth grade students to pass state examinations. You didn't know your grades or whether or not you passed until the exams had been graded and you were notified by the county superintendent of schools by mail. Passing the eighth grade was special. If you passed you got an invitation to attend eighth grade graduation ceremonies held in Sundance for the whole county. Kids from all over the county with their parents and teachers would come to Sundance. Most of them brought their picnic lunches and spent the day. I didn't know about graduation ceremonies in Sundance or find out if I passed the state exams until after the big day was over. Milt decided I shouldn't be told because I would expect to attend and he couldn't spare me from working that Saturday. I spent that day on a grain drill planting oats.

After we got all the crops planted it was time to start putting up hay. Milt made a deal with Merrit Barton to trade help with him during haying. We helped Merrit first, then he was to send a man with a mower to help us. The Thompson place had a lot of good hay land on Beaver Creek. The Barton place joined the Thompson place to the west.

By working for Hewes, Howard had paid off most of the loan that was past due last year when we had mostly a crop failure.

Eunice was going to college in Spearfish to upgrade her teaching certificate. She had a steady boyfriend, named Joe Haberzetle, who worked at the John Guidinger ranch, the place where Eunice boarded when she taught school.

Helen worked for Mrs. Barton, Merrit Barton's mother.

Buck, Duane and I went to Barton's ranch to put up hay and each night we came back home to do our chores.

Barton had a young 17-year-old kid working for him by the name of Bruce Jameison. He was nicknamed Omaha because he came from there. It was the first time he had ever been out of the city and it showed. I think it was the first time he ever worked anywhere. He got blisters on his hands even wearing gloves. I don't think Buck, Duane or I ever owned a pair of gloves to protect our hands from blisters. In the winter maybe to keep our hands warm but even then it was usually mittens. Before Bruce could pitch a fork of hay he had to stop and put on his gloves.

Buck had to show him how to put the harness on the horses. When Bruce hitched his team to the hayrake, he had the horse on the right that belonged on the left and the left one on the right. It is only natural a city kid wouldn't know that the inside lines you steer horses by need to be longer than the outside lines. When Bruce drove the horses and pulled up on the lines to change direction, he pulled their heads together. When we saw what he had done everyone had a good laugh at Bruce's expense.

"You think it's funny," he said, "giving me two horses that are in love."

The next morning Bruce tried to put the harness on the wrong end too. After a few more of his dumb stunts Buck decided it wasn't funny. The poor guy needed help if he was going to keep his job. He still tried to bluff when he didn't know how to do something, so Buck and I helped him without being wise about it. Bruce was the "Man" Milt got in return for our helping Barton. Anyhow, the team and mower were what we really needed.

Bruce was very interesting to talk to. I learned a lot about city life. He bragged a lot but when we got to know him better you could forgive him for that. He was an orphan with one sister. His mother had died when he was small, his dad had married again and he too had died a couple of years ago. His family in Omaha consisted of a sister he didn't like, a stepmother and a court-appointed lawyer guardian. His guardian was a friend of Merrit Barton's uncle who lived in Omaha. They sent Bruce out to the Barton ranch in Wyoming before he got into any real trouble with his drinking buddies in the city. Merrit was using Bruce for free help—he didn't pay him one cent.

Bruce smoked and was running low on cigarettes. He wanted to know how far it was to the closest store so he could walk in after work.

Duane told him, "It's about 20 miles." (It was only about 12) "Why don't you cut your cigarettes in two then you'll have twice as many?"

Bruce took Duane's advise and after he took a few puffs he burned his fingers. We all had a good laugh.

"You're a wise little runt," Bruce told Duane.

"Yep. Wise enough not to smoke cigarettes."

When it was time to start haying at our place, Bruce stayed with us and we passed and kicked a football around in the evenings. Both Buck and I intended to turn our for the high school

94

football team, that is if we could afford to go to high school that fall. Bruce said he wasn't going back to Barton's. He wanted to stay with us and go to high school in Sundance and play football. Sundance was always recruiting players for football and basketball. Bruce said he was a good basketball player too.

Otis Reynolds, a lawyer friend of ours, had papers drawn up so Milt was Bruce's limited guardian. He could go to high school in Sundance that way without paying tuition and would be eligible to play football and basketball. He would be staying with Buck and me. Bruce had a trust fund controlled by his lawyer guardian in Omaha who agreed to pay 15 dollars a month for Bruce's room and board while he attended high school. That was enough money to pay for groceries for all three of us. This meant Buck and I would be going to high school for sure, whether Milt paid us anything for our summer's work or not.

Milt thought he had everything under control and could run around on rubber tires, as the Boss called it, while the rest of us stayed home and did all the work. Not so.

Howard decided to quit working for Milt and signed up for the Civilian Conservation Corps. I guess after Howard had paid off the government loan he wanted to get out and see the world. The three C's, as it was sometimes called, was a government program where young men worked in the woods, built parks, roads, fire trails and fought forest fires and such. Howard quit Hewes and left immediately for the Jackson Hole area. Buck saw it was his chance to take the job Howard had at Hewes's. Hewes always paid well and you got your money while Milt never paid.

With Howard and Buck gone that left Duane and me to put up all the hay with only Bruce for help. Milt sold part of the hay to Scotchy and it had to be baled in order to haul it in one of Scotchy's trucks. Scotchy found a horse-powered hay baler that belonged in a museum. It was a stationery model where the horses went around in a circle. The hay had to be pitched in with a hand fork and the bales were tied by hand. Grace drove the horses that powered the baler.

I was 15 and more or less in charge unless Milt or Buck were around and that wasn't much of the time. Milt arranged it so we would bale hay on Sundays that was Buck's day off working for Hewes. Buck would run the crew when he was there. Duane and

I worked until dark many times during the week in order to have the hay ready for baling on Sunday. Bruce was some help until he had an operation for appendicitis. He was in the hospital in Deadwood for a week before he came back to our ranch. He wasn't allowed to do any heavy work for another month. We treated him like one of the family. He didn't know how to milk or much of anything else we did on the ranch but I didn't mind because at least I knew, because of Bruce, I would start high school. We weren't through haying when we had to start running the binder for cutting wheat. Duane had to finish the haying with only Grace's help. Duane was 13 and Grace was 10.

One of the wheat fields next to a county road was half a mile long. The John Deere tractor wasn't new anymore and sometimes it was hard to start. Milt would crank it by turning the flywheel. After cranking awhile he would swear while he rested. Then it was my turn to crank while he swore at the tractor and me. After about fifteen minutes of this the tractor finally started.

Milt got on the binder and yelled at me, "Let's go, damn it!"

I was about to let out the clutch when I noticed the oil gauge showed no oil pressure. Milt had drilled it into me when I first started driving the tractor, that if the oil pressure indicator didn't show oil pressure to shut the tractor off without asking questions. I shut the tractor off as I had been taught. I think Milt swore at me a solid five minutes before I could tell him there was no oil pressure.

When we checked we found there was no oil. Someone must have stolen it during the night. Milt said he knew who would do such a thing but there was no way to prove it.

"Some damn high school kid," Milt said. "If he can't afford to buy his own gas and oil he has no business to drive a car."

When Milt realized I had shut the tractor off before any damage had been done he looked at me and smiled. I was expecting to be complemented for not burning up the tractor's engine by running it without oil.

"I guess I did a pretty good job in training you," was all he said.

I had my first day of high school to look forward to the next week.

Chapter Twelve

Bruce was our paying boarder when I started high school in the fall of 1933. Four of us lived in three rented rooms in the back of Mickey Farrel's gas station. Buck was a junior in high school as was Bruce. Helen was going to high school (post graduate training) so she could teach grade school and she did the cooking and housekeeping. It was a new phase in my life to be away from my mothers cooking. Buck had his own money for clothes from his job working for Hewes during the past summer. Eunice gave me enough to buy the clothes I needed when school started.

It had been four years since I had lived in Sundance and I knew many of the kids and we were friends. When we had the election of freshman's class officers I was nominated for treasurer. Rachel Canfield, nominated a girl to run against me. I thought since Rachel and I were from the same country school she would support my candidacy and vote for me. Maybe because she knew me, and thought she was better than me, was her reason for not wanting me elected? I was elected without her support and my feeling was, to hell with Rachel Canfield. It was good to be accepted again by my Sundance friends.

Bruce turned out for the football team as did Buck and me. Bruce bragged a lot better game than he played and wanted to play quarterback. The first day or so the coach let us try out for whatever position we wanted. It wasn't until about the third day before we did any tackling or blocking. The first time Bruce got a chance to run with the ball someone tackled him hard and he didn't get up right away. I think football was a lot rougher game than he thought it would be. Some of the kids said they could tell he had never played the game before. They nicknamed him Windy because he couldn't play football as good as he could talk. That night he quit and turned in his football uniform. He said his appendix hurt. It had been six weeks since his operation. His game was basketball anyway, he said.

I met several new friends that turned out for football. It was a good way to get to know the upper classmen as well as the freshman that weren't big babies. I didn't make the first team but got to play some. Buck played on the first team most of the time. His position was end on offense and linebacker on defense. I was a backup guard. Only about 25 were still out for football after the first week. In those days we all played both offense and defense.

One freshman, Hally Oudin, who played second team backfield, was pretty good and plenty tough. When the second team scrimmaged against the first team Hally and I liked nothing better than to break up the play. We planned it between us how one of us would take out the blocker so the other could get the tackle. Hally and I became the best of friends all through high school.

Our first game was against Spearfish, a town in South Dakota about 30 miles east of Sundance. I didn't get to play but it was a great experience for me since it was the first time I had ever been to Spearfish. Our team lost, six to seven, but our school had never beaten Spearfish and we usually played their football team every year. Later that year we played Deadwood, another school we had never beaten, and we lost to them by the same score. Every time we played an away from home game, it was in another town where I had never been.

The first time I got in a real game we were playing Newell and were so far ahead, Mr. Knoddings, our coach, let almost everyone play. I got to play again in the Newcastle game. I think the coach thought the regular player wasn't trying hard enough so he put in a freshman to make him mad so he would try harder. The last game of the season we played Gillette and the player I was the backup for had chicken pox, so I got to start. We would have won except for a dropped pass. Our would-be receiver was in the open with no one within ten yards of him, or between him and the goal, and he let the ball slip through his fingers. He came back to the huddle with tears in his eyes. I thought maybe some of the guys would give him hell for not catching the ball. They all felt as I did and told him not to feel bad or blame himself since it could happen to anyone. That game taught me a lot about teamwork and how it felt to be part of a team. The game ended in a tie. It was the first football game I got to start but not the last. I was a starter in every football game Sundance played the rest of the time I was in high school.

Another good thing about turning out for football was that we got to take a hot shower after each practice and game. That was important because our living quarters, as well as most houses in Sundance at that time, didn't have an inside bathroom.

After Bruce dropped out of football he played in the school band. Helen gave up the idea of becoming a teacher and dropped out of school after six weeks.

After Helen left, Buck and I did all the cooking, laundry and housework, if you could call it that. Bruce's favorite dish was a large bowl full of breakfast cereal, Wheaties or corn flakes with milk. We ate lots of eggs, pancakes, and fried potatoes. I missed not having any pie or cake. I had made a rhubarb pie once so I knew how to make pie crust. I wanted to surprise Buck and Bruce with a homemade pumpkin pie. A can of pumpkin dumped into a pie shell without adding, milk, sugar, eggs or anything else was sure a good way to surprise them. It was the most awful tasting concoction you could imagine. It tasted like eating a cooked ground-up jack-o'-lantern.

My next bust at cooking was when I stewed some dried peaches using a syrup can for a kettle. If you ever get the urge to try it don't put on a tight fitting lid. When it blew, there were stewed peaches all over the ceiling and walls of our apartment. Mickey Farrel, our landlord heard the explosion and made me try to clean up the mess. Buck and Bruce still let me cook. I guess they thought I should stay with it until I got it right. They thought it best I stick with fried potatoes, eggs, pancakes and open cans that contained food ready to eat.

Eunice was teaching the same school she taught the year before. I had seen her boyfriend Joe, only once when he rode a horse over to our ranch to see Eunice. One day she and Joe stopped at our rented rooms in Mickey Farrel's gas station and she said she was now Mrs. Joe Haberzetle.

I looked for the ring.

Eunice said, "I don't have a ring yet. Joe is getting his mother's ring to give to me. They haven't sent it yet."

I asked them to have dinner with us. I fried some potatoes and opened a can of beans. We had bread and peanut butter and I opened a can of peaches for dessert. There was something about the way Joe talked and looked at me and stared at the food I prepared that I thought was strange. I couldn't put my finger on what it was, but I got the feeling he was laughing at the food, or at me. It was the first time I had really talked to him. He was not too tall but had broad shoulders. It was hard to be sure how old he was because he was short on hair except for a fringe over his ears and the back of his neck. Eunice was 21 and I guessed Joe to be between 25 and 30. By talking to him I found he was a friend of Mickey Farrel and Gaylord Zane, the guy that married Miss Canoy, my teacher at the Canfield school.

Mickey was small in stature but with a big heart. Some called him Runt Farrel. They said he was the kind of a character who would beat you out of your last dollar and give it back to you, even if it was his last dollar. He had been a school teacher and encouraged Buck and me to plan to go on to college. High school kids hung around his gas station just to talk and keep warm by his pot belly stove.

Sometimes Mickey's friends would join him in a poker game. They played for money, only small stakes, usually about a nickel limit.

Prohibition was over but Mickey usually had part of a gallon jug of moonshine whiskey cached in the station rest-room. Bruce watched where he hid it and one night we helped ourselves. Bruce poured each of us a glassful and put back the same amount of water so Mickey wouldn't know. I took one big swallow and almost choked so I let Bruce have the rest of mine. Bruce got so silly Mickey knew what was the matter with him and hid his jug in a better place. I guess you could say it was my fault he found out. If I had drunk mine Bruce wouldn't have had so much. If Buck had known what we were going to do I'm sure he would have stopped us.

One Friday when Buck, Bruce, and I came home for lunch there was a poker game going on in Mickey's gas station with Joe Haberzetle, Mickey, I think Gaylord Zane, and some others. When we got home from school that night they were still playing cards. Buck and I looked on awhile. Joe was so drunk he didn't know what he was doing and the others were taking advantage of him. There was no longer a nickel limit and Joe was losing. When the others saw Buck and me watching our brother-in-law being taken advantage of, the poker game broke up. We took him to our quarters in the back of the station and put him in bed so he could sleep it off.

Joe had been asleep awhile when Mickey came into our place

100

and said we couldn't have a drunk in our rooms. I never could figure out why he wanted Joe out of there so bad. I knew his aunt, who owned the station, didn't want Mickey to drink. She had put up the money for Mickey's station after he lost his teaching job. Mickey insisted on waking Joe up and for me to take him home. For me to agree to ride home with Joe was one of dumbest things I have ever done, and at times that night I thought it might be my last. There was no way he would let me drive Eunice's car. When we left town he tried to cross Sundance creek where there was no bridge. Dumb me, I warned him before he drove into the creek, telling him there was no bridge across the creek on that street. It would have been better if I had let him get stuck. When we got on the country road he drove off several times and had to back up and turn where the road turned. I know it was embarrassing for Eunice to have me bring him home in that condition, but we made it without wrecking Eunice's car.

I didn't know then my sister had married a guy who had operated a whiskey still for John Guininger. Later Joe told me all about it and he liked to brag about the time he sold a barrel of whiskey to the sheriff. He delivered it to him in broad daylight hidden inside of a load of wood. The sheriff sold it to some bootlegger in Deadwood, South Dakota.

Buck and I were always interested in doing odd jobs to make some spending money. I met Mr. Donaldson on the street one day and he asked if I wanted to cut some wood for 25 cents an hour. I told him sure. He said he would be getting a load in a few days and would let me know when I could start. A few days later he told Buck he had the wood for him to cut. After Buck finished cutting all the wood, Mr. Donaldson said he would pay him when he got his paycheck. In a few days he saw me and handed me a couple of dollars and said it was my pay for cutting the wood. I let Buck stew awhile before I gave him his money because I was a little upset about Buck taking my job. Buck paid my way to a show that night that cost 25 cents. We both thought it was funny because Mr. Donaldson couldn't tell us apart.

Most of the high school kids went to a show once a week with their girlfriends. Neither Buck nor I could afford that, but Bruce could. He had a steady girlfriend and his lawyer guardian in Omaha sent him five dollars spending money, and the 15 dollars each month to pay for his room and board.

As freshman class treasurer, it was my job to collect 50 cents from each of my classmates to pay for a party we were planning. I hid seven dollars of class funds in our bedroom, only Buck, Bruce and I knew where. When I looked for the money to put it in the bank it was gone. Bruce at first denied knowing anything about it, then he said I should know better than tempt him. I desperately insisted he give it back. I had no way of replacing it. Bruce agreed to give me the money even though he denied taking it. His allowance check from Omaha was late but when it came he gave me back the money I knew he had "borrowed."

After our last football game came basketball practice, and Buck, Bruce, and I turned out for the team. Bruce had been shooting off his mouth to anyone who would listen what a good basketball player he was. He didn't have to quit basketball as he did football because the coach made the decision for him. When the squad was cut down to 15 players, Bruce was one of those cut. Buck and I both were still there after the cut. Bruce was disappointed at first when he didn't make the squad, but after a while he didn't seem to mind so much. He had more time for his girlfriend and could play in the band. I don't think Bruce had any idea Sundance would be such a strong contender in our basketball conference.

I got my first chance to play in a varsity game when we were playing Whitewood in a non-conference game. The score was 35 to O at half-time in our favor. Our coach had his first team take a shower, get dressed, and let us subs play the second half. We knew it was up to us to win the game with the first five watching the game in their street clothes. I didn't get to travel with the team that year. They only took the first ten when we played the conference games. Buck traveled with the team most of the time and we both got to practice against the first team.

Duane rode a horse into Sundance to see the Tri-County basketball tournament and stopped at our batching quarters. When he changed clothes he left his billfold on a dresser in the bedroom. Duane was doing well trapping so he had his own spending money. By the time he thought about where he had left his billfold the money was gone. We all knew Bruce had taken it, but he never owned up to it. I felt bad about Duane losing his money because I hadn't warned Duane about Bruce being light fingered. I knew he couldn't be trusted after he had "borrowed" the class treasury funds. The one thing about us Kaisers, we might argue or fight among ourselves, but we never stole from anyone. It was hard for us to believe someone else would.

Sundance won the Tri-County tournament and lost only one conference game all year. Before the district tournament, our coach scheduled a game with the Black Hills Teachers College at Spearfish so they would be used to playing tough competition, he said.

Eunice and Joe came through Sundance on their way to Gillette where the district tournament was being held. They invited me to go with them. Sundance had already won three games and was playing that night for first place. When Eunice was in high school she was the captain of the girls' basketball team, a cheerleader, and was very interested in school sports.

Even though I didn't suit up with the team they let me into the dressing room. I remember the pep talk the coach gave our players on the Gillette team and how they would play and how to play against them. As I watched the game I could tell he knew what he was talking about. We beat them, thus winning first place in the Powder River Conference tournament. I will always remember how everyone was so happy in the locker room after the game that night.

One of our star players looked at me as he held up the first place trophy and said, "I want you freshmen to keep the tradition of what our basketball teams have going for Sundance."

I already knew the tradition he was talking about as this was the third time Sundance had won first in the district in the past seven years. The other four years they had always been in the running. One year they beat Casper to get fifth place in the state.

Eunice and Joe stopped by our living quarters in Sundance one day to visit. "I'm not going to be teaching around here next year," she said. "Joe and I are selling all our furniture. When my school is out we're going to Indiana."

"Indiana?"

"Yes. Indiana, That's where Joe's family lives."

"Maybe you can get the diamond ring that was his mother's wedding ring as he promised."

I could tell Eunice didn't want to talk about the ring.

The next time I saw Helen she told me the wildest story. Someone told her Eunice and Joe had sold most of their furniture, and Joe lost all the money in a poker game down in Deadwood.

Eunice told the story a little different. She said Joe had an accident with her car and wrecked the other man's car. Joe had to give him all the furniture money so he wouldn't sue.

When Eunice and Joe stopped to tell Buck and me good-by before they left for Indiana, I couldn't tell that the car had been in a wreck.

I wasn't happy to see my first year of high school come to an end. Without any more help from Eunice I knew it could be my last. Buck and I had decided next year would be without Bruce. Besides the money that he stole, he was coming in drunk and hadn't paid his last month's board. I wasn't sure if I was unhappy because I liked school that much or I dreaded the thought of working for Milt one more summer without being paid.

Chapter Thirteen

After school was out for the summer of 1934 it was back to working for brother Milt on the Thompson place for me. With Buck working for Hewes and Howard still in the CCCs, that left Duane and me to do most of the work on the ranch. Milt had signed up for a government program where he got paid not to farm. While we didn't have the usual spring planting, there was still plenty to do. Duane had the trapping on Beaver Creek all to himself the past winter and did very well. Milt got a permit from the owner of the ranch so Duane could trap beaver. Duane and Grace traveled one additional mile each way to attend the Canfield school. Five miles was a little far in the cold weather with all the snow. Duane was ready for high school that fall so Grace would be the only one left to attend the country school.

Milt was working on a deal to buy a sawmill but there was one catch, they wanted mostly cash. Howard was sending home 25 dollars a month for our mother to bank for him. Duane had to sell his beaver pelts through the landlord because a trapping permit was required to trap beaver. The land owner had to claim the beavers were damaging the land in order to get the permit. He gave the check for the beaver pelts to Milt to give to Duane. Between the money Howard sent to our mother to bank and Duane's beaver money, plus 50 dollars of Duane's muskrat money, Milt had the cash he needed to close the deal to buy the sawmill.

Milt bought four milk cows after we no longer had the Schloredt cattle we had been paid to take care of. Buck came home Saturday nights and we sometimes went to the country dances at Ealy's. The dances lasted until daylight so we would milk the cows in the morning after we got home and before we went to bed, that way we could sleep in on Sunday, the only day we had off.

Different friends came to our place on Sundays to go swimming or fishing for chubs in Beaver creek. Buck, Duane, and I would go to the picture shows in Sundance, getting a ride with Milt, or we rode our horses. Although we didn't have to worry about grain to harvest that summer, haying kept us busy.

Milt was sweet on Sadie Grubb, a girl who attended the country dances. She was 10 years younger than Milt. He spent a lot of time at Grubbs, he said making arrangements to buy timber from Sadie's dad.

After we had finished with most of the first cutting, Duane and Grace stayed on the ranch to finish with the rest of the haying while I worked at Milt's sawmill located on the Grubb ranch. Milt had never run a sawmill but had worked around one once. The first boards we sawed had to be used to build a cook shack and a lean-to to sleep in. It was too far to commute each day from the ranch.

Eunice and Joe didn't go to Indiana as Joe said they would. Joe got a job in Denver so they decided to stay there. Helen was working for Mrs. Grice in Sundance at a motel where she met some people from Indiana who knew Joe Haberzetle. They said the Haberzetle who married Eunice wasn't really named Joe. His name was Andy. He had a brother named Joe who owned a tavern in Indiana.

Milt hired Frank Platner and Bill Cottonburger to work with me at the sawmill and cut down trees. Milt was the sawyer. The mill was located in the woods near the log supply. Many times Milt would leave me with Frank and Bill to fell and buck trees while he delivered lumber with a Model T Ford truck. It might be several days before he would come back. I had no idea where he went or when he might return. I did all the cooking for the crew but never tried to bake another one of my famous pumpkin pies. When not preparing meals or washing dishes, I would off-bear (removed the lumber from the saw as it was sawed) or work in the woods with Frank and Bill. I was supposed to be in charge when Milt was gone.

Milt usually took us back to the ranch on Sundays, our day off. Frank and Bill sometimes spent Sundays at Frank's home. Buck would come home from Hewes's and our mother did the laundry for both Buck and me.

It was about time for high school to start and we hadn't made any arrangements for a place to stay in town. I had about given up hope of going to high school until I talked to Buck one Sunday. Buck saw Mickey Farrel in Sundance and he asked Buck, when were we going to move in for school.

"We don't have a place to move to," Buck told him.

"Oh yes you do," Mickey said. "Otis Reynolds told me to save the rooms for you."

Otis was the lawyer friend that had fixed the guardian papers so Bruce would be eligible to play school sports. Buck and I both knew Otis wanted us back to play basketball and football again. Buck had money he was earning working for Hewes. Duane had very little left after Milt used what he earned from trapping to buy the sawmill. I knew I couldn't count on Milt for the money he had promised me for working at the sawmill. He had already told me I could forget going to high school anymore.

The big surprise of the summer was when our mother announced she had decided to leave Milt and the ranch and move into Sundance. I knew it would have been hard for Grace to go the five miles to the Canfield school by herself. Our mother always stressed the importance of an education. Besides being a hardship for Grace to attend the Canfield school, I guess she could see Milt was arranging things so that none of us four younger kids would be able to go to high school or college as she had always said we should. One Sunday she asked me to go to town with her in the wagon loaded with our household belongings. She was moving into the rooms Otis Reynolds had Mickey save for us so we could go to high school. She had no intention of returning to the ranch with Milt. She asked me to take the team back to the ranch without her because she was staying in Sundance.

Our mother signed up for a government program where we got free food vouchers that were good at a regular grocery store. She said later she would seek work at a WPA sewing center. It wasn't much, but we could get by. The important thing, she said, was Buck, Duane, and I would get to go to high school and Grace wouldn't freeze another Wyoming winter traveling five miles to a country school. Before our mother took charge, Milt had almost won the battle to keep us from continuing our schooling. I know our mother had to be desperate to accept welfare, something our family had very strong feelings about. I had never known her to take a stand like this before, unless it was when she refused to let our dad put the four younger kids up for adoption. There was no argument or bickering, with Milt, to my knowledge. She could have asked him to move us to town in his truck, but she didn't. The wagon was piled high with beds, blankets, dishes, pots, pans, some furniture, and all our clothing. We were loaded like pioneers crossing the prairies going west.

I was back working at the mill the next week and we were getting low on groceries. Milt had been gone for several days and didn't show up. Besides needing something to cook for the crew, I wanted to go to Sundance so I could join the others and start high school. It was Tuesday and school had already started.

I was helping Frank and Bill fell trees when I heard Milt drive up to the cook shack. I came in to start lunch for the crew as usual and Milt drove away before I had a chance to talk to him. He knew I wanted a ride to town so I could start school. He had left a sack of apples but nothing else and we were almost out of food. I was so mad I felt sick. I fried some apples, stewed the last of the dried prunes I had soaking, sliced the last of our bread and called Bill and Frank for lunch. I took quite a ribbing for the sad lunch, after all Milt was my brother. They blamed me for not having anything better to eat. I felt so bad I had to force myself to go back to felling trees that afternoon.

When it came time to fix dinner, I told Frank and Bill I was sick and they could fry their own apples. There was some pancake flour and syrup, besides coffee, but nothing else to eat. They didn't believe me and said it was my job to do the cooking. I couldn't blame them for feeling that way, but I knew both of them would get paid and I would be lucky if I could get a ride to Sundance. I really was sick, it may have been mental but I felt bad.

I didn't want to argue with Frank and Bill so I pretended as if I was going to the spring for a bucket of water. As I went by our sleeping lean-to I put down the water bucket and grabbed a quilt off my bed. I didn't stop until I was sure I was deep enough in the woods so if Frank and Bill came looking for me to try to make me cook their dinner they would never find me. I heard them looking, but they soon gave up. I wrapped up in the quilt and went to sleep still trying to figure out what I would do.

I woke up early in the morning knowing exactly what I should do. I returned to camp and built a fire in the stove and fixed a breakfast of pancakes and coffee. I bid Frank and Bill good-by and apologized for the skimpy breakfast. Sundance was 20 miles away and if I started right away I knew I could make it before dark. If I was lucky, I might catch a ride after I got on the main road.

"Where are you going?" Frank asked me.

"To Sundance to start my second year of high school."

I can't say as I blame you, the way Milt's been screwing you guys. I thought you, Buck and Duane would have had your bellies full of old Milt a long time ago."

"When You're a little kid, if someone takes advantage of you, you more than likely don't know it. Even if I had known there was nothing I could have done about it."

"So why now?"

"I know, as you say, Milt's been screwing me for years and I'm going to do something about it. I'm leaving and I'll never be suckered in by his promises again."

It was about five miles out the main road, from there I thumbed a ride and was in town in time for lunch. I still had time to sign up for my high school classes. I met our new coach, Mr. Rickard, and checked out a football uniform.

Buck had the coach save one for me.

Howard returned from the CCCs so Milt was able to keep the mill going, not that I cared anymore. Howard thought even less of Bill Cottonburger than I did. They couldn't fire him, Milt said, until he got the money from lumber sales so he could pay him off.

Buck and I walked out to the ranch on weekends. We would cut a wagon load of wood on Saturday and haul it to Sundance on Sunday. Bill would ride back to town with us and return the team of horses to the ranch. One weekend when it was Duane and I who cut the wood, Bill rode to town with us as usual. He refused to take the team back by himself. When I returned to the ranch with Bill and the team, Howard wanted to know why I didn't stay in town. I told him Bill wouldn't take the team back. Howard paid Bill off with his own money and fired him on the spot. Howard gave me a ride back to town and told Bill he could walk. We never heard from Bill again.

Our new coach, Mr. Rickard, was a real disappointment. He had never played football in his life. We were in the Great Depression and he must have been desperate for a job trying to coach a sport he knew nothing about. After a couple of weeks some of our good players refused to play for him. Wilford Reynolds quit school so he could play someplace else. Sundance didn't score a single touchdown all year. Teams that we had romped over previous years beat us badly.

When we played Gillette, Buck and I were playing on the first team. When the Gillette band came on the field there was Bruce Jameison, the kid that stayed with us the year before, playing the big bass drum. When he saw Buck and me, he got a big smile on his face and beats on the drum extra hard. After the game we had a chance to talk to Bruce. He was paying room and board and staying with a teacher who used to teach in Sundance and was then teaching in Gillette. Bruce, the orphan kid, seemed to have found a good home.

In spite of our football team losing all its games, I liked high school even more than the year before now that our mother was doing the cooking. I think Buck liked it better too because he didn't have to try to eat a ground up jack-o'-lantern in a pie shell.

We paid for our groceries with food vouchers we got from the government until they started a WPA sewing center. Women were paid for sewing and the clothes they made were given to the needy. Our mother was a good seamstress and had made most of our shirts and our sisters' dresses, when we lived on the ranch. She went to work at the sewing center. This way she could pay for our food instead of getting a free hand out. It wasn't too long before she was the assistant supervisor and then promoted to being in charge of the sewing center.

Buck took a chance on a raffle for a suit of clothes and won. He needed the suit to wear to the senior prom and graduation. He also wore his new suit when he had a leading part in the senior class play.

Coach Rickard knew even less about basketball than he did football. The Tri-county tournament had always been played at Sundance and he let Moorcroft take it away from us. Tom Hooper, a good player, quit. One kid who played on the first team was a brother of the coach's wife's best friend, while another was the son of a judge. Buck was the only one of the Sundance team selected first team all tournament when Sundance took third place in the Tri-county tournament, yet our coach had Buck playing second team.

Howard sawing lumber at Milt's mill.

When we were playing a conference game at Gillette I got to play because the game was already lost. Gillette was also playing its second team because Gillette was so far ahead. One of the Gillette players faked as if he was going to give me the ball then pulled it back and stuck his tongue out, and gave me the Bronx cheer while spitting on me.

I found basketball different from football because it didn't help my game to get mad. I remembered the kid's name was Keck and I promised myself instead of getting mad someday I would get even.

My biggest disappointment was I didn't get to play very much on the same team with Buck his last year in high school. A couple of our players could best be described as clumsy as they usually fouled out. At the district tournament held in Gillette that year

Buck was sick with chicken pox.

We were playing Moorcroft when our two clumsies fouled out. The coach was desperate and had to put me in along with Wes Huckins, another sub who was a better player than some of the first team. When Wes and I first got in the game we were behind. I think Wes felt the same way I did so the two of us looked for each other to pass to. To our coach's embarrassment our team won the game. I didn't realize it at the time but a lot more was decided that day than winning one basketball game. The next year we would have a new coach.

Buck was able to make up for the semester he lost the second half of his sophomore year and graduate with his class. He not only graduated but he won the scholarship given each year by the University of Wyoming to the boy with the best high school grade average.

When one of the ladies at the sewing center where our mother worked congratulated her for having such a bright son, she said there wasn't much competition. She spoke before she thought. The other lady had a son in the same class. Our mother was never one to take the blame for anything she did, nor did she brag about her kids to us or other people. I could only tell whenever one of us did something that especially pleased her by her smile since she hardly ever told us. I guess it was her way of being modest.

Buck's winning the scholarship put a different outlook on education for him. It also gave Duane and I hope in setting our goals to go on to college. Further education after high school no longer seemed like such an impossibility. With our mother working on WPA, in charge of the sewing center, our finishing high school seemed a lot more likely.

Chapter Fourteen

May 1935, Buck graduated from high school with plans to work one year and then attend the University of Wyoming. The scholarship he won would pay his tuition for four years. A job at a large cattle ranch seemed to fit into his plans, that is, until he got rocky mountain spotted tick fever. While he ran a high fever he stayed with our mother in Sundance. It took several days before the fever was down and he was well enough to work again. Milt convinced him he could make more money working at the sawmill than on a ranch.

Helen was in Denver staying with Eunice and Andy. He no longer used the name of Joe. They told her she could stay with them and go to a beautician's school.

Duane joined Buck and Howard at Milt's sawmill at the Kelly place on Irish Divide.

I refused to work for Milt anymore, he never paid when he said he would and last year he wouldn't even take me to town when school started. I did let him soft talk me into moving his cattle from the Thompson ranch to a place he was renting where they ran the sawmill. My pay was a sack of potatoes that I made him leave at our place in Sundance before I did the job. It was too far to drive the cattle in one day but Milt told me he would meet me at Grubb's ranch where he had made arrangements for the cattle to stay the first night. I rode Babe and got the cattle as far as Grubb's as planned and waited for Milt. Mr. Grubb didn't know anything about Milt's arrangement for me to leave the cattle there and Milt never showed up that night. I had dinner with the Grubb family and they put me up for the night. After breakfast the next morning I continued on to the Kelly place on Irish Divide where I delivered the cattle as agreed. When I asked Milt why he didn't show up as he said he would at Grubb's ranch, he said he didn't have time to tell them I was going to stay there but he knew they wouldn't care.

"Since you are here you might as well work for me at the mill this summer," Milt said.

My answer: "Go to Hell!"

I was 17, over six feet tall at the time and no longer considered Milt a physical threat.

I was in Sundance only a few days when Scotchy Roberts gave me a job driving a tractor doing some custom farming for Merrit Barton. Barton had made arrangements for someone to cook for the man Scotchy would have to do the farming. When Merrit saw it was me, Milt's kid brother, he sent the cook back to the main SY ranch and had me cook for myself. Another thing Merrit did that I didn't like at the time, was his calling me the Sundance Kid. I guess it was because the SY ranch was closer to the town of Moorcroft.

After the custom farming job was done Scotchy hired me to tear down an old building in Sundance. It had been Frank's grocery store and the first bank in Sundance that was built when Wyoming was only a territory.

When I completed dismantling the building, pulling the nails and stacking the lumber, I got a job working on a ranch run by Bob Ganze. Everybody warned me that he was known for not paying his help. He told me he would pay me when he sold the wheat in the fall.

I cut my foot with an ax while chopping wood and lost a few days work. Ganze took me to Sundance where Doc Clarenbach took several stitches to close the wound. He wouldn't take any pay, saying he hoped he fixed me up good enough so I could play football and basketball again for Sundance High School. I knew he never got paid the 25 dollars, his usual fee, when I was born during the night he got lost in a blizzard.

School started before Ganze sold his wheat so I didn't get my pay when I left. Scotchy bought the wheat and hauled it to Moorcroft, the closest railroad, for shipment. Before Scotchy paid Ganze he asked me if Ganze had paid me for my summer's work.

I told him, "Not yet."

"Did you agree on what you have coming?"

"Yes, he promised me 60 dollars."

Scotchy had a pleasing smile on his face. "If you have time to wait, I'll write you a check and subtract it from what I'll pay Ganze for the wheat."

"I got time."

I was in my junior year in high school with all my summer wages for the first time.

Rickard, last year's coach, was hired back as a teacher, but Mr. Tracy was our coach. It seemed like a major victory when we scored our first touchdown, the first in two years.

Mr. Tracy did more for me than any teacher I had before or since. He worked with me in class as well as in sports helping me build confidence in myself. If I did something right he told me, on the other hand he was just as quick to tell me what I did wrong and how to do it right. If he told me I could do something, he made me believe I could.

I remember when we were playing basketball in Buffalo. Their team was built around their big left-handed center. It was a three-day trip and we had been beaten by Midwest the night before. Buffalo had just beaten Midwest by a considerable amount and their big center scored most of their points. Tracy took me aside and told me if I could keep the Buffalo center from scoring more than one field goal he would buy me a milkshake. He said he knew I could do it if I played up to my ability. That's all it will take, he said, for us to win this game. He must have known how much I like to eat, especially milkshakes. I won that milkshake, their big center never scored a single field goal that night. Mr. Tracy bought milkshakes for the whole team. We won the game and their total score was seven points. The next night we beat Sheridan, the third largest town in Wyoming. Sundance was a town of less than 500 people and our high school had about 100 students. Sheridan had a population of around 10,000 with about 300 students in the senior class alone.

I mentioned earlier a Gillette basketball player, named Keck stuck his tongue out and spit at me the year before. This year when we were playing Gillette, they were one point ahead with only seconds to go. I didn't know exactly how much time was left because we didn't have a clock we could see. All Gillette had to do was hold the ball the few remaining seconds and they would have won the game. I came up from my zone, which was near the basket, to challenge their guards who were playing keep away between themselves. Keck stuck his chin out with a cocky expression on his face daring me to try to get the ball. When he tried to pass it to the other guard in front of me I intercepted the ball with one long jump. When Keck moved over to get between me and the basket, our forward, Swede Erickson, broke for the basket. I passed Swede the ball and he scored about a second before the whistle blew ending the game. Score, Sundance 33, Gillette 32. Thanks to Keck, we went on to win the conference that year by one game.

We started the school year living in the rooms behind Mickey Farrel's gas station but when the station was sold to Scotchy Roberts, we moved to the Sawyer place a couple of blocks away. Our mother was still working on WPA, in charge of the women's sewing project.

Helen had to send for money to get home from Denver. Eunice and Andy got a job herding sheep and left Helen in Denver to fend for herself. For the second time she didn't attend a beautician's school as she had been promised.

Helen said, "While living with Eunice and Andy, Andy made her feel like a horse-turd shit in the wrong pasture."

She lost her high school class ring in their apartment. She figured Andy had hocked it. After returning to Sundance, she worked at a few restaurants and Mrs. Grice's motel for a while before going to California to marry Fred Schock. She had been writing to him off and on, but hadn't seen him since they first met when he sold tickets on the merry-go-round at the Sundance fair. They made their home in California.

When Tom Sawyer, the man who owned the house we were renting, wanted to stay nights at our place when he was in town we moved out of his house and rented a couple of rooms in a house that belonged to Mrs. Schloredt.

During Christmas vacation I helped Howard make lumber at Milt's sawmill. My pay was some slabs from the mill, which Duane and I cut up for firewood. Slabs are waste from the outside of the logs that can't be used for lumber.

When Milt came to town, he sometimes stayed all night and parked his truck in front of where we lived in the rented rooms. Sometimes he would leave his truck there and run around with his car. Our mother would always fix dinner for him when he stopped although he never contributed anything for food. Once when he stopped he had Orian Platner with him. Orian worked for Milt at the sawmill at the time. When our mother was preparing dinner she couldn't find the can opener. We looked every place we could think of but we couldn't find it anyplace. Milt helped us look. We finally had to open the can of tomatoes with a butcher knife. Orian told me later they had lost their can-opener at the mill and Milt put ours in his pocket when no one was looking so he wouldn't have to buy a new one that cost about 35 cents.

Our mother was notified she was no longer eligible for working on WPA because they said Milt was living with us and he made enough money with the mill that he could support us. There was no way we could live on Milt's promises. I knew I would have to quit school and get a job if I couldn't get them to give our mother her job back. I went to Otis Reynolds and told him my problem. He told me not to worry he would take care of it and for me to concentrate on playing basketball.

Our mother was back supervisor of the sewing center without missing a single day's work. I guess Mr. Reynolds and Mr. Tracy, my coach, stirred things up pretty good at the WPA office. They even gave me a job after school and on Saturdays in the assessor's office. The money for my job came from the Federal Government, a division called the (NYA) National Youth Administration. I got about $10 a month, which was more than I needed for spending money. We asked Milt not to park his truck in front of our house anymore.

That spring before school was out Eunice wrote and told us she was going to have her first baby. She came back to Sundance and stayed with us. Andy came with her but he left after a day or two, returning to Denver, he said to look for a job. Eunice was going to stay at least until the baby was due in August. She had talked about coming back to Sundance the fall before. She even had a job teaching school but had told them at the last minute she wouldn't take the job.

We had been getting by with what our mother made on WPA, but now there wasn't enough to pay all the bills. The unpaid balance at the grocery store grew a little each month. Eunice had loaned Milt money and he never paid her back. Milt had borrowed the money to send to our dad when he was stranded in Arizona. Dad had repaid Milt but Milt never gave it to Eunice. It embarrassed Eunice to stay with us without her paying her share so she asked Milt for that money she had loaned him several years before.

Milt told her, "You got yourself in that shape," he had to be

117

referring to her being pregnant, "so you can get yourself out of it."

What Milt didn't tell Eunice was that he had hired Andy to drive the tractor doing some custom plowing, before they left for Denver. When Andy asked Milt for his wages, Milt told him he would have to wait until Milt got paid for the plowing. Andy collected and kept all the money for himself. Milt didn't even get the expenses for the tractor fuel.

Since Eunice would be staying with us at least until the baby was born, we rented a different house. It was a few blocks closer to school. When the weather got warm enough to sleep outside, Duane and I slept in a tent in the back yard.

After school was out in the spring of 1936, Duane went to work for Merrit Barton and he rode Babe so he could come home on Sundays. Babe came in heat when she was at Barton's and the Nefsy stud got to her. Merrit wouldn't pay Duane anything for two month's work, claiming Duane owed him the stud fee. Merrit has since inherited a great part of the SY ranch and became a millionaire. Millionaire or cowboy, I will always remember Merrit Barton as the guy that pimped for the SY stud horse and never paid my little brother the money he had coming.

When Duane couldn't get the pay he had coming he rode Babe to a horse sale in Upton, sold her and sent Helen all the money. All he got for most of the summer was the experience.

Buck had been working for Milt for several months without drawing any pay. When he threatened to quit, Milt told him he had to stay. Milt said no one else could find the logs Buck had cut down that were still out in the woods. Buck stayed when Milt promised him he could have a percentage of the money when the railroad ties were sold, plus part of the lumber that was always trimmed from the logs when they sawed ties. This would be enough money so Buck could attend the university as he had planned.

I didn't have that much faith in Milt's promises so I was in town several days after school was out before I got a tree pruning job working for Hewes. When they couldn't agree on what they would pay their regular hired man for the summer they asked me if I would stay on after the pruning was done. They were paying me a dollar a day for pruning. I told Mrs. Hewes I would like more than a dollar a day if I worked through haying. She assured me I would get more than that and they always paid better than most ranchers in the county. I knew that was true. The last time Howard worked there he got two dollars a day. Buck didn't get quite that much. I was embarrassed for having brought it up. I knew my dad worked for them once and so had Milt. When Milt worked for Hewes, the horses he was driving got stung by some hornets and they ran away and wrecked the mowing machine. It seemed that one Kaiser or another had worked for Hewes for years.

Mr. Hewes told me I was the first hired man he ever let spend the evening in the house with the family. Some of the neighbors said Hewes had an air about him and he thought he was better than most people. When I think back now I know he probably felt that way because he was better than most of them. Once Mr. Hewes told me how much the grocery bill was a month. I think he meant I should eat less. I was told by a man who used to work for Hewes they didn't feed you very well. I never had that problem. I have wondered since if the Hewes family had to eat less when I worked there. Anyhow I knew I was supposed to stay in the bunk house after supper and talk to myself but I liked to read the daily paper each night before I went to bed. They let me spend my evenings in the house as long as I didn't sit in Julius's chair. They were friends of Governor Smith and sometimes spent the day as guests of the governor at his ranch.

Once when they had some important company, Mrs. Hewes explained to them I was the star on our basketball team and Mr. Hewes was president of the school board. She made it sound as though they were obligated to hire me because of Mr. Hewes's position. She told them that I would be going to the University of Wyoming after I finished high school. I had no intentions of attending the University of Wyoming at the time. I thought then I would never be able to afford college and it sounded as if she was apologizing for having me spend my evenings in their house and eating dinner with the family. I think now I was too touchy and dumb in not seeing she was trying to build up my confidence and encouraging me to go on to college.

I thought I was working for them because I was doing more work than any hired man they ever had. They had always hired

119

two men before during haying. One on the stack and another on the ground to pull the rope sling from the stack and set it in place for the next load of hay. I did both jobs. After spreading the hay on the stack I would climb down a ladder and pull the ropes and have them ready when Julius brought in the next buck-rake load of hay with a tractor. After we pulled it upon the stack with the tractor I'd climb back upon the stack again and spread it out while shaping the hay stack. I got up each morning before anyone else, milked the cow and did some other chores before joining the family at breakfast.

The Hewes ranch, in my opinion, had the best herd of registered Hereford cattle you could find anywhere. Accurate records were kept of all breeding stock and Julius and I usually took the bull out to serve the cows that were ready each morning. We also had to check for new born calves and when the calves were small the cows sometimes gave more milk than the calves could handle. We had to rope the cows and milk them out. If we didn't, the cows might have a tit or two dry up because the calf couldn't use all the milk when first born. The calves needed the extra milk when they were older. Julius taught me how to rope. The cows were so strong if we roped them around the neck our horses would have trouble holding them. We always aimed our ropes for the horns only, that way we could hold them. After we got two ropes on a cow, one holding her each way, we called for an older calf, named Swede. All we had to do was yell "here Swede" and he would come on the run and nurse out the cow. It was better he got kicked by the cow than one of us. This part of my job was lots of fun. They let me drive their pickup truck so I could go home to Sundance each Sunday. The water in Sundance was a lot better tasting than their well water so I would bring back a load of fresh drinking water to last the next week.

Duane, Buck and I talked about how foolish it was that we had always had to pay rent when we lived in Sundance to go to high school. With all the unsold lumber at the mill and Milt owed us all wages we would probably never collect. Why not buy a lot and build a house? If we had a large enough lot we could build a small house at first and later we could rent it and build a larger house. Buck said we could have his share of the tie lumber he had coming from Milt. He would still have enough money to go

120

to college when the ties were sold. When I inquired around town, Scotchy sold me three lots for 35 dollars, the same price he had paid for them. I had the deed put in our mother's name.

After Duane couldn't collect his wages from Merit Barton, he was back in town helping Lew Wane dig ditches. Lew was a carpenter of sorts and he would trade Duane's labor digging ditches for carpenter work and he would show us how to build a house. Duane and I had both taken a course called farm shop in high school so we knew how to use carpenter tools. We had finished a desk for the school that another kid had started. After that we built all kinds of furniture for the school, several desks, bookshelves for the library and several tables. I had helped another kid, Edgar Partlow, build a chicken house, as a project in the farm shop class. It was decided between Duane and me, we would start building a small house as soon as Hewes was through putting up hay.

Chapter Fifteen

Mr. Hewes wanted me to repair some fences after the hay was all stacked. I needed the money, but I also had to get started on building our house in Sundance if we were going to have it ready to move in before the weather got cold. I agreed to work the rest of the week, that would give me about three days to get the house started before school started. I told Mr. Hewes I needed the three days to attend to some business. I knew better than to tell him that Duane and I were going to build a house. He would have thought I was lying or, worse yet, laughed at me. Who would believe two high school kids could build a house in their spare time, go to school and still play football? We had to do all this between September 1 and December 1.

Mr. Hewes asked me, "What business could you have that is more important than working on my ranch?"

I was both embarrassed and angered by his question.

"Any business that I might have is more important to me," I told him, "than your whole damn ranch." I was sorry I said that but I never apologized because I knew what I said was true.

When they took me back to Sundance, Mrs. Hewes told me my check would be left at Ralph's store. Ralph Partlow ran the grocery store where they did their grocery shopping.

I don't know why Mrs. Hewes didn't just give me my check. When I picked it up a few days later I noticed she wrote on it, wages in full, one dollar per day except during one month haying, 30 dollars for that month. With four Sundays in a month it didn't require much knowledge in math to figure out the difference between a dollar a day and thirty dollars a month. We had been haying more than one month. I never said anything because I knew they were having trouble selling their bulls. I thought I had been shorted about 35 dollars, enough to pay for the building lots. I was thankful Ralph didn't ask me to pay our grocery bill when I picked up my check.

When Joanne, Eunice's baby was born that summer, Andy wasn't there. He was still in Denver looking for a job, he said.

The one thing I wanted most that would cost money besides the house, was a new suit of clothes to wear to graduation and the school prom. I never had a new suit of my own. Last year

Buck let me wear the one he had won in the raffle to the junior senior prom. Our school only had about 25 kids in a senior class so our proms always included the junior class. I put aside 20 dollars as though I didn't have it. My mother and I thought the safest place to hide it was in an envelope marked "Link's money" inside the lining of her purse. We would leave it there until I needed it so I wouldn't spend it for building materials.

In order for Duane and me to get started building our house we needed lumber. Buck told us we could have his, that was stacked and dry, ready to use, but we had to find a way to haul it to Sundance. Although Milt came to town with his truck empty many times, he told me if I wanted Buck's lumber I knew where it was. I had worked for Floyd Hawkins on weekends the year before in his gas station. He agreed to haul a load of lumber for us and I could pay by working at his station.

When we drove out to where Buck's lumber was located, we had to cross a rickety bridge that was more than 100 feet above the ravine it crossed. Mr. Hawkins was afraid of the bridge, but I told him they always hauled across it. The mill had been moved to another location but Buck's lumber was still there. We loaded the pile of lumber that belonged to Buck, it must have been around 5,000 board feet. On our way back to Sundance, before we crossed the ravine Mr. Hawkins got out and examined the old bridge. He was afraid to cross but there was no other way out of the canyon with the load of lumber. As we drove across the bridge I could hear the cracking of planks as they were breaking under the heavy load. I was sure we were going to end up in the bottom of the deep ravine.

The next time I saw Milt he asked me how I got the lumber. I told him it was Buck's tie lumber and Floyd Hawkins had hauled it for me.

"How the hell did you get it without crossing that old bridge?" That bridge is no longer safe to cross you know."

I realized we all could have been killed and we would have wrecked Hawkins' new truck for sure. Milt didn't warn me when he told me if I wanted Buck's lumber I knew where it was. He must have thought we could never get it out of that canyon.

You can't build a house with only two by fours and one by eight boards so I traded with John Grice. He ran a lumber yard in

Sundance and he needed clear grade boards for his customers. We needed floor joists, rafters, finished lumber and siding so we traded. Duane and I figured we had enough lumber, by trading, to build a house 14 feet by 20 feet plus a kitchen 10 feet by 12 feet. It may sound small by today's standards, but some high school kids rented cabins where two kids lived in one room 10 feet by 14 feet. We decided to put the chimney in the middle of the house so later, after we built the big house, it could be divided into two rooms. We could rent rooms to school kids and each room could have its own stove.

We had ordered the windows from Sears and they were there when I finished working for Mr. Hewes. A house had been built in Sundance that had some sand, gravel and cement left over. They sold it to us real cheap. Duane and I used it for our foundation, mixing it with a hoe in a borrowed wheelbarrow. The city of Sundance had some brick left at one of the springs that supplied city water. Scotchy was the mayor, he sold me the leftover brick for a penny a brick and lent me his new pickup to haul them to our building site. Mr. Kokash agreed to build the chimney for five dollars.

Duane and I got up mornings at about daylight so we could work on the house before school, then we worked after football practice until dark each night.

Our big problem was Lew Wane, the carpenter, who was supposed to work with us. He wouldn't work the same hours we had available. He had dismantled an old school house and had the lumber piled in his yard that was across the alley from where we were building. He let us keep the nails we pulled from his old lumber. We could also have any we found on the ground. They had to be straightened before being used but it saved us from buying new nails at seven cents a pound.

When Lew Wane was working on our house, he would stop whenever anyone came to buy used lumber he was selling. I could see at the pace he was working we would never get moved in before cold weather. I didn't blame him for not working with us at our weird hours, but he was charging us for eight hours work when we couldn't see what he had done. Because we weren't there when he worked, I asked him how many hours he had put in the day before. He told me eight. I asked him what he had accomplished.

"You don't understand carpenter work," he said. "If you don't think you're getting your money's worth, why don't you fire me."

He spit tobacco juice in my direction as if warning me not to press him. I dodged it but some landed on Duane's shoe.

"How about the wages Duane has coming for digging ditches?" I asked him.

"I'll pay him off in cash at 50 cents an hour."

I could tell he didn't mean it and he didn't think we could build the house without him.

"Consider yourself fired," I told him.

I thought the old man was going to have a heart attack. He got so mad he almost swallowed his chew of tobacco, but he stuck to his word. We didn't even have to take wages in bent nails, he paid Duane off in cash.

When I found out our teacher who taught farm shop knew less about building a house than Duane and me, I went to Mr. Ruggles, a carpenter. He was building a house so I knew he knew how. He was married to the same Mrs. Ruggles that had been my first grade teacher. When I went to him for advice he came over to our house and showed me more in five minutes than Lew Wane knew. He told me I could ask him for advice anytime and he would be glad to help.

Working on the house never interfered with my playing football, but once Duane had to miss a Saturday game scheduled for the junior varsity. Mr. Sampson, who replaced Mr. Tracy as our coach, told me Sundance lost the game because Duane couldn't play. We had to work on the house every day or it would never be ready to move in by the time the weather got too cold to work outside. Duane also subbed on the varsity football team.

We lost our first varsity game to Belle Fourche after we scored a touchdown on our first offensive play of the year. We also lost to the Sheridan team and who were usually state champions. When we played Deadwood the referee wouldn't count our first touchdown because it was a sleeper and he thought our man might have been off side, although he wasn't watching. We beat them anyhow, the first time Sundance had ever beaten Deadwood in either football or basketball.

Sampson, our coach, had gone to high school in Spearfish and his younger brother played on their football team that year. Sampson said if we could beat Spearfish he would consider us champions. Our school had never beaten Spearfish. Spearfish had already beaten Belle Fourche by about four touchdowns and Belle Fourche had beaten us by two touchdowns earlier in the season.

We scored first and missed the extra point. When they scored a touchdown I figured we had to block their extra point. They had a good kicker and we knew they would try a kick. In our defensive huddle I said we could block their kick by grabbing their linemen and pulling two of them out of the way, that way one of our guys would have a clear shot at their kicker. I was reminded we might get a penalty for holding.

"It's a night game," I said, "and they have only two officials, who might not see it. Besides how does a penalty hurt you on an extra point? They'd only get to try it over or they may be foolish enough to try to run it." I felt sure we could stop them on a running play.

We agreed we had to block the kick. Jim Fraser and Frank Dinkins, our center and left guard, said it was worth a try. I played the other guard position. Since it was my idea Jim and Frank agreed to clear the way for me to get to the kicker.

When the ball was snapped the officials had their eyes on the ball as they always do. Our plan worked. I got the ball in my belly just as it left the kicker's foot. It was one loud thud and the ball disappeared. I was wrapped around the ball and everyone but me was looking to see where the ball went. I knew where it was.

As I lay on the ground holding the ball and trying to get my breath back, Frank Dinkins reminded me, "Remember it was your idea."

Before the season started, Hally Oudin and I were elected captains. I guess I took the job pretty serious during this game. We were behind eight to six when we had the ball, fourth down and one yard to go for a touchdown. I told Hally, our quarterback, we could open a hole for him in the center of the line, but when we tried that play the last time he didn't go where we had the hole.

"The play goes over the center," I said. "Remember we run the play with an unbalanced line, both of our guards are to the right of our center."

"Okey dokey," Hally said, "but you better have a hole opened for me."

Frank, Jim and I had bodies pushed aside far enough you could have driven a truck through. My baby sister could have scored a touchdown. What did Hally do? He missed the hole, same as last time we tried this play, only he plowed his way through anyhow, over their bodies and down the other side into the end zone for a touchdown.

We were defending that 12 to 8 lead when somebody hit our big right end pretty hard and he started to cry from pain. When Hally asked our coach for a substitute, the coach wanted to know why. I told him we wanted someone who wouldn't bawl. Our coach put Duane, my little brother in to replace the injured player. I went over and kicked Duane in the butt to make him mad. I told him they would try to run the next play over him. Duane weighed 70 pounds less than the man he replaced and his size always fooled the other team. They have never yet made a tougher football player. My prediction was correct, but we were expecting it. Duane got there first and smeared them for a loss. They left him alone after that. I kept going from one of our players to the other either patting them on the back or kicking them in the butt. We were all shouting encouragement to each other so loud the other team could hardly hear their signals. Our coach's brother who was playing for the other team complained to an official.

"What are they doing wrong?" he asked.

"Can't you tell? They're all crazy," he said, unable to hold back his tears of desperation.

We won that game, but Spearfish went on to win their South Dakota conference. They had been rated about five touchdowns better than Sundance.

Otis Reynolds asked our coach, "What did you do to get the team up so high. Spearfish had a much better team."

Sampson looked at me and grinned, "I know, I know," he said, "Everybody knew they had a better football team, but somebody forgot to tell Link."

Duane and I had our new house ready to move in Thanksgiving day. It took a lot of hard work and all the money we could scrape up. We didn't have the wall board on the inside yet, but we could stop paying rent for the first time in years. There was no inside plumbing, the same as most houses in Sundance. We had to carry our water from a neighbor's outside spigot. The outhouse was a separate house you entered from inside the wood shed, this made it possible for anyone to return after nature's call with an arm load of wood.

While Duane and I were kept busy building the house and playing football, Buck was having his financial problems away at college. The few dollars he had collected before he left were spent. Milt was supposed to send him the rest of the money he had coming for his year's work when Milt got paid for several carloads of railroad ties. Every day or so Buck would write and ask Milt to send him some of the money he owed him, if not all at least part. Milt sent Buck ten bucks or so but didn't even answer most of Bucks letters. Duane and I had spent all the money we had on the house, except I still had the 20 dollars hidden in the lining of our mother's purse for a new suit of clothes.

Buck had a NYA job (National Youth Administration) that paid 15 dollars a month. His roommate, Ward Smith, got him a job where they worked for the railroad. They unloaded the fresh meat from the express car one night a week and Sunday mornings. They were only extras so the work wasn't steady. Some days Ward and Buck had to pool their money to see if they would eat that night. This was all happening to Buck when Milt owed him almost a year's wages. I wasn't able to give him any help. I might have sent him the money I was saving for my first suit, but at the time I didn't realize Buck was so desperate for money.

Eunice and Andy's baby were doing fine and Andy finally got a job at a logging camp near Keystone, South Dakota. Andy decided he would go to work on his new job and send for Eunice after he got his first paycheck. He asked me if I would loan him 20 dollars and borrow my friend's car and drive him to Newcastle where he could catch a bus. I told him I didn't have 20 dollars to loan him. I didn't think much of borrowing someone else's car, but I did it anyhow. I had ordered my new suit of clothes to be shipped COD from Sears, so I didn't really have 20 dollars to loan Andy. I wasn't used to driving at night and it rained so hard I had trouble seeing the road. Andy didn't pay me anything, not even money for gas. I was glad just to get back home alive.

When I got the notice from the post office that I had a COD

from Sears I was as excited as I was on my first date. I had to wait for my mother to get home from work because she kept the money to pay for it hidden inside the lining of her purse. I was waiting for her when she got home, but there was still time to pick up my first new suit before the post office closed. Eunice had gone to a friend's house to show off her baby.

I waited impatiently as my mother rummaged through her purse looking for the envelope she had put there marked, "Link's money." The envelope was missing. The money was gone. There was no way it could have fallen out the way it was tucked in behind the lining. We examined the purse looking for holes where it could have slipped through. There were no holes. My mother started to cry.

"I can't believe it," she said. "How could he?"

"How could who what?" I asked.

"I came in the house the other day and I thought Andy had been going through my purse. He acted so strange."

I was bewildered. I had been so excited, about to get my first suit, now I felt so let down. I remembered how Andy had asked to borrow 20 dollars. Why would he even think I had 20 dollars. Why not 10 or 25 or what I could spare? I was sick. I also knew my mother would never take the blame if somehow she had lost it.

"We'll just have to take the money I was going to pay on the grocery bill," my mother said. "Don't say anything to Eunice."

It may seem strange to anyone who hasn't done it, but a good fit on a suit from a mail order house all depends on your size. If you could wear clothes off the rack you got a lot more for your money from Sears than a tailor-made suit from a Sundance merchant. Mine couldn't have fit any better.

Buck wrote and told me he had given up hope trying to get any more money from Milt. If I could get anything out of him we could use it to finish the inside of the house.

Milt said he could get a good deal on some wallboard at a building supply store where he sold lumber in South Dakota. He agreed to get the wall board we needed for the little house Duane and I had built.

After finishing high school in May we could start building a bigger house for our mother. Duane and I had already leveled the area for the foundation with a pick and shovel. When we bought the lots we had the deed put in our mother's name because neither Duane nor I were of legal age. I overheard Milt telling our mother she would have to sign the deed to our lots over to him before he would help us. I told her in front of Milt not to sign anything over to him. He then demanded the money for the wallboard. Buck had sent me an account of how much Milt owed him. I told Milt when Buck was paid off we would pay him for the wallboard. We didn't see anything of Milt for a few weeks.

While Howard had a man helping him fell trees, Milt was trying to strike it rich with a coal mine south of Upton.

A widow who lived up the canyon above Sundance asked me several times, "When will Milt be back in town?"

She seemed a lot more interested in Milt than a mere acquaintance. Milt showed up in about a month. A friend of mine told me they saw Milt's car parked at the widow's place all night.

When I kidded Milt about it he asked me, "How the hell did you know?"

I told him, "One of her neighbors told me."

"Tell her to mind her own damn business," was his reply.

I know the neighbor's suspicion must have been correct. In a few weeks Milt married Ethel who had three kids and another on the way.

They rented a house across the alley from us and the next morning after their wedding Milt was over to our place bumming firewood. It was worth the loss of a little wood to see Milt chopping it. It had always been one of his younger brothers or the hired help that cut his wood.

There were many things about Milt's life that changed after he got married. I like to think God has a way of giving people what they have coming.

Chapter Sixteen

To play in a state basketball tournament was one of my childhood dreams. The Sundance team I played with my junior year in high school got first place in our conference but the state tournament was canceled by the health department because there had been several deaths in Wyoming caused by spinal meningitis.

Teams that placed first, second or third in the district tournament got to compete in the state tournament. My senior year we had won our first two games and were playing Gillette for second place and the opportunity to represent our district at the state. When we got 10 points ahead we decided to sit on our lead. We kept the ball almost the entire last quarter. There was no rule that required us to shoot after so many seconds. I still remembered when I was a sophomore how Keck, one of the Gillette players, gave me the Bronx cheer and sprayed me with saliva. Now it was my turn. When I taunted this same kid, with words not spit, he started crying. The Gillette home crowd booed us for stalling, this I also enjoyed. The win gave us second place in our district and a trip to Casper where the state tournament was held.

Although our basketball team didn't place in the state tournament it was a happy experience to be a part of what was to me a great event. We stayed in a hotel for four days and met players from all over Wyoming. After the tournament we went to a school dance. I never quite understood, or appreciated it at the time, why girls stopped me from time to time and asked for my autograph. I knew it was fun and I enjoyed every minute of it. Just to be in Casper, one of Wyoming's largest cities was exciting. Casper boasted having the only traffic light in Wyoming at that time.

That state tournament was a happy climax to a four-year struggle for me. I looked forward to graduation, like winning another basketball game. Seeing my high school days coming to an end was in a way frightening. It was knowing a more important game lay ahead, only it wasn't a game, this was for real. I was 19, a kid by most people's standards and like most high school graduates, it was time for me to make decisions that would affect me the rest of my life.

Buck was writing to me from Laramie telling me I should join him at the University of Wyoming in September. He assured me

Link leaving for state basketball tournament.

we would get by somehow. He had a summer job working for the Union Pacific Railroad in the freight house. He had no intentions of ever returning to Sundance, except for a visit from time to time. I knew by then there was no chance of building our mother a house or doing anything with Milt. This was even more apparent since he was married.

Mr. Tracy, who had been my coach and teacher had taken over his father's grocery store in Sundance and was always available for me to go to for advice. He had gotten me the part-time government job in the assessor's office when I was going to high school. He told me they were going to have many jobs poisoning crickets that summer working out of Sundance and I should apply. When I got the job I knew I could earn enough so I could join Buck in Laramie and go to school at the University of Wyoming. The job would pay me around 300 dollars if I worked most of the summer, more than enough to go to college. This was about three times more than I could earn working on ranches.

Going to college was something I had hoped for but never thought I could afford. In Wyoming, at that time, if you had enough credits to graduate from a Wyoming high school, you also had all the requirements to enter the university. I remembered when I took some kind of a pre-college test I thought it was a joke because an entrance test score wasn't required and I couldn't afford college anyway. I was so sure, I didn't even take time to try to answer all the questions.

When I told my mother I had a job poisoning crickets and would be going to the university next fall she seemed pleased, yet I could tell something was bothering her. I guess because I was overjoyed with excitement I thought she would be too. She showed me a letter she got that day from her mother, my grandmother. Grandma wanted to send my mother money for her train ticket if she would spend the summer with her in Seattle. This was 1937 and our mother hadn't been back to Washington since she left to marry my dad in 1907. It had been 30 years since she had seen all her brothers and sisters.

"You are going aren't you?" I asked.

"I don't think I should." She put her hand up half covering her mouth as she spoke, as if trying to hide her true feelings. I knew she wanted to go.

"This is great news. You should be happy."

"I'm happy for you getting the job because it means you will be joining Buck in Laramie. But I can't be gone this summer."

"Why not?"

Have you forgotten? We're behind about 100 dollars on the grocery bill. It'll take me all summer to catch up."

"I always thought you wanted to go back to Washington."

"I do."

I'll be able to pay the grocery bill now that I got this job."

"The most important thing is your education. You'll need all your money for college."

"I'll have enough to do both. Grandma wants to see you and so do your brothers and sisters."

"I'll think about it."

I knew that meant she'd go.

Several of my friends also got jobs poisoning crickets and would be able to afford college. For some men around Sundance this was their first job that paid that much since the start of the depression.

I have always hoped that humans benefited from that government project. I know the effect on bird life was devastating. We dusted powdered arsenic on the crickets with a hand-cranked blower. I think we killed every insect-eating bird in that corner of Wyoming. When I first learned to shoot a 22-caliber rifle, I liked to bring home wild prairie chickens for dinner. I don't think prairie chickens have returned to that corner of Wyoming to this day.

Milt let me use his car to drive our mother to Moorcroft where she boarded a train for Washington. I don't think I had ever seen her this happy. With Duane and Grace both working, I stayed by myself and cooked my own meals in the house Duane and I had built. Duane wasn't old enough to work at the same job I had since it was considered too hazardous for anyone under 18. He was working for Hewes. Grace worked the first part of the summer for Fredie Oudin, baby-sitting while Fredie helped her husband run the bowling alley in Sundance.

One day when I came home from work, I found Milt had moved his wife and three kids into the house as though it was his. When I confronted him about his intentions he assured me it would only be for a short time. During that short time Milt's wife got in a fight with a neighbor lady. They were throwing rocks and swearing at each other when I broke it up. It was something over their kids playing together. I was glad I was able to separate them before they got to pulling hair because Milt's wife was several month's pregnant. A few days later I took a knife away from Bernie, Milt's stepson, who was only four or five years old. He was going to use it on another kid about his age.

One night when I came home from work I found Milt's stepdaughters, Bernice and Clarice making mud pies. Bernice was Bernie's twin sister, and Clarise was a couple of years older. They were in the kitchen mixing dirt with sugar, flour and water in one of my mixing bowls. They had made the most awful mess of the kitchen you could ever imagine. Their mother was asleep in another room. I discovered Bernie had taken his nap in my bed and it stunk because he had wet the bed. I told Milt he would have to find another place for his family to stay.

I was corresponding with Buck and he had a temporary place for me to stay when I got to Laramie to start college. Buck lived in a basement room in a four-plex where he worked out his rent by doing some janitor work in the rest of the building. He told me I could stay with him at least until his room mate came back after summer vacation. It was possible his roommate might not come back.

The first thing I did when I got enough money was pay off the grocery bill in full. It came to a little over 90 dollars. From then on I saved everything above bare living expenses. Buck told me I would need about 200 dollars. I could see I was just about going to make it.

The letters I received from our mother were all about Washington state and what a wonderful time she was having. For her birthday Duane and I went in together to buy her a new dress and a hat to match. We saw just what we wanted the Sears catalog. We knew her dress size but the hat was a different problem. I found one of her old hats and put it on me and had to guess how much bigger it was than my head. Her presents got there in time for her birthday and she said they both fit perfectly. One of my aunts in Seattle thought it was a strange thing for two boys to give their mother such a birthday present. The strange part she said was they both looked fine on our mother and she couldn't have done better if she had spent all day shopping in a Seattle department store. I guess what she didn't know was that our mother had such strange kids.

My summer job was going fine as far as saving money was concerned, but it seemed like the more arsenic we put on the crickets, the more would hatch. It was an endless job as we tried to head them off before they got into grain fields, hay meadows or whatever. They would almost cover the ground in places and eat everything in front of them as they moved like an army destroying ever bit of vegetation but the trees. The alarm went out they were headed for Sundance and some said they would even eat the paint off the houses if we couldn't head them off. People acted afraid as though a fire was approaching town.

It was decided we would dig a trench and put sheet metal fastened to a board on the far side so the crickets couldn't climb out. Every so often we curved the ditch and metal covered fence and dug a hole that was filled with crude oil. It worked. The crickets had to be taken out and burned as the holes filled with dead ones.

When we were defending dear old Sundance we didn't pay any attention to days off or eight-hour days. The government wouldn't pay overtime, so we had to take time off instead. I had several days off coming I had to take before the end of the month or I would be donating my time.

In one of the letters from our mother she told about getting in a car accident. Grandma had a heart attack and was in intensive care. Uncle Gus had been taking them to see one of my mother's old school teachers when their car got hit broadside at a stop sign. It wasn't important whose fault it was because Grandma was over 80 years old and a nurse said she probably wouldn't live.

When I got home from work one night there was a message pinned on my door telling me there was a telegram for me at the telephone office. My grandma died a thousand deaths before I got to that telephone office. The telegram was from Ethel, Milt's wife. It read, "I am not well stop come at once stop signed Ethel." It was sent from some town in Kansas.

I knew she wanted Milt to take her to Kansas and see her first husband's family. Her first husband had committed suicide by drinking strychnine. I couldn't understand why she wanted to go there, especially in the heat of the summer. I wasn't sure she was sick or if that was her way of getting Milt to come and get her. I knew Milt, if he said he would be back to take her home in a week, it meant when he got around to it. I couldn't decide if I should try to get word to Milt or not.

The next morning I was trying to decide what to do about the telegram when a man who Milt had promised some lumber to, came to the house and asked me if I knew when Milt would be in town. The man was building a new store in Sundance and he urgently needed the ceiling joist as it was delaying the job. He told me he couldn't just buy them at a lumber yard or he would. They had to be long enough to span the width of the building. He had specially ordered them from Milt and had been promised them a couple of weeks ago.

I told him I would like to see Milt myself, now that I had a telegram for him. He told me if I could tell him how to find Milt he would deliver the telegram. I knew about where the sawmill was but it was hard to tell anyone how to get there because I had never been there myself.

Since I wouldn't be working the next few days I told the man, "I'll try to find the mill if you'll drive me out there and bring me back."

"I'll pay you for your time if you will," he said, "because those ceiling joists are holding up the whole job."

"It won't be necessary to pay me, I only hope I can find him. I don't like lying around town doing nothing anyhow."

We took a short cut through the Bear Lodge forest reserve. It was a beautiful drive as the road wound its way around the pine trees and over the many hills and ravines. I always liked the smell of pine. When we finally came out the other side of the forest, we stopped at the first ranch and asked directions

"I know Milt Kaiser and where the mill used to be," I was told by the rancher, "but the mill has moved or will be moved soon."

He told us how many gates we would have go through and how many bridges to cross and how many roads not to take ending up with, "You can't miss it."

I had a piece of paper in my pocket and a pencil and had him draw me a map or we might have been looking for it yet.

With the aid of the map, we found the location and Howard and Milt had just finished unloading the last of the sawmill off a truck.

When the man asked Milt about his order of lumber, Milt explained to him how he knew those joists had to be top grade. They had to move the mill to find the right kind of trees without knots and they had to be strong enough to carry the roof.

"We have found the very best trees at this location and your order will be the first we will cut," Milt told him.

I thought the guy would be mad when he could see the mill wasn't even ready to cut lumber. He seemed happy that Milt waited until he could find choice trees. I couldn't believe it, he went for Milt's line of bullshit.

It reminded me of the time Milt couldn't make the payments on an old Dodge truck and the dealer asked him to bring the truck back. When Milt took the truck in he explained to the dealer the old truck wouldn't do the job. If he just had a new Ford truck he knew he would soon be making plenty of money for the payments. The dealer sold new Fords and Milt went on how much better Ford trucks were than Dodge trucks. You guessed it. Milt drove away with a brand new truck and the only down payment was the old Dodge he was about to lose because he hadn't been making the payments.

I gave Milt the telegram from his "sick" wife. He read it and smiled.

"I guess she's had enough of Kansas."

"I thought you were supposed to be poisoning crickets," he said to me.

"After we saved Sundance from the big cricket invasion, they gave us all a few days off," I told him.

"This man needs those ceiling joists real soon and..."

"Yea. He told me, he needed them weeks ago." I interrupted Milt and knew what he was leading up to.

I turned my back on him and walked away. He followed me. He never gives up, I thought.

"I have to go to Kansas and pick up Ethel," he said.

Here it comes. I thought. It was like waiting for him to drop the other shoe. I knew what he was going to say next, as sure as I knew he wore two shoes.

"How much will you take to work for me until you have to go back to work on your cricket job?"

"Since you are going to be gone and I'll be working with

138

Howard and I don't like to lay around town doing nothing. I can help Howard until Sunday. But please, don't promise me anything. I'd rather we both know in advance that I'm donating my time."

He had a silly grin on his face. Like I said, he was about as hard to insult as a hungry stray dog.

"Make damn sure you are here Sunday to take me back to town." I added. "I have to go to work on my job Monday. Okay?"

"Okay," he said and went over to his lumber customer who had been out of hearing range. Milt fed him some more bull.

With Milt gone the next few days, Howard and I set up the mill and had everything under control when Milt showed up late Sunday afternoon. The three of us got in the pickup and headed for Sundance. We hadn't had supper yet, but Howard said we'd eat at Whitie's greasy spoon in Sundance.

By the time we got to my house in Sundance it was dark. I thought it was strange there was a light on since the house wasn't wired for electricity.

"What the hell," I said, "there must be someone in my house."

"Oh that's my family," Milt said.

"What the hell are they doing in there?"

"I didn't think you would mind."

"If you had asked me you sure as hell would have found out."

We sat in the pickup, for an instant no one moved or said anything.

"Get them out of there," I said. "Tonight!" When Milt got out Howard and I drove downtown to the restaurant. Howard could see I was mad. I could tell by the look he gave me he approved of what I had said to Milt.

"I'm buying," Howard said as we sat down to order supper.

When we got back to my house, Milt loaded his wife and kids in the pickup.

His only comment was, "I wished you'd have told me you were going to a restaurant to eat. I haven't had my supper yet either."

The next letter I got from our mother said Grandma was out of danger and back home with Aunt Myrtle. Our mother said she would be coming home a little later than she had planned because she wanted to wait until Grandma was a little better. It would be after I left for Laramie. Duane didn't like the idea that she wouldn't be home when school started.

My job ended sooner than I had expected because the government was running low on funds. I was told they would keep only the married men with families. It was sort of like being penalized for being young and single. I knew that money meant as much to my future as it did to the family men, but I was used to depression talk.

I phoned a rancher that had an ad in the Sundance paper asking for help thrashing. I agreed to work for him for two dollars a day until the first of September. It was twice as much as I got paid the summer before working on a ranch.

Buck wrote and told me he had a job for me that started soon after the first of September. I could work for a couple of weeks at the college farm putting up silage before school started. It paid more than what I was earning running a bundle wagon on the thrash run. I was eager to be with Buck so I told him I'd join him when it was time to start the silage job.

I stayed with the thrashing run until the first of September, as agreed, driving a team of horses on a bundle wagon. Never in my life had I seen so many rattlesnakes. The grain had been cut for some time and field mice were under almost every shock of bundles. The snakes were there after the mice. I would carefully check each shock of grain for rattlesnakes before I started to pitch bundles onto the wagon.

"There are rattlesnakes everywhere," my boss warned me. "Always shake the shock before you pitch. They don't always rattle before they strike. Like some people, the ones that don't warn you are the ones to watch out for the most."

I think his warning was intended to be as much about people as snakes. He was telling me how he managed to successfully cope with the Great Depression.

As the man said, "You will find a lot of rattlesnakes and some will strike without warning." This bit of philosophy came from the last rancher I would ever work for in Wyoming.

Chapter Seventeen

The University of Wyoming is located in Laramie in the southeastern corner of the state, some 300 miles from Sundance. With most of my worldly possessions in one suitcase, I got a ride with Mr. Ruth who had been my boss that summer. He took me as far as Cheyenne where he had to report to his supervisor at the state capital. I rode a Greyhound bus from Cheyenne to Laramie. In Buck's last letter he gave me good directions so I could find the basement apartment where I would be staying with him, at least until his regular roommate returned when school started.

Buck had lined up a temporary job of putting up silage at the university's farm for both of us. Some of the silage workers were college students, some were not students who worked steady at the farm. They had a rule that students couldn't drive the beautiful pedigreed Percheron mares that pulled the wagons hauling the sunflowers we used to make into silage. I had never seen better draft horses anywhere. It was understandable why they wouldn't let just anyone drive them.

One morning, when a regular driver failed to show up for work Buck, was asked to drive the horses. It was evident to me that the foreman in charge of the farm knew and trusted Buck as did the professors that came around while we were working.

I hadn't registered for classes yet so I had to make up my mind as to what subjects I would be taking. When I started college I had the same feeling I had before my first day of grade school. Except then I didn't have any decisions to make.

When most boys start kindergarten they leave home, where they are king, only to find many other kids who are also used to being king. It sometimes took a bloody nose or some other kind of peer pressure to shape their actions. When they start high school they find they are no longer eighth graders who the little kids look up to.

I had left a high school where I knew everyone in school. I had been co-captain of a winning football team and high scorer on our basketball team both my junior and senior years. One year we took second place in our conference and first place the other. I knew I wasn't good enough nor could I afford to take an active part in varsity sports at the University of Wyoming. Instead of a big frog in a little pond I had become a little frog in what to me was a very big pond.

Buck was taking agriculture and his grades were near the top. He got along well with his professors. He had financial problems at first, but with hard work he was now getting by okay and had bought his first car, a Model A Ford.

I wanted to become a lawyer, maybe because I had always admired Otis Reynolds. I would have to take two years of pre-law and if my grades were good enough to get in law school I would need to complete three more years in the law school. I knew I could always change my major after the first year or so without losing any college credits. My second choice was to become a high school teacher and coach football and basketball.

I was only supposed to stay with Buck in the basement apartment until his regular roommate returned for the summer. Mr. Holiday, who owned the four-plex, said he didn't want the other guy back because he never did the work that was supposed to be done without being reminded all the time. It was agreed that I could stay and help Buck with the janitor work that didn't amount to much. We had to keep the lawn mowed and watered, wash the apartment windows on the outside every two months, some vacuuming and dusting in the halls and some other little jobs around the place. Compared to pitching bundles and stacking hay it was like getting free room rent.

Buck got me a job with the Union Pacific railroad where he worked at the freight house one night a week and Sunday mornings. We moved the fresh meat from the express cars when the passenger trains arrived. Everyone got called for work according to their seniority and I would get to work only when they were short handed.

I got another job for needy students. It was federally financed through the National Youth Administration (NYA) so I could earn 15 dollars a month for 40 hours of work. I sometimes did janitor and gardener work on campus and sometimes I worked at the college farm. By working eight hours Saturdays at the farm I only had to work two hours during the week. With three jobs I came close to paying my board. Tuition was 15 dollars per quarter that included passes to all the home football or basketball games. I wasn't required to use any of my meager cash for room rent but two meals a day at a boarding house cost about 20 dollars a month. Buck and I both skipped breakfast to save money.

Sometimes I had trouble staying awake in class after working a night at the freight house or when I stayed up all night studying. One five-hour accounting course took much of my time. Because I had taken bookkeeping in high school they put me in a class with others that were supposed to know the basics. It took only one week to cover everything I had been exposed to in Mr. Rickard's class in high school. It was important that my grades were a B or better in order to get into law school.

Our sociology professor would lecture about the study of history, development, organization, and the different problems people had living together as social groups. We covered various theories of people and how they reacted toward each other in different cultures. He told the class a story about what he had discovered last summer when he was on vacation as he toured the state.

"People can learn a lot by observing birds, animals and insects," he said. "Last summer while up in northeastern Wyoming near Sundance I drove up on this high grassy hill called Warren's Peak in the Bear Lodge National Forest Reserve. On this peak the ground was covered with literally millions of little insects. The natives called them crickets. They were actually the genus Gryllus belonging to the order Orthoptera, related to the locusts and grasshoppers. I asked one of the natives why all these insects had converged on top of this grassy hill. He told me it was because their legs were shorter on one side than the other. They had to walk around the hill because they couldn't go down hill. So they all converged at the top where I observed them."

He concluded his story by saying, "People are like these insects, you need to understand why they act as they do. It may be due to physical of mental reasons that we don't understand. When you can figure out what makes people do what they do, you can solve many of the world problems."

I couldn't believe what I had heard. Here was an educated man telling this story for the truth. I think he had a B.S. degree. He made it sound as if a group of bugs belonged to fraternity called Orthoptera. It had been my job most of the past summer poisoning these crickets, these cousins of the grasshoppers maybe

143

uncles of locusts, he didn't say. I still knew they were crickets. I knew the area he was talking about and the reason they were on the grassy peaks. It was because they fed on grass and the area below the peaks was all covered with timber.

It was a big joke, like selling someone the Brooklyn Bridge, to tell some dumb tourist that story about their legs being shorter on one side than the other.

I knew he used the story to make a point, but when you use information without checking out its accuracy you don't solve human problems. You will more than likely create more problems than you solve.

How do you tell someone when he has been foolishly duped? That was my question. I knew I couldn't say anything in front of the class because it would have embarrassed him to make him look dumb and he would probably flunk me. If I didn't say anything and he found out I knew, he could likewise be unhappy with me. I waited until the classroom was emptied of all students.

"Could I speak to you for a minute sir?" I asked as he started to leave.

"If you're sure it's not more than a minute," he grumbled.

"I'm from Sundance," I began, "and I'm afraid that the character that told you about crickets having legs shorter on one side than the other was pulling your leg."

He looked at me fuming, "Mister are you telling me you think I'm stupid?"

He grabbed his grade book and stomped off. As I watched him leave, my heart sank because I knew that grade book would never show an A for me in Sociology 101. We had been told much of our grades depended on class participation. I guess I hadn't learned how a student can participate in a class discussion with a professor who only wants to make a point. You have to agree with his theories. I'm afraid I have never learned to agree with someone when I know he's stupid.

Political science for pre-law students was a lot different from what I had expected, especially when we got to reviewing briefs on supreme court cases. The United States Supreme Court, I found out, was the basis of all law in our country. It didn't seem to matter if the congress or the state legislators, who were elected by the people, passed a law. If the supreme court, whose judges were all

144

political appointees, didn't agree with those laws they could change them or kill them altogether. The congress and legislators had to answer to the people who elected them, while the supreme court judges who were appointed for life had to answer to no one. The courts were made up of lawyers whose main concern, we were taught, was to win their cases. It didn't matter if they knew the person they were defending was guilty of murder or whatever. It was a "good" lawyer's duty to get him off if at all possible. They called it justice and seeing that your client got a fair trial. At home I was always taught justice meant the guilty party should be caught and punished and it was the duty of every good citizen to help bring him to justice.

It was hard for me to take part in class discussions that taught there would be times you or your fellow workers might knowingly help a murderer or some other criminals go free.

Before I left Sundance to go to the university, most of my knowledge of the outside world was from reading and the movies. In the movies the guys in the white hats always won and whenever a guy in a black hat killed someone, he died before the end of the movie. My firsthand knowledge of a lawyer was Otis Reynolds, who I had gone to on several occasions for help when something was bothering me. Without his help I never would have finished high school.

I told Buck I wasn't so sure anymore I wanted to be a lawyer. He told me I should switch over to agriculture because I didn't have the background to be a lawyer anyhow. I was starting to believe more and more he was right but I wouldn't admit it to him. Besides, if taking agriculture meant farming or ranching, I had seen enough of that.

There were several university students who had gone to high school with me in Sundance. Dick Smith was one who used to come down to our apartment from time to time and we would have what we called a bull session. Dick had always been a good student and he wasn't sure what he wanted to do in life either. In our high school geometry class when our teacher didn't understand something she was trying to explain, Dick would help. When Dick explained to me how and why a radio worked, I told him that if what he said was true then if the aerial wire touched a certain tube it would complete the circuit and cause a short. That's

145

correct he said and when he showed me, it blew a fuse. The lights went out in our apartment. It convinced me Dick knew what he was talking about which was a lot more than some of my professors.

Dick had run away from home and rode the freight trains when he was in high school. He spent one summer with an aunt who lived in Tacoma, Washington. When I told him about the professor and the short-legged crickets, he said he learned more sociology riding a freight train to Washington than they could ever pretend to teach in a college classroom.

"Aren't you afraid of the bums?" I asked.

"There's a world out there you'd never believe exists unless you've seen it," he said. "The bums are nothing to be afraid of. It's like anything else, you got to know what you're doing."

"I've always wanted to go to Washington."

"Riding the freights is a good way to save money. Look at it this way, if it takes four days to get to Tacoma by freight and the ticket would have cost you 60 bucks, you've made 15 bucks a day."

"I never thought of it that way."

"Why don't you go with me next summer? Didn't you once tell me you have relatives around Seattle? My aunt can get me a job out there making more than what I'd make in Wyoming."

"I have several aunts and uncles that live in or around Seattle I've never seen, but I'd be scared to ride freight trains."

"We could go together as far as Auburn, Washington and I can show you the ropes."

"It all depends if I can find work around Sundance. I do plan on going to college next year if I can afford it."

When I told Buck what Dick and I were thinking about he told me I was nuts. "I don't intend to try to find work around Sundance anymore," he told me.

"You still sore at Milt?" I asked.

"I should be, but I don't think it's altogether him. I just don't see any future around there. I can make as much working part time in Laramie at the freight house as any full-time ranch job up there."

"What about our mother, Duane and Grace?"

"What about them?"

146

I could see what Buck meant. We had to look out for ourselves, but I hated to think of our mother spending the rest of her life on WPA in Wyoming. I knew she always wanted to return to Washington someday. Her mother was over 80 and after the car accident last summer she wouldn't live many more years.

I had been writing to our cousin Roger who lived near Arlington, Washington. He invited me out to see him. Roger said we should all move out to Washington. His mother had several places around there. We could buy or rent one and the colleges in Washington were as good as those in Wyoming.

Duane would be finishing high school in May and he wanted to go on to college some place. He might have a lot better chance in finding work in Washington.

I knew Dick's idea of riding a freight train sounded crazy. I wrote Duane and told him what I was thinking and warned Roger we might be seeing him in the summer.

After I had lived away from Sundance for several months for the first time, the whole world looked different to me. It was a world I always knew existed but never had been a part of. I knew Buck was right, there was no future in Sundance anymore for our family or me. It had been like living in a ghetto. I realized that as kids, we had been raised in poverty maybe even worse in some ways than most kids raised in the slums of a big city.

A teacher of mine in grade school once talked about the poor people that lived in our big cities. I wondered why they didn't just get up and leave. Would getting a college education be my way of leaving? Buck thought so.

If I could achieve success for myself, would I enjoy it knowing my mother was still in Sundance working on WPA? Should she be left to live out the rest of her life wishing she was in Washington state? I wasn't sure what was the right thing for me to do. I only knew a wrong decision would affect the rest of my life.

The way things were going, it was doubtful my grades would be good enough to get into law school. Attending school without playing basketball or football seemed flat, like the way oatmeal tastes when cooked without salt. I guess I felt like the way it smelled the time Milt put manure in my oatmeal on April Fools' Day. I was having trouble separating the manure from the oatmeal before biting into it. I didn't fully understand the grading system. I got good enough grades on the test but I was told class participation was also part of my grades. This meant the professors had to like you to get a higher grade than average. It seemed there was nothing I could do to improve my grade in sociology after I tried to explain that crickets didn't have legs shorter on one side than the other. I still had a chance to get into law school if I could get a high enough grade in my political science class.

Our political science professor said he would be teaching summer classes in California and would be leaving early. A student intern would be giving us our final exam and it would count as most of our grade for the course. He said he would make out the exam before he left and it would be all true or false questions. That was good news to me because I got an A in the only test we had taken so far that quarter. My whole future as a lawyer depended on that final. I burned the midnight oil as we called it, studying most all night cramming for that final. A friend of mine who had always been an A student in that class was well liked by the professor. I thought the exam was easy and after my friend and I both finished we compared papers. It was easy to do with a student intern giving the exam. I didn't change anything on my papers because we agreed on all the answers except two out of 100. We looked them up later, my answer was right on one and he was correct on the other. When we got our final grade for the quarter my friend got an A and I got a C. When I complained to my advisor, naturally I couldn't tell him how I knew I should have had the same grade as my friend. He shuffled some papers before answering.

"You did do well on the final," he admitted.

"According to your pre-college test scores it's unbelievable you lasted past the first quarter," he said.

"I can't understand what that test has to do with my grades now in college. When I took that test I didn't think there was any chance I would be going to college. I didn't think it meant anything so I didn't even finish it."

"If what you are telling me is true you should take that test over. I can't say anymore about it now but when you return for the fall quarter remind me and I'll arrange for you to take your pre-college test over."

"How about this grade I got in political science?"

"I'm sorry. I'm afraid I can't change that."

I thanked him for his time and left. If I understood him correctly he was telling me some professors check on the score we got in our pre-college test and arrive at out college grades accordingly. I couldn't believe anything so unfair was possible.

I got a letter from my cousin Roger in Washington and he was expecting me out to see him in the summer. Duane said if he couldn't get a job around Sundance that paid enough so he could go on to college, he wanted to go with Dick and me. When I got to thinking about it, the idea sounded exciting. I could see Washington state and like Dick said, learn my sociology without listening to stories about short-legged crickets told by narrow-minded professors.

Left; Buck and Link, receive reserve officers training while attending the University of Wyoming.

Chapter Eighteen

After my first year at the University of Wyoming, life took on a new meaning for me in planning my future. The coming summer vacation was not really a vacation but a time to find a job and earn enough money to return to college next September. Buck's plans were to stay at Laramie taking his chances on getting work at the railroad freight house. I didn't have enough seniority to get more than a few hours work now and then.

A friend of mine from Sheridan asked me if I knew anyone that was staying in Laramie for the summer that could hold his job for him until school started in the fall. He did the cleaning in a little restaurant every night after they closed. The pay was a week's meal ticket for a week's work. I agreed to take the job and Buck agreed to take over after I left. This gave Buck a job for his meals, he also had the one at the apartment where we stayed that paid the rent. With his job at the freight house, Buck was set for the summer.

My plans were to find work around Sundance, if possible, and return to school in the fall. If I couldn't find work that would pay enough to go to college, I would go to the state of Washington by freight train with Dick Smith.

On my way back to Sundance I hitchhiked rides as far as Lusk, Wyoming the first day. As I was standing by the side of the road trying to catch a ride toward Sundance, a friend named Bill Watts recognized me. He stopped and invited me to spend the night at his house in Lusk. I had met Bill when we worked putting up silage at the university farm last September. He had finished law school fall quarter and had passed the bar examination. We had a good talk about his new law practice and how hard it was for him to get started. The only steady money he earned was from legal work for the city of Lusk. It paid about the same as working on a ranch. He and his wife had a baby only a few months old. This baby, of this struggling young attorney, I believe is the same James Watts that later became the Secretary of Interior for President Reagan.

After having breakfast with Bill and his wife we wished each other luck and I continued on my way home using my thumb as my only mode of transportation. I had been by the side of the road for a while before two men in a Lincoln Continental stopped and gave me a ride. One of the men asked about the letterman's sweater I was wearing. When I told him I played football he was more than a little interested.

"Did you win any games?" he asks.

"We beat Deadwood and Spearfish." I told him.

He said he had heard of those two towns but never realized Sundance even had a football team.

"Neither did Deadwood or Spearfish," I told him, "but they found out."

He seemed to like my confident answer. "How would you like to play football for me?" he asked.

I realized I didn't know who I was talking to. It could have been the Deadwood coach.

"I guess I should have introduced myself," he said. "I'm Lawrence Jones and I coach football for the University of Nebraska. My friend here, is a professor there."

I had heard of Jones, the Nebraska coach. Nebraska's football record was one of the best. Only a few years ago they had played in the Rose Bowl. I didn't take the coach's offer seriously. Was he actually recruiting me to play football for Nebraska? It would have been easier for me to believe President Roosevelt wanted me for his vice president.

"I'm not good enough to make the Nebraska football team," I told him and he didn't press the subject further.

I think it was his way of letting me know who he was. He was on his way to a publisher's summer home on Sand Creek, near the little town of Beulah. Annenberg, the publisher, was known for his national sport Publication. Beulah was about 20 miles east of Sundance. Annenberg was a millionaire that invited big-shot friends to stay with him and go fishing.

Duane had graduated from high school that May and had been looking for a job for a couple of weeks. He had decided he couldn't make enough around Sundance for college so he wanted to go with Dick and me to Washington.

Duane told me about one rancher who offered him a job. He explained to Duane their day would start a little before five in the morning. The rancher was proud to say he got up with his men and helped with the chores including milking, feeding the pigs, getting the horses in and tending to the calves, etc.

"After we have breakfast we are in the field by seven," said the rancher. "I always let my men take a full hour at noon when the horses are eating. We quit at six and all have dinner together, that is after we take care of the work horses. After dinner I always help with the milking and the rest of the chores. We are usually through by nine."

"What do you pay?" Duane asked him.

"You young punks are all alike. The first question is how much do you pay."

"When you sell your cattle or your wheat," Duane asked, "do you know the price they are paying you or do you find out when they hand you your check?"

The rancher didn't answer Duane's question.

"My second question. How much do you pay?"

"I pay the going wage. A dollar a day."

"From five in the morning until nine at night, I would like two dollars a day. I need to make enough to go to college."

You don't work all the time from five to nine. I feed you three meals too you know. And you get an hour off at noon while the horses are eating.

"It sounds like you take good care of your horses, but they don't need to save for college. I can't work for a dollar a day and have enough for college.

"I hope you starve to death if you turn down a good job like I'm offering you," he interrupted.

"If I worked for you, I might as well starve."

Duane told me that was about all we could expect from working on ranches around Sundance. I was offered a job that was about the same as the one Duane turned down.

Milt was still running his sawmill but working for him was out of the question. He never paid Buck, Duane and me for the times we had worked. The last time I worked a summer for Milt, I not only didn't get paid, I even had to hitchhike a ride back to town when school started.

Duane and I had never put running water in the little house we had built for our mother. We decided we should do that before we left for Washington. There was no way of knowing when or if ever we would be back in Sundance, and our mother and

Grace would still be living in the house. The ditch for the water pipe had to be at least six feet deep to get the pipe down far enough so it wouldn't freeze in the cold Wyoming winters. While we were digging the ditch and installing the water pipe, several ranchers tried to talk us into going to work for them. It was always the same, they wouldn't pay enough for us to go to college.

People around Sundance didn't seem to believe or understand the three little pigs, as Eunice use to sometimes call Buck, Duane and me. We were not going to be satisfied to live on other people's scraps like pigs and chickens for the rest of our lives. Leaving Sundance meant leaving a lot of happy memories and a lot of good, friendly people. The way I looked at it, it was as my teacher had told us in grade school.

"Kids that are raised in the slums of our big cities have to leave. They should realize there is no future for them as long as they stay in their old neighborhoods."

I wrote to our Cousin Roger who lived in Washington. He said there was farm work as well as work in the woods out there. He was expecting us and the plan was we could stay with him and his mother until we found work.

Dick had ridden the freight trains as far as Tacoma, where a relative of his lived. He told us what we could expect. Duane and I both had small day packs we could strap on our backs. It was important to have our hands free while riding freight trains, Dick said. We carried only the bare necessities with us and had one suitcase mailed to Spokane, Washington where we could pick it up at the post office.

Duane and I wore our high school sweaters with the big S for Sundance on the front. Mine had three stripes on one sleeve with a star. The star was for being captain of our football team. The few dollars we had we tucked inside where the letters were sewn to the sweaters, like a money belt. Dick warned us it wasn't safe to have money where anyone could find it. We had room in one of our packs for food, a loaf of bread and several small cans of deviled ham. A small loaf of bread cost a dime, a can of deviled ham a nickel. In the other pack we had one change of clothes. Dick had some sweet rolls and fruit in with his change of clothes. Dick told us we wouldn't need blankets, besides they would make us look too much like bums.

153

It was decided to hitchhike to Moorcroft and catch a freight train from there that headed west. It was sad telling our mother and Sundance good-bye. We didn't tell anyone but our mother and Grace where we were going. It was exciting and scary.

My mother gave me the same advice she always did before we played a football game. "Be careful."

She would never watch Buck, Duane or I play football because she was afraid we would get hurt.

Our first ride was with Frank Mitts in a wagon pulled by horses. Just why we accepted a ride with him I don't know, maybe it was better to sit down and Dick was tired of walking. I know it gave me too much time to think about what might lie ahead. I no longer had Buck to worry for me.

Mr. Sigg, the county superintendent of schools, gave us a ride but his back seat was so full of books and papers there wasn't room for all three inside. Two of us stood on the running board of his car and held on to each other's hand across the top of his car. We didn't tell him where we were going because we were afraid it might sound like a stupid thing to do and we didn't think he would believe us anyhow. I guess you could say he was helping us run away from home and didn't know it.

When we got to Moorcroft, we found out the freight train didn't stop there except when it dropped a car off or picked one up. We hitchhiked a ride to Gillette, the next town to the west.

Gillette was where the district basketball tournament had been held. I hadn't been back since I played for Sundance High School. The last night of the tournament we were in the finals and won the right to represent our district in the state tournament. I had happy memories of how it was then. It seemed everyone in town knew me or at least was friendly and spoke when we met on the street. It wasn't only me, our whole basketball team and the town of Sundance were in the spotlight. I remembered how the papers wrote me up when we got into the finals as if I was something special. I was hoping when we got into Gillette, people wouldn't find out their basketball hero was about to catch a ride on a freight train headed for Washington state.

The man who gave us a ride let us off near the tracks and Dick spotted a brakeman and asked him about freight train schedules. He told Dick it would be a couple of hours before the next freight would stop that would be headed west.

We didn't have a pocket knife among the three of us and Dick said we would need one with a can opener. I remembered from tournament days where there was a hardware store. I knew they sold knives and the two guys that ran it had been so friendly.

When we entered the store with our small packs the two men who operated the store were talking to each other. I spoke first with a big friendly howdy and a smile, happy to see them both again. They both gave me the weirdest look, I could tell they didn't recognize me. That was good, I didn't have to explain what I was doing back in Gillette. Dick knew what kind of a knife we would need so I let him pick it out while I looked around the store. One of the men waited on Dick and the other followed me. I told him I was just looking, but he stayed with me anyhow.

When another customer entered the store and asked to be waited on, the guy who was following me said, "I'll be with you when this hobo leaves. I have to watch him."

It hadn't occurred to me I was being watched because he was afraid I would steal something. Hobo was what a railroad bum was called. I had my ego deflated, from a basketball star to probable thief with one short sentence. It was like one minute being a proud shining balloon and the next minute I felt like crumpled garbage. This was the same town that only a little over a year age treated me like a celebrity. I was too crushed to respond. I left the store feeling like a dog that had been kicked.

"Did you hear that guy's remark?" I ask Dick when he joined me outside.

"I would have to be deaf if I didn't," Dick said. "As a railroad bum you're going to have to get used to that."

"How could he tell I was planning on catching a ride on a freight train?"

"He could tell we are railroad bums by the packs we are carrying."

We found an outside water spigot, Duane, Dick and I had a drink of water and washed the sweat off our face and arms while we were waiting for the west-bound freight.

We were ready to climb aboard when the smelly freight train came rattling to a stop hissing steam and belching coal cinders. "Don't get on until after it starts to move," Dick told Duane and

155

me. "The bulls may kick us off if we don't wait. It will always give two short blasts on its whistle before it pulls out."

We spotted a box car with the door open and waited for Dick to give us the word. I had never been on any kind of a train before, freight or passenger.

When the giant locomotive jerked the long freight into motion, Dick gave us an okay so we jumped into the empty boxcar. Our forward progress was a crawl at first, like someone taking slow steps walking on ice. When the engineer gave a little too much throttle I could hear and feel the wheels spin so he had to slack off and wait for the wheels to take hold. We slowly picked up speed until the click of the wheels passing over the track ends became a steady hum.

The smell of burning coal that powered the long freight train filled our rattling boxcar. The ride was so rough that when I sat down my butt would bounce on the floor and the side to side swaying made it hard to stand up. Dick told us we'd stay on this train until we got to Laurel that was near Billings, Montana.

I couldn't have been more excited if we had been heading into a band of hostile Indians while going west in a covered wagon. I was heading into the unknown, and at last I was on my way to Washington state.

After leaving Gillette we crossed open spaces covered with sage brush. There were no ranches or farm buildings in sight. It looked as though it hadn't changed since the pioneers crossed this same area in covered wagons. I wondered if those people were as carefree as we were. We were so taken in by the adventure that we didn't worry much about the dangers that might lie ahead. The pioneers had to be on the watch for savage Indians who would kill them for the provisions they were carrying. Unlike the pioneers we didn't have enough provisions for even an Indian to bother us, if there had been any Indians. I had one dollar in my pocket and three dollars sewed under the letter of my football sweater. I think Duane had about the same. Dick said we didn't need money and we would be safer without it. He promised he would show us how to get day-old rolls for free from the bakeries and fruit from the markets. I had known Dick for a long time and one thing I knew for sure was that he was not dumb. I was sure he would show us how to get to Washington state.

Chapter Nineteen

As the freight train slowed for a stop in Laurel, Montana, I climbed down the ladder on the front of the car until my feet touched the ground. By running while hanging onto the ladder I was able to let go without falling, finding myself in a world I never knew existed. I guess I had never thought much about it before.

We were in what Dick called a jungle, the place where railroad bums stay. The people we saw were pathetic. Most were unshaven and dressed in all kinds of ill-fitting clothes. Some were dirty, some in rags, some wore old suit coats with pants of denim or wool that looked like army surplus. The hollow looks in the eyes of most said they could use a good meal. The shelters they called their shacks were made of all descriptions of material: packing crates, scrap boards covered with tarpaper, sheet metal, I guess anything they could find. I had studied different cultures in college, but no one ever mentioned anything like this.

There was something about the smell of the jungle fires cooking stew and boiling coffee that took on an atmosphere that I could not only see and smell, but also feel. Since there were three of us I wouldn't say I was afraid, but it was an exciting new experience. Most of the hobos seemed to be in their own world without anyone they could call a friend.

One friendly young man, about 18, was eager to get acquainted with us. I guess he felt safer to be with someone about his own age. It was a little scary he said to be by himself. He was on his way to a relative who lived in Oregon. We shared our food with him, which consisted of canned deviled ham sandwiches, sweet rolls and oranges. I wasn't hungry, I guess all the ragged sad-looking people got to me.

Our new-found friend, Bun, was from the same town in South Dakota where Mr. Severson, one of our high school teachers, had taught and coached. Mr. Severson had told us how he lost his job there because he played a black kid on the basketball team instead of one of the school board member's kid. Bun told us it was the other way. He wouldn't let the black kid play when he was the best player they had. Without the black kid playing they lost out in the tournament and that was why Mr. Severson was fired.

Mr. Severson was fired in Sundance too and I don't think he ever knew how the school board found out what he did. Mr. Hewes was president of the school board and when he wanted to know about coaches or teachers he would ask one of us Kaiser kids, Buck, Duane or myself. As I said, our ranch was next to the Hewes ranch and we had all worked on his ranch at one time or another. He had respect for how we always told him the truth. Mr. Severson didn't like the football coach, who was a friend of Julius Hewes. Severson coached basketball and he made it difficult for the football coach by starting basketball practice before football season was over. Because Sundance was such a small school most of the football players were also the best basketball players. Duane and several others couldn't turn out for basketball practice until football season was over. That's why Duane and others were never given a chance to make the first team in basketball their senior year. When Mr. Hewes asked Duane what was going on, Duane told him how Mr. Severson was making it rough for the football coach. That was the end of Mr. Severson's job at Sundance.

With Bun, there were four of us traveling together. Dick picked out an empty box car on the next freight heading west and pulled the door shut to keep out the bums, this way when the train pulled out we had our own private car. After we moved out of the freight yard and were bouncing along at full speed, Dick opened the door that let in the smell of burning coal that powered the huge locomotive.

The train moved so slow on some of the mountain grades you could almost walk as fast as the train was moving. It was on one of these grades where an old man jumped in the open door of our box car. He seemed surprised to find four of us in the car and I think a little afraid. He apologized for intruding and I'm sure he would have left if we had complained. He explained he had a low-paying job herding sheep and liked to go to town once in a while. If he had to pay for a ticket, he wouldn't have anything left for himself come winter when the sheep herding job would be over. We let him know he was more than welcome to ride with us.

Dick had us change cars when the train made a stop. He found a berry reefer for us to ride in. He said they had the same springs

158

as passenger coaches. Berry reefers were cars used to haul berries and soft fruit from the west coast. In each end were compartments they filled with ice to keep the fresh fruit from spoiling. Going west they were empty and we could ride in the ice compartments. The center of the cars where they hauled the berries had doors that locked only from the outside like a home refrigerator. They were always locked when the train was moving so it wasn't safe to get in the center compartment at anytime.

Dick left Duane and me in the car to watch our packs while he and Bun went for provisions. We knew it would be an hour or so before the train left. When they returned they had two quarts of milk, day-old sweet rolls, some overripe and under-ripe oranges, and some green bananas.

Dick was very proud with his success. "It didn't cost us a cent he announced."

"I can understand someone giving you the stale rolls and cull fruit," I said. "But how did you get the milk?"

"I borrowed it off a porch," Dick said.

"Don't you call that stealing?"

"I call it night farming, besides there were six bottles and I let them keep four."

"That was mighty big of you."

After we had eaten we decided it would be more comfortable for two of us to sleep in separate ends of the car, two in each compartment. Duane and I stayed in one end while Dick and Bun went to the other. That night it rained but we were inside with the soft springs of the berry reefer under us. Even with the flashes of lightning, the constant hum and rattle of the train and the mournful sound of the whistle at grade crossings, I don't think I have ever had a better night's sleep. When it was daylight and the train had stopped I peeked through the overhead hatch and could see a capital dome. I knew we were in Helena, Montana. Dick had said we would stay on this car until we got to Missoula some distance further west so I went back to sleep.

We all got off the train before it came to complete stop in Missoula because Dick had warned us Missoula had many railroad bulls (railroad police). Dick said it must have been some kind of a railroad police training school.

While in Missoula we stayed out of sight the best we could

until we heard the two blasts from the train's steam whistle. That meant the train was pulling out so we got on the first open box car we could find.

When we stopped near a post office in Sand Point, Idaho, I wrote and sent a quick postcard home letting our mother know where we were and that everything was going okay.

Our train pulled into the freight yard in Spokane during the night. We had to walk several miles until we came to a highway bridge that crossed the Spokane River in Spokane. Dick knew we could sleep under the bridge in a little park. When we awoke the next morning it was Sunday. The post office wasn't open so we had to stay until Monday when we could pick up the suitcase we had mailed ahead. On this hot July day, what we all needed most was a good bath. We had our swimming trunks with us and Dick knew where there was a city park with a free swimming pool. After a good swim we returned to the little park by the end of the bridge.

Next morning Dick thought I should go to a bakery that was not to far away and ask for some day-old rolls. He said I had to get used to it sometime. I had never done anything like this before. As poor as we were in Wyoming, I had never asked anyone for food although many a time I would have liked to have had more to eat.

"You get used to it after a few times," Dick said.

Duane went with me and Dick stayed with our gear under the bridge. We had no trouble finding the bakery where Dick said it would be but I couldn't get up the courage to beg.

After everyone else in the bakery had been waited on and left, the fat jolly man behind the counter asked me, "What can I do for you son?"

The thought of begging scared me almost speechless. I pulled the one wrinkled dollar out of my pocket and asked him, "How much are your day-old rolls?" I'll never forget the look in that man's eyes.

"Keep your last dollar son," he said and he handed me a paper bag full of bakery goods.

I let Dick think I had begged and thinking about it now I guess I really had.

We picked up our suitcase at the post office and were returning to our home under the bridge when a Spokane policeman walked along with us and got Dick in conversation. He was very friendly and we talked freely with him and told him where we were from and where we were going. He seemed satisfied that we were telling him the truth and when we parted he told us to be careful and wished us luck. He sounded like my mother when we left Sundance. At the time I couldn't see what there was to be afraid of. We were having such an exciting good time, it was like discovering a new world, learning things they never taught in any school.

Dick said it was his turn to forge for more food. We needed oranges to quench our thirst because it would be hot before we got to the Seattle side of the Cascade mountains. Duane and I agreed to stay with our packs under the Spokane River bridge. I stretched out in the shade of some bushes where I could watch our gear. I hadn't gone to sleep yet when some bum ran up and grabbed one of our packs. I stood up so he could see me for the first time and yelled at him. He put the pack down and said he was looking for his pocket knife he had lost in the park. He thought it might be under our stuff. I helped him look but I knew we wouldn't find anything. The little guy left without finding his knife. I think the fact that I was over six feet, three inches tall and twenty years old, may have influenced his decision to leave in such a hurry. It was decided we might as well wait for a west-bound train in the freight yard. When we got there we talked to a man to find out when our train would be leaving. We could tell he was a railroad crewman by the way he was dressed. He wore the kind of cap that almost all brakemen, firemen and engineers wore. He was carrying a railroad lantern even though it was mid-afternoon. He said he was a brakeman. This friendly stranger told us it would be several hours before our train would be leaving. He seemed in no hurry so he stayed and talked with us, telling us they were hiring men at the Grand Coulee Dam and they should be needing cherry pickers in Yakima. We quizzed him for more information about jobs in Washington.

This friendly "brakeman" pulled a deck of cards out of his pocket and started playing solitaire. The cards were small, about half the size of regular cards. He asked if we ever gambled and I told him I never did. He said he never did either but he liked to

161

play solitaire to kill time. He told us he was waiting for a friend that would be coming in on the next train. He asked if we four were together. I don't think Dick heard his question and told him no.

While we were having a friendly conversation with our new friend, a rough-looking unshaven rude character came up and butted in.

"How would you like to play some poker?" he asked.

"I never play poker," our friend told him hardly looking up from his game of solitaire.

"I'll bet you on what the next card you turn up will be if you give me some odds."

"You don't look like you would have any money to bet," our brakeman friend told the rude character.

"The hell I don't. What do you call this," he said as he opened his billfold so we all could see. It appeared to be full of twenty dollar bills.

Our friend gave me a wink and whispered. "We should teach this bum a lesson."

"How much do you want to bet on what the next card I turn over will be?" Our friend asked the shaggy one.

"I'll bet a hundred bucks the next card you turn over will be the ace of spades."

"I haven't got that much."

"How about your young friends? Their money is as good as yours.

While this rude stranger was trying to get Dick to bet, our brakeman friend slipped the ace of spades out of the deck and put it face down behind him. "Help me teach this guy a lesson," he said as he winked at me showing me where he put the ace of spades.

"I don't want his money," I said. "Besides I don't have much to bet."

"You must have a buck or two. It's not the money, help me teach him a lesson."

"Maybe betting a couple of bucks would teach this obnoxious character some manners," Dick said.

After Dick bet two dollars, Duane and I each put up two dollars. We dug it out of the compartment under our letters where they were sewn on to our sweaters.

"Remember," our friend said, "the bet is, the next card I turn over will be the ace of spades. Does everyone agree?"

We all nodded.

Our so-called "brakeman friend" reached around behind his back and turned over the ace of spades.

I realized almost at the same time he turned the card over we had been conned. My first impulse was to grab his wrist on the hand he was holding our bet money. I got a good grip on him and I wanted to slam him to the ground like I had done many a time while playing football. I decided it was best to keep him in my grasp.

"You dirty sons of bitches," Dick said.

The guy with the billfold full of twenty dollar bills answered Dick with, "Somebody ought to cut your damn throat, somebody ought to, somebody ought to, by God I think I will," and he started for Dick with a knife.

Dick was able to run away from the guy with the knife.

I still had a grip on the other guy's wrist.

"Hey Dick," I said, "go get that cop we saw at the flour mill."

There was a flour mill a block or so away.

Dick took off on the run with the guy still chasing him with the knife. There was no way he could have caught Dick.

I don't think he could have caught me either if he had been chasing me with a knife after threatening to cut my throat.

"Hold it you guys," our "brakeman friend" shouted, with me still holding onto his wrist. "Come back or you'll get us all in jail. You can have your money back if you don't call in that cop."

"I'm going to get the cop," Dick said. "We'll get our money back too."

"Come back," I shouted to Dick. "All we want is our money back."

"Get the money first."

Our "brakeman friend" handed me the money and I let loose of my hold of him. I stuck the money in my pocket while he rubbed his wrist. Dick and the other con-man swore at each other at a distance.

Our "brakeman friend" and the rough character left together. "Why didn't you find out the four of them were together," I heard the shaggy one complain, as they disappeared behind some freight cars.

Duane gathered up our stuff and said, "Let's get the hell out of here."

"I still think you should have let me get the cop so they can't pull the same thing on someone else," Dick said.

Bun said, "I think I know why he called you back. You've heard it said there is never a cop when you need one." Bun turned to me. "That's the fastest I ever saw a cop invented. Whatever gave you the idea?"

"You're right," I admitted. "I never saw a cop. I guess I invented him because we needed one. Sometimes you have to improvise."

I was shaking I was so mad, first at the con-men, then at myself, because I was so dumb I didn't see through their scheme sooner. I realized we had almost gotten into a fight over six lousy bucks and the other guys were armed with a knife and ready to use it. Six bucks is a lot of money when it's almost all you have and you're a thousand miles from home.

"Like Duane says," I said, "let's get the hell out of here and get on that freight headed toward Seattle."

Bun agreed, "That guy with the knife was so mad he may be back to get even, but I don't think he'll try anything until it gets dark."

We watched as they were making up the west bound freight train. When they connected on the road hog, a big locomotive with two white flags on the front, we got in the first open box car we could find.

We rode the bouncing box car the rest of the night getting very little sleep. If I sat down my butt would bounce on the floor rattling my teeth. Standing up with my knees slightly bent absorbed the shock but it was too tiring for very long at a time. By laying down I put my jacket under my head for a pillow. When it got daylight the train stopped and Dick suggested we look for another reefer with softer springs. I agreed it was a good idea.

We were walking along the tracks when we met the train crew coming from the other direction.

"Where the hell do you punks think you're going?" One of the train's crew asked. "If you're looking for a place to ride you've already passed up several empties."

"We're looking for a reefer with softer springs," Dick told him.

"You punks are getting pretty damn particular don't you think."

"Jesus mister, you ought to try it some time," was Dick's reply.

The other crew members had a good laugh and paid no more attention to us, letting us find the kind of a car that we were looking for.

Chapter Twenty

The freight train we were riding pulled into Pasco, Washington during the heat of the day. A hobo told me it was 105 degrees in the shade and there was no shade. I had never felt such hot weather in Wyoming. We got off to make sure we were on the train that was going to Auburn, Washington and not Portland, Oregon. The Portland train left first. We bid Bun, our new friend, good-bye.

We had to wait for a train that would be going to Auburn. There was a young mother with a baby in her arms and her husband waiting for the same train. They told us they would be stopping in Yakima to work in the fruit harvest.

When the train started to leave the station, Dick, Duane and I jumped into an open boxcar. The woman who was carrying the baby was having trouble boarding the moving train. She handed Duane her baby and even then she was just barely able to climb aboard ahead of her husband as the train picked up speed.

I asked Duane, "What would you have done if they had missed the train?"

"I guess you would just have to get used to being called uncle by your brother's baby."

We stopped in Yakima and I talked to a hobo who said he was looking for a job picking cherries. When I told him we were headed for Auburn and would be staying with relatives north of Seattle, he laughed at me.

"I've heard that story before," he said. "No relative will want to see another relative that is a railroad bum and when you think about it you won't want them to see you either."

I understood what he was saying was that even hobos have pride. I might have agreed with him if I had been his age, but I didn't consider myself a railroad bum. I thought of myself as a college kid out discovering a new world and having lots of fun while doing it.

When we arrived in Auburn it was past midnight so the three of us found a place to sleep in a big hay shed. I fastened my suitcase to my belt with a piece of bailing wire before going to sleep. After our experience in Spokane I didn't feel so trusting.

The morning sun was peeking over the Cascade mountains

when we awoke, finding ourselves in a valley with green vegetation everywhere we looked. After our usual breakfast of sweet rolls and oranges, Dick left as planned hitchhiking toward Tacoma, where he would stay with an aunt.

Duane and I were on our own for the first time without Dick showing us the ropes. We found a service station and a friendly attendant who let us wash up and change into clean clothes. Our plan was to hitchhike to Lake City, a district north of Seattle, where our grandma was staying with Aunt Myrtle and Uncle Clyde Musser. We would next catch a ride to Arlington where our Cousin Roger and his mother, Myrtie West were expecting us.

If there ever was a first day of the rest of my life it was Wednesday, July 20, 1938 in Auburn, Washington. Duane and I actually started a new life as we walked away from that service station on our way to the edge of town to catch a ride to Seattle. I was excited just to be in the Washington I had heard our mother talk so much about. As she had said, Washington was like being in a different world. The entire landscape sparkled in the morning sun. The smell of freshly mowed hay combined with the multitude of flowers that decorated the yards with their freshly painted houses made me feel as though I was truly in God's country. The constant singing of the many songbirds were in perfect harmony with each other as they welcomed us into their valley. The air was clean and fresh as though it had been rinsed by God's own hands especially for our arrival. The area between Auburn and Seattle was appropriately named the Green River Valley.

We hadn't been waiting very long by the side of the road when a young man about my age stopped and gave us a ride in a Model A Ford. He said he was a milker and was on his way to milk a string of cows. He was very friendly and let us off at a roadside produce stand where he knew the manager usually went to Seattle every Wednesday morning. The manager was of Japanese descent and he welcomed us to ride with him. On our way to Seattle we passed through the little town of Kent where our mother's family had lived and Granddad Perrigoue had been buried.

My first view of the Seattle skyline from the south included the Smith Tower, the tallest building at the time west of the Mississippi River. This was our first time to be in a city the size of

Seattle or one that was a seaport. We had a map of Seattle and knew what bus to take to get to Lake City. We walked from near the King Street train station to Lake Union taking in the sights along the way. Two oceangoing ships were tied up at a dock like horses at a hitching rack. They looked just as they should from pictures I had seen. We stopped at a little grocery store and bought some food and had lunch before catching our bus.

We didn't know Aunt Myrtle would be expecting us, but our mother had written telling her we would be showing up after riding a freight train from Wyoming. She seemed surprised and relieved to see us in clean clothes. I guess she was expecting a couple of railroad bums like the guy in Yakima had warned me. It was good to meet her and Uncle Clyde and see our grandma again. We hadn't seen Grandma since September 1930 when she was in Wyoming. We enjoyed the first home-cooked meal we had had in about a week and stayed there that night.

Duane and I started hitchhiking for Arlington the next morning, our first ride taking us as far as Bothell. When we were walking out of Bothell we noticed a sign by the side of the road asking for cherry pickers. We decided to apply for the job, after all, we were looking for work. We talked to a lady who seemed to be doing the hiring. We told her we both wanted a job. She asked where we lived. I told her we had just arrived from Wyoming and would look for a place after we got a job.

"Oh you poor boys," she said. "You cannot earn your salt picking cherries."

I told her I didn't understand. "You are hiring cherry pickers, yet you don't pay enough for us to earn our salt?"

"I'm sorry for you poor boys. We hire kids mostly around the neighborhood. We can only pay two cents a pound. The kids earn a little spending money. This is not a real job. It takes many cherries to weigh a hundred pounds."

I thanked her and we were soon back on the road catching another ride toward Arlington. Two rides later we were in Snohomish. We found a little grocery store at the edge of town where we bought a can of beans and some sweet rolls for our lunch.

We finally caught a ride with a man that said he was going to Arlington. When we told him who we were going to see, he informed us Roger and Aunt Myrtie didn't live at the same place anymore. He told us where they lived and how to get there. This man turned out to be the same lawyer that handled Aunt Myrtie's legal affairs when she made off with most of our Dad's and the rest of the Kaiser family's inheritance. I had heard our mother talk about him, referring to him as a real shyster, whatever that is supposed to be.

Duane and I walked out from Arlington to the place by the Stillaguamish River where the lawyer told us we would find Cousin Roger and Aunt Myrtie. There were kids all over the place, some by the house, others out in the orchard picking cherries. I asked one of the kids by the house if this was where Roger West lived.

"Oh you might find him around here some place, maybe out in the orchard, who knows, he could be around here some place. I guess you'll just have to look for yourself and find out."

My thought was, what a wise-ass kid.

After Roger and Aunt Myrtie both welcomed us, Roger said, "I would like you to meet another cousin you have never met, Walt Hass."

Walt turned out to be the same wise-ass kid we had already talked to.

Roger took the day's picked cherries to market in Everett that night and came back with the news he didn't get paid because the cherries were wormy.

Roger and his mother were selling milk from a few cows and Roger was working on WPA. The prospect of finding any kind of work that would pay enough to go to college didn't look any better here than in Wyoming. While Roger worked days, Duane and I kept busy around the place weeding their corn and other little jobs. Roger's dad had died a few years before so what he earned on WPA and the little money from the farm appeared to be their only income. They did own several places that were left from the Kaiser estate but money to spend was quite another thing.

Roger seemed glad to have us as guests and showed us around. He took us to the beach once, the first time I ever saw someone dig clams and another time we went on a picnic up the Stillagumish River near Verlot.

169

Duane and I wanted to see the rest of our relatives while in Washington so we wrote to Aunt Myrtle in Lake City. She invited us down so we could meet some more of our aunts, uncles and cousins. They arranged a picnic for us at Uncle Elmer's place on Angle Lake. I heard later Uncle Hank had expected to see us looking like railroad bums or wearing coonskin hats. When we showed up dressed like college kids wearing our letter-man sweaters I think he was disappointed.

Next, Aunt Myrtle and Uncle Clyde took us to see Uncle Gus and our cousins in Carnation, or Tolt, as the old timer's called it. This was the area where our mother had lived from 1899 to 1907. Uncle Gus was a fun sort of guy. He and Aunt Bell and our Cousin Jack couldn't have done more to make us feel welcome. They showed us some of the places where our mother had lived and where our granddad had farmed and ran a sawmill. The more I saw of Washington the more I could understand why our mother talked so highly about it. As I said, Jack and Gus treated us great, but whenever I mentioned getting a job, or them helping us find one it was as if I had said a dirty word in church.

For some reason I had a feeling our Washington relatives thought of Duane and me as a couple of hicks or hillbillies and couldn't hold a job if we found one. Maybe it was as the hobo told me in Yakima, in their eyes we were a couple of railroad bums. They didn't say so, not to my face at least, but they gave me that feeling. Duane and I talked it over and decided if we found a job in Washington we would have to do it on our own.

We both returned to Arlington after our visit in Tolt as the summer was coming to a close. Neither of us had found a job. Duane wanted to stay in Washington because he had nothing in Wyoming to go back for and I wanted to return to the University of Wyoming in the fall. Buck had found me a job at the University farm, the same one I had last fall, helping put up silage. I could make enough in two weeks to pay my tuition and maybe the first month's board. Duane decided to stay with Roger and his mother and look for work.

I didn't look forward to the freight train ride back to Wyoming all by myself but it seemed like the only way. I could have borrowed the train fare from Grandma Perrigoue as Helen had, but I would have had to pay her back with money I would need for college. The way I looked at it, it would be like earning more money in a week by not paying for a railroad ticket, than any job would pay. I didn't feel comfortable leaving Duane without a job because I felt responsible for his being in Washington.

Roger's mother fixed me a lunch of two liverwurst sandwiches and a banana and Roger took me as far as Lowell near Everett where the freight trains left heading east.

Duane gave me, I think the last dollar he had, which made two I had to get me back to Sundance.

I inquired from a hobo in the freight yard and found out my train didn't leave until after midnight. This meant I had to kill about 18 hours. At least I had someone to talk to or I should say listen to. He was cooking a pot of stew over an open fire. As he talked he whittled on a stick of wood with a butcher knife. Every once in a while he would stop, check his stew then sharpen his knife and whittle some more. He gave me the greatest lecture on sociology I had ever heard. I don't think I believed much of what he was telling me at the time but I didn't believe much of the lectures I heard from college professors either.

I remember him telling me, "Man is a vicious animal and can't be trusted. He is always looking for a chance to take advantage of another man."

I couldn't help but think of the warning about rattle snakes. I had been told to watch out for the ones that don't rattle and warn you. I don't remember all he said, but he impressed me as a man that had been walked on so much by other people he was completely defeated. He took me into his confidence because I listened, I guess, and he told me all of his life's problems. I knew I would soon be back in college again and the life this man was suffering from would only be a learning experience for me and soon forgotten. He told me the stew was ready and offered to share it with me. I thanked him but gave the excuse I had to look for a friend. The truth was he was starting to make me feel depressed and I thought it was a good time to leave. After listening to his outlook on life I didn't feel the least bit hungry. After I left him I found a place fifty feet or so away from the railroad tracks in tall weeds where I wouldn't be seen and went to sleep.

It was late afternoon when I was awakened by some loud talking. I could tell by the excited tone of the voices something terrible had happened. When I peeked and saw some of the men wearing police-like badges I thought I should stay hidden. As they came closer I was sure they hadn't seen me and I could hear what they were saying.

"Why would anyone want to kill that old man?" One said.

"And left him with his throat cut with a butcher knife."

I had heard all I wanted to hear. They came from the direction where I had left the old man with his pot of stew. I was sure they were saying someone had murdered him. I didn't want to answer a lot of question and maybe be accused of a murder so I stayed hidden in the tall weeds. I didn't leave my hiding place until after it got dark. When the train was about to leave I got in the first empty gondola car I could find, afraid they might search the train before it pulled out. They didn't so I guess no one cared enough to try to find if whoever killed the old man was on that freight train. Maybe they had already found a suspect.

It was already starting to become daylight when the train started climbing the Cascade mountains heading for Wenatchee. A couple of men in the same car with me talked about the old man who was murdered back in Lowell. His throat was cut, they said, with his own butcher knife and all the guy wanted that did it was his pot of stew.

"Did they catch the guy that did it?" I asked.

"The cops won't waste any time looking for someone who killed a bum," he told me.

These two guys had packs for camping out saying they would get off as the train slowed on the mountain grade when it passed through the huckleberry area. After a few days they would return and sell the berries. It was their way of earning a little money until they could find a real job.

The clouds were closing in around us spitting a fine mist as the train approached a tunnel through the mountains. I was feeling lousy, like the weather, thinking how I had wasted the past summer. It had been a great experience but I had earned no money for my second year of college. Trying to see the cheerful side, I knew Buck had a job waiting for me that would start about the time I would be returning to Laramie. Buck wrote and told me he would be driving up to Sundance for a short visit so I could ride back with him and stay with him where we could work out our room rent the same as last year.

Washington state was such a beautiful place to live. If I could only find a decent job I knew I would rather live there than in Wyoming. I could see why our mother always talked about it the way she did. Her mother, my grandma, was over 80 and would like to live with us if we moved out to stay in Washington. Aunt Myrtle and Uncle Clyde who lived in Lake City had a house with two bedrooms on the main floor. Dottie, my cousin, had to sleep with Grandma or in an attic room that had a ceiling so low she couldn't stand up. If Grandma wasn't there, Dottie would have her own bedroom.

Our other aunt Myrtie, Roger's mother, had another farm she was renting and she told us she would like to get the renter she had to move out. Maybe we could work out an agreement to rent her farm she said. She also had a beach house on Camano Island, a house in Arlington, a 160-acre place mostly timber and two 20-acre places. One of the 20-acre places had a house that could be made livable. I tried to get her to say what kind of an arrangement we could work out. When it came to talking business she always went into a lot of double talk. Her favorite saying was, oh this, that and the other, which didn't make any sense or answer my question. I figured she knew I didn't have any money and she wasn't parting with any of her ill-gotten inheritance. Anyhow, it had been nice staying with her during the summer while seeing Washington state.

The light drizzle added to my gloomy feelings as the two huge locomotives tugged the long freight train up the mountain grade. I pondered my options as the train entered a long tunnel that took it through the Cascade mountains. It was spooky, being 1,000 miles from home with the smell of hobos beside me in total darkness. It was sometime before I could see the light at the east end of the tunnel. When we broke out into bright sunshine it seemed like breaking out into a different world again. Maybe it was, but at the time I couldn't but wonder, what would I be doing in five or ten years? Trying to guess what was in my future was like riding a freight train in a dark tunnel. Would there be sunshine at the end of the tunnel as I found this day when we passed through the Cascade mountains into eastern Washington?

In Wenatchee, I waited by the Columbia River near the freight

173

yard as our train took on ice. I opened a can of beans from my pack but for some reason I wasn't hungry. I left most of them, wishing I had a hungry hobo to give them to. It wasn't any fun travelling alone. I hurried to catch the train when I heard the two short blasts of the train's whistle. We followed the Columbia River a ways as we headed toward Spokane.

While waiting for the east-bound freight to be made up in Spokane, I felt a lot less confident than when I had Dick and Duane with me. I talked to a brakeman to find out what time the east-bound train would leave. He could see that I was alone and he told me this was a rough place to be by myself. He took me to a box car that he said would be heading east.

"When you get in," he said, "pull the door shut and if I see any bums get near you I'll kick them out."

I wasn't sure if I should trust this man. He seemed sincere so I did what he told me. It wasn't too long before I found out. I could feel the jolt when my private car was connected to the train and I was on my way home again.

The weather was nice but the car was so rough to ride I decided, when the train made a stop, to find a berry reefer with softer springs. The thing I hadn't thought about was while going east they would all be loaded with produce and the compartments were stocked with ice. I rode on top of one for a while until I was afraid of falling asleep. With the train on the move it would have been dangerous, if not impossible, to get into an empty box car from the top. I settled for an open gondola that had many hobo riders. The train stopped out in the country before it got to Missoula where an ornery brakeman was going to kick us all off. I think he thought better of it when he saw how many of us there were. He waved a pistol to show us his authority.

"Well I'll be damned," he said. "All the way from an old man in his eighties," he looked at an old gray-haired man, "to a punk kid not dry behind the ears yet, and everything in between, all bumming a free ride."

When he looked at me, I knew he meant I was the punk kid.

"I'll tell you one thing," he said as he waved the pistol, "if you want to see the scenery buy a ticket on a passenger train. I'm going to let you stay, but if I see a head sticking above the sides of this car there's going to be a bullet hole in it."

I know there were about a dozen hobos who would have torn him apart if he didn't have that gun. I wondered if he realized how lucky he was to have a job, the stupid jackass. None of us were riding his train by choice. In a way he reminded me of the professor telling the class why all the crickets were on that grassy hill. If that railroad bully had no gun I wanted to tell him we were riding his train because one of our legs was shorter than the other. We damn sure weren't there to see the scenery.

When our train was going full speed through Hardin, Montana, some guy desperate for a ride tried to board the moving train. When he grabbed the ladder on the back end of a car, he was jerked off his feet and swung under the train. By the time the train stopped he was ground to bits. I felt as if I was going to throw up but I hadn't eaten anything in over a day. I was no longer hungry.

I got off the train to get a drink of water when it made a short stop in Sheridan, Wyoming. It started up before I was ready and I had to catch it on the fly. I was careful to catch the ladder on the front end of the car. Dick had warned me not to try catching a moving train by the back ladder like the guy tried that got killed in Montana.

I had planned to get off in Moorcroft and hitchhike to Sundance from there but because we didn't leave any cars or pick any up, the train didn't even slow down. I knew it would stop in Upton for water where I could get off and thumb a ride home, about 30 miles away. A couple of hobos riding with me on a flat car were discussing what a desolate looking country this was as we approached Upton.

"Who the hell would ever want to live here?" One said.

"Look." The other said. "A jack rabbit actually lives here," as a rabbit scurried away from the moving train.

"He must be carrying his lunch," was the returned answer, and they both laughed.

I didn't say anything, as the train slowed for a stop. That sagebrush and jack rabbit looked mighty beautiful to me just then, but I knew Wyoming would never seem the same again. Getting off that train was like leaving a classroom. I had heard everything the professor had said but would I have the correct answers for the test. I would just have to wait and find out.

Chapter Twenty-one

It was great to be home again after My freight train trip to the state of Washington. The summer was almost gone and I had nothing to show for my time but the experience and that wouldn't pay any of my expenses for college. Buck was in Sundance when I got there so I could ride back to Laramie with him. He had a couple of week's work and a room waiting for me so I could at least start the fall term.

Before leaving for the university, Buck and I went to a baseball game near the Devils Tower. It was great to again see many of the kids we went to high school with. After the game we went for a drive with a couple of girls in Buck's Model A Ford. Buck was driving with the girls sitting on the front fenders. We drove down to the Belle Fouche River on a road that was only wide enough for one car to squeeze between the tall grass on both sides that formed a barrier. We caught up with a skunk in the road that stayed ahead not wanting to get out of our way. When we got close to the skunk the girls screamed. When we slowed down to give the skunk a chance to get further away the girls stopped screaming. When we speeded up again and got closer, the girls would scream again. It was like riding in a fire engine, the girls were the siren until the skunk got tired of our little game and took off through the tall grass. I guess you could say it was clean fun since no one got perfumed. We all went to a dance in Hulett that night.

I know I never would have been able to start that second year of college without Buck's help. I arranged my class schedule so I would have time to work the several jobs I needed to stay in school. All my classes were in the mornings so I could either study or work all my afternoons and evenings. Sometimes I worked for the Union Pacific Railroad on Thursday mornings between midnight and daylight and Sunday mornings when the express train arrived. Buck and I both worked for the railroad. We unloaded the fresh meat shipments for Laramie and rearranged the rest of the load in the order it would be unloaded farther up the line. I usually only worked two or three hours once or twice a week. I had another job on NYA (a federal government financed work program for college students) for 40 hours a month. I worked

Saturdays and two hours during the week. The work at our apartment where we worked out our room rent could be whenever we could work it in. The job my friend wanted us to save for him, cleaning up each night in the restaurant, turned out different than I had planned. Buck was doing a much better job than my friend had been doing so the restaurant didn't want my friend back. I complained to Buck that it wasn't right to keep my friend's job and he told me they wouldn't have him back, even if Buck quit. Buck was getting a lot more work than I at the freight house so I did the clean up job at the restaurant. Because he liked to eat at different times, Buck used the meal ticket that was the pay for the restaurant job. He paid my board at the cooperative where I ate. The cooperative was formed by a group of us college boys. We rented a house, hired a cook and took turns with the other work, like peeling potatoes, setting the table and doing the dishes, etc. Our meals cost us only what it took to pay the bills. We got a lot more to eat for less money.

After I finished the silage job at the university farm that paid my tuition for the fall quarter, I worked (NYA) for the university, cleaned up at the restaurant, moved freight for the Union Pacific railroad, did janitor work for my room, and helped with the chores at the cooperative.

All college sophomores were required to take two hours of physical education. I found out even though I was no longer a freshman I could turn out for freshman basketball and if I made the squad it counted for PE credit. I missed not taking part in sports as I had in high school. Since I might want to coach someday, I signed up for freshman basketball. When the freshman basketball squad was cut, I was one of the 15 left. Freshman basketball practice was in the afternoons. When I registered for classes I knew I would have to work a lot to make enough money to stay in school so I only took the minimum required hours. I had a tight schedule, but outside of not getting enough sleep at times, everything was falling in place. That changed when my typing teacher wanted only girls in her morning class. I couldn't see how I could change my schedule around to please her. It was only a two-credit class and since I had done so well in typing in high school it was what you could call a cinch course to help my grade average.

I can still picture Miss French in her dark skirts and white blouses with lace cuffs and lace collars that fit up almost to her ears. She was nearly 60 years old and always walked so stiff and straight. She could have easily taken the part of an old maid in a Hollywood picture.

She wanted only girls in her morning typing class. When I told her I couldn't change to her afternoon class she drew her face up like the wicked witch of the East, as in the Wizard of Oz.

"You can't or you won't," she snapped at me.

I told her it would interfere with my several jobs and playing basketball. I didn't see any reason for me to change from a morning class to one in the afternoon.

"Typing is a very exacting science," she told me. "Girls are just more adept to being better typists."

I knew better than to tell her how I had done better than most of the girls when I took typing in high school. I felt like asking her, how would an old maid know how exacting men are. In my politest voice I told her that my work schedule was already set and I had to work. The only way I could change was to drop typing altogether. I didn't think it was necessary to explain to her I couldn't drop the class because I was already down to the minimum credits. I knew she simply didn't want men in her morning class. Miss French had the final say, but I found out too late. My final grade in her typing class was a F. The first and only time I failed a class in school. Did I learn anything from this experience? Possibly, but not enough to change for unreasonable people when I know I'm right.

Duane and I kept in touch by mail and he had found a job feeding cows on a dairy farm near Arlington, Washington. The job paid 50 dollars a month but now that he was earning money, Aunt Myrtie wanted him to pay 30 dollars a month for his board and room or move out. This would only leave him 20 dollars for himself. He would have been better off working for 30 dollars a month as they had offered him in Wyoming. There was another reason why she wanted him to move out of her house Duane said, but he didn't want to put it in writing. He had me curious as to what was bothering him. I was sure Duane wouldn't do anything to be ashamed of but why couldn't he write and tell me. The next time I heard from him he had found a second job where he was working for his board and room. His mailing address would be the same, in care of Aunt Myrtie.

After the argument with my typing teacher I had been doing a lot of thinking. My political science teacher the year before didn't give me the A I knew I had coming and I was told by my advisor that I should take the college entrance exam again. That dumb prof who thought crickets' legs were longer on one side than the other didn't give me the grade I had coming either. I knew I should do some serious thinking about whether or not I should continue at the University of Wyoming. I could see that after getting a failing grade in typing I wouldn't have a grade point average high enough to get into law school.

I knew our mother wanted to move back to Washington before Grandma died and I felt responsible for Duane being almost stranded out in Washington by himself. Our mother was working on WPA, with no hopes of anything better. It didn't seem that any of my brothers or sisters were willing or able to help her get off welfare, that is what WPA really amounted to. Maybe I should quit college after the winter quarter and join Duane in Washington? We could find a place, perhaps rent or buy one on time, maybe one of Aunt Myrtie's places around Arlington would be available? We could send for our mother and Grace after we found a place for them to stay. Our mother could find work out there and Grace could go to high school. After we were established, Duane and I could finish college in Washington. I wrote our mother and told her what I was thinking about doing. She was overjoyed with the idea. I knew how she had always put our getting a good education above everything else so I had explained to her we could move to Washington and go to college out there. She said she would try to sell our house in Sundance and could be ready to move in the spring.

Duane and I had talked about it before so he was more or less expecting it. If we were ever going to make the move it might as well be after I finished the fall quarter.

I had been keeping in touch with Roger and his mother, Aunt Myrtie. She wouldn't give me a straight answer whether or not we could rent her farm where she wanted to change renters.

"There is this, that and the other we have to talk about," was about all she would write in her letter.

179

Since I couldn't get a straight yes or no from her, I wrote and asked Duane to see if we could buy one of her 20-acre places and what her terms would be. For some reason Duane ignored my letter altogether but Aunt Myrtie finally wrote and said we could buy the 20 acres with the house that could be made livable. We shouldn't worry about the price or terms, she said that could all be worked out when I got there. That sounded good enough to me so I decided to finish the fall quarter, and leave for Washington after Christmas. We hoped to sell the little house Duane and I had built in Sundance and get enough for the down payment on the 20-acre place near Arlington that belonged to Aunt Myrtie. Howard agreed to move Grace and our mother in his pickup in the spring. Grace would have to get permission to complete that year of high school early but that would be no problem.

Buck and I spent Christmas of 1938 in Sundance that made it possible for me to discuss the details of our move. I would stay with Roger and his mother until Duane and I could get located, then Howard would bring Grace and our mother out to join us.

I left Laramie by Greyhound bus on New Year's Day, 1939, feeling bad about leaving college, yet excited and I looked forward to making Washington my new home. It was around -20 degrees Fahrenheit in Wyoming and ice on a pond west of Laramie was nearly two feet thick. Roger had told me it was in the upper 40's in Washington and the lawns were all green. When my bus crossed over the Columbia River into Washington it was raining a soft gentle rain. I liked the contrast of the green lawns compared to the snow and ice.

I stayed overnight in Lake City before going on to Arlington. My aunt, uncle and grandma were glad to hear our plans to relocate with our mother in Washington. Grandma wanted to live with us after our mother got there. Aunt Myrtle (our Lake City aunt) said we could count on Uncle Clyde and his truck if we ever needed anything hauled.

When I got to Arlington, Roger welcomed me as a long lost brother, but his mother went into her, this that and the other act when I tried to talk business with her about buying or renting one of her places.

When I gave Duane hell for not answering all my letters he told me he hadn't received those letters.

"And what is the problem you didn't want to put in writing?" I asked Duane.

"You remember the house Roger and Aunt Myrtie used to have in Arlington?" He asked.

"What do you mean used to have?"

"It burned down."

"What has that got to do with you not telling me something in a letter?"

"Roger asked me to burn that house for him, but I refused, so I can only guess Roger set it on fire for the insurance money."

"You're kidding."

"It was after that they told me I had to pay $30 a month for board and room."

"And that is when you moved out?"

"Do you blame me?"

"No. That makes everything different. Then I guess she didn't give you all the letters I wrote."

"You always sent my mail addressed in care of Aunt Myrtie?"

"Sometimes I put your letter in the same envelope with one for her. I guess it doesn't make any difference now that I'm here. I've asked her to draw up a contract for the 20-acre place."

I walked into Arlington just to get acquainted with some of the people trying to decide if I wanted to live near there. I met a young man named Peterson who was very friendly. After we talked a while he asked if I ever played basketball and I told him I did. He invited me to turn out for the Arlington town team. I did and we played against such towns as Darrington and Mukilteo.

I met Mr. Murphy, another friendly man in Arlington who ran a hardware store. I asked him if he ever knew A.J. Kaiser. I didn't tell him he was my granddad.

"Did I. Back when he was alive everyone in Arlington knew and loved old A.J.," he said. "If there was ever a better man on God's green earth, I've never met him. What I can never figure out is how come such a nice old man could have such an old witch for a daughter." I knew he was referring to my aunt Myrtie, Roger's mother. "Not only that," he continued, "how could he have a grandson like Roger, who has shit for brains?"

I hadn't told Mr. Murphy my last name, so I left before he

181

asked me.

I had been staying with Roger and his mother about a week when she presented me with a real estate contract for the 20 acres I had told her I wanted to buy. She had already told me she wouldn't charge me any interest because the place was just something she had to pay taxes on. I could pay her the down payment after we sold our place in Sundance she had told me.

I couldn't believe my eyes when I read the contract her lawyer had drawn up. It was for more than we had agreed on and the interest was twice the going rate. I knew I could never make the $50 a month payments. When I told her I didn't understand, she said that was the way her lawyer told her it had to be. It had my mother as the buyer and not me, so I asked her why.

"You know," she said, "the down payment will come from the house that's in your mother's name. You're not 21 yet so a real estate contract wouldn't be legal my lawyer said."

"I'll be 21 in less than three weeks. Can't we make that the effective date?"

"Oh there's this, that and the other. You can send it to your mother to sign."

I handed the contract back and told her it was no deal.

It looked to me as though she wanted it in my mother's name because my mother would have an inheritance in a few years. After she got all the Kaiser estate now she was after what my mother might inherit someday from her mother.

The next day I was pondering over what I should do. The "old witch," as Mr. Murphy had called her, decided things for me. She told me I would either have to pay for my board and room or get out.

Was she one of the rattlesnakes I had been warned about? I wondered if this was how a pioneer would have felt when the Indians burned down his cabin? I realized I was in hostile territory and no longer had a roof over my head. Like those early pioneers, I had no intention of going back to Wyoming. I was determined to make Washington my new home.

Chapter Twenty-two

When my aunt in Arlington told me to pay board or move out I couldn't blame her, after all she didn't owe me anything, but it's hard to explain how I felt. I had no job, very little money and was over a thousand miles from what I used to call home. I couldn't just claim a plot of ground and build a cabin as the pioneers did because the tillable land was already taken and I had no intentions of returning to Wyoming. I talked things over with Duane and we concluded there was no reason to restrict our new location to the Arlington area. Maybe it would be better to locate near Seattle where we could find jobs other than farm work.

You aren't really broke if you're out of money and you still have a friend. Our Aunt Myrtle and Uncle Clyde, who lived in Lake City, had told me if there was a way they could help us relocate, just let them know. Since I couldn't stay with Roger and his mother any longer I needed a friend more than anyone could realize.

I don't think Roger knew his mother had told me to leave because when I told him I was hitchhiking to Lake City to see my aunt and uncle where Grandma lived, he seemed surprised.

When I got to Lake City I found out Grandma was temporarily staying with Will Perrigoue, another uncle who lived near Granite Falls. Aunt Myrtle and Uncle Clyde drove me to Uncle Will's home. Grandma got Aunt Leola, Will's wife to drive us around looking at places we saw for sale in newspaper ads. Grandma said she would loan me money for the down payment until we sold our house in Sundance. She was looking forward to my mother moving to Washington so she could live with us. Duane agreed to make the monthly payments if they weren't too big. I was looking for a place we could afford with a few acres and a chicken house big enough to go into the chicken business at least in a small way. We wanted room for a vegetable garden, some berries and fruit trees. We looked at about all the places we could afford, but none of them seemed to have what I was looking for. The ones that were within our price range were located so far out in the country it would have been difficult for Grace to go to school or Duane and me to find work. Grandma suggested we should look closer to Seattle. She knew Clyde would take me around or realtors were always willing to show what they had for sale to a potential buyer.

My grandmother owned one farm near Monroe. She had part interest in another in the Snoqualmie Valley near Carnation. I knew it would have caused concern among my mother's brothers and sisters to even think of us moving onto either one of Grandma's farms. After the trouble over inheritance in my father's family I didn't want to do anything that might bring on hard feelings among my mother's family.

I hitchhiked to Lake City and stayed with Aunt Myrtle and Uncle Clyde while realtors took me around showing me what they had listed. The Seattle papers were full of places for sale, some by owner and some by realtors. A realtor named MacPherson, whose office was near Lake City, showed me several places north of Seattle and around Bothell. Everything he showed me was either not what I wanted or it cost too much. One morning he told me he had found just the place for me if I didn't mind living on the east side of Lake Washington. This place, he told me, was near a little unincorporated town called Bellevue.

We drove around the north end of Lake Washington and the road turned south before we got to Bothell. We passed a golf course where everything was so green and fresh. Geese were honking at each other as they grazed on a fairway. They hadn't bothered to go south for the winter. Giant fir trees were scattered throughout the landscape bordering the golf course. Huge stumps were in evidence of past splendor before the trees had been cut to make room for the many neatly kept small farms. We passed a couple of dairy farms with their painted barns where most of the stumps had been removed to make room for the green pastures.

Before we got to the place the realtor wanted to show me near Bellevue, we went through a little town named Kirkland. There was something interesting about the beauty of the area and this little town located on the lake shore. I noticed a high school on the right as we drove down a street that made a sharp turn to the left. Had we continued straight we would have ran into the lake. There was a movie theater on our left before we turned south again on a street that took us by several stores, a bank and a post office. I saw several feed stores, which told me they must raise chickens in the area.

The place Mr. MacPherson showed me near Bellevue was a few miles south of Kirkland. The total price was 1,750 dollars, 500 down. It had a small house we could get by with, a big barn that could be fixed into a chicken house, about five acres and with enough cleared land for a garden. The rest was in native trees. The water supply was a well. It was the nearest to what I had been looking for so far but the closest public transportation to Seattle was by ferry boat from Kirkland. Kirkland also had bus service. The down payment was a little more than I wanted to borrow from Grandma because 500 dollars was more than our house in Sundance would sell for.

On our way back to his office the realtor was trying to get me to make up my mind, telling me it was the only such place he had to show. There aren't any more like it he said. As we passed through Kirkland again he was giving me the hard sell. I guess he could tell I was more interested in seeing Kirkland than hearing what he had to say.

"Are you sure you want to buy anything?" He asked.

"I'm sure," I told him.

There was something about Kirkland. It was like the first time I saw my wife. I knew she was different from anyone I had ever met but don't ask me to explain what it was. I guess you could call it love?

I was thinking about what the realtor had said, "I don't have any more like it."

I noticed a sign on a Kirkland building, Hozel Realtor. I told Mr. MacPherson I had to sleep on it.

That night I asked Aunt Myrtle about the town of Kirkland. She knew it well. It was where my mother stayed when she went to sewing school. My Aunt Minn went to high school there because they didn't have a high school in Tolt at that time. My Uncles Elmer and Gus had run the first stage ever, that ran between Kirkland and Fall City. There was a ferry boat that went to Seattle and back about every hour during the day and a bus that ran between Kirkland and Redmond that made connections with the ferry. Redmond was a small town five miles to the east.

I hitchhiked a ride to Kirkland the next morning and stopped at the place where I had seen the Hozel Realtor sign. I was tired of looking at real estate but I knew one thing for sure, I had to see more of Kirkland. I thought the realtor that had been showing me around no longer believed I was going to buy anything. The Hozel real estate office was run by a lady named Bertha Hozel. She had so many listings similar to the place I had seen the day before near Bellevue it was confusing. She showed me several that I liked, but none had everything I was looking for at the price and down payment I could come up with.

The more I looked around Kirkland the more I was sure I wanted to live near there. By talking to people that ran several of the feed stores I found out they had many chicken ranches in the area. The ferry boat to Seattle made it possible to live in Kirkland and work in Seattle. It cost a dime or three rides for a quarter to take the ferry and the same price to ride the Seattle street cars that met all the ferries.

I didn't want to wear out my welcome with the Kirkland realtor as I had with Mr. MacPherson. I asked Mrs. Hozel if I could look over the cards that had the descriptions of her listings. If I found one I thought I might like, then I would have her show it to me.

She handed me a stack of cards and told me I was welcome to sit at a desk and take my time. If I was interested in any she would be glad to answer any questions to help me make up my mind and show me the ones I wanted to see. I went through the whole stack and set three cards aside I told her I would like to know more about.

The first was located near Juanita. It had three acres with a small house and some other buildings. Mrs. Hozel told me I wouldn't want to live near Juanita. It was an impoverished area and because people didn't like to live there, was why it was priced so cheap. It was also way out in the sticks and not near a bus route.

My second choice Mrs. Hozel told me I would like. She called it the frog farm.

The past owner had raised frogs for the market. I would be in on the ground floor of a new and up and coming business, she told me. "Some day there will be as much demand for frog legs as fried chicken. The past owner had failed because he was lazy. It is owned by the bank that had foreclosed and the price is low because the bank is anxious to sell."

"There is one other I would like to know more about," I told her. "It has two acres and a clean house, a chicken house with room for a thousand chickens, near the bus line, school, church and about two miles east of Kirkland."

"I'll show it to you. It's on the way to the frog farm but not near as good a buy as the other place."

We drove by the place I asked her about with the chicken house. She stopped the car and pointed out where the corner property lines were. She didn't show me the inside of the house because she forgot to bring the key.

"You can see the house will be needing a new roof soon," she said.

Next we drove through Redmond to the frog farm. If the place in Juanita was in the sticks I don't know what she called this.

When I mentioned it seemed a little swampy she said, "This is January, the wettest time of the year you know."

The house was livable but with the moss on the roof I couldn't tell what shape the roof was in.

"The wild blackberries make good jelly," she explained.

I told her they would have to be cleared out before I could plant a garden. When I asked her about schools she told me the kids all rode buses and one went by the house on the road we drove in on.

I was trying to think over everything she had told me about the places we had seen. "How about the house in Juanita?" I asked her.

"You won't like it, believe me."

"I would like to see more of the place with the chicken house."

"I have to get back to the office. My mother is there alone to answer the phone when I'm out."

"I have to think it over, but I still like Kirkland."

"You take your time. After you think it over I know you'll choose the frog farm."

"I'll be back, maybe tomorrow," I told her as I left.

I did a lot of thinking and that night I dreamed about frogs and was sure I knew more about raising chickens than frogs.

Next morning I hitchhiked back to Kirkland. I took the ferryboat to Seattle and back and found out it took only 20 minutes each way. I got on the Redmond bus and got off so I could see the chicken farm again. It was only a quarter of a mile from the bus line. I talked to the people who lived in the house next door and asked them about the well.

"It is one of the best in the neighborhood," Mr. Miller told me.

"How is the soil for raising a garden I asked."

"None better," I was told "and it holds moisture so well in the summertime it doesn't need to be watered.

"How about drainage, is it swampy?"

"Have you noticed there is a small creek that runs through the back corner? You might have to clean out the ditch, but there is good drainage."

I thanked Mr. Miller and took a walk around the neighborhood. There was a church within walking distance; also a school for the first six grades, and I was told by another friendly neighbor, Mrs. Belts, the bus for the high school was a block away. I could tell by the mail boxes, mail service was on the next street.

I peeked into windows of the house and it looked about the best I had seen yet for the price. The asking price was $1,100, $300 down and 6% interest on the unpaid balance with payments of $15 a month. The seller would hold the contract so there would be no closing costs.

The chicken house was painted red. It was over 100 feet long and about 25 feet wide. It was in good condition, big enough to

Our Washington home on Rose Hill near Kirkland.

188

house 1,000 laying hens with a feed room on one end. I took a stick and dug in the ground where a vegetable garden could be planted. I never saw richer-looking soil. The more I looked and asked questions the better the deal sounded.

I knew I had found our new home in Washington. I think I felt like a prospector who had been looking for gold all his life and at last struck it rich. My problem now was not to look too anxious when I went back to the realtor. Grandma had warned me that they never expect to get the listed price. I knew I should take her advice since she would be loaning me the down payment and at the same time I was so excited I could hardly contain myself.

When I went into the real estate office Mrs. Hozel asked me, "Would you like to see the frog farm again?"

"Could I see the inside of the house with the big red chicken house?" I asked her.

"It's on the way to the frog farm," she said. "You are right. If you see that place first you'll be more satisfied with the frog farm."

The house I wanted to buy had a porch the full length of the back side, under the main roof. I could see it would cost very little to enclose and have more rooms inside.

Mrs. Hozel reminded me, "It didn't have inside plumbing."

I had already found out most of the houses in the neighborhood had outside toilets.

"The well hasn't been used for some time," she told me. "You'll have to clean it out."

The well was cased with three feet cement tile and covered, so I knew it only needed to be bailed dry a few times. The neighbor had already told me it was ten feet deep and although the water level rose to near the ground level there was no need to worry of it being surface water. The electric power line was on the street in front of the house and the house was all wired with plenty of wall plugs. Most of the houses or ranches around Sundance didn't have electricity or inside plumbing.

"Have you seen all you want to see here before we drive out to the frog farm?" Mrs. Hozel asked.

"This house is for sale?" I asked her.

"Would you like to make an offer?"

The way she said, make an offer, made me think she would

189

accept less than the asking price. Was she going to turn down my offer and still try to sell me the frog farm?

"Would they take 1,000 dollars instead of 1,100 with 200 down instead of 300 and the interest on the balance five percent instead of six?"

"I'm sure they will." She said. "The payments will be 15 dollars a month."

"And the interest on the unpaid balance will be five percent?"

"I think we have a deal. I can tell you're no longer interested in the frog farm," she said, regretfully. "I can see this is the place you really fell in love with. We'll go back to the office and draw up the papers."

How could she tell how I felt about this place, but it was like paying only $200, because it would have cost at least $15 a month to rent the house on a city lot. Besides a house, this place had two acres and a chicken house. I never told Grandma how quickly the realtor agreed to my offer. She might have thought I should have offered less.

"Since I won't be 21 until the 25th of this month, will it be okay to date the contract ahead?" I asked.

"No problem, but I'll need twenty dollars for earnest money before I draw up the contract and take it off the market."

I didn't want to tell her I didn't have twenty dollars on me. I never carried more than a dollar or two in my pockets when I hitchhiked. She didn't need to know my thumb was my mode of travel. I asked if it would be okay to have my grandmother see it first before I decided.

"That will be fine," she agreed. "

"When can I move in?" I asked.

"I'm sure it'll be okay with the seller for you to move in as soon as you put up the earnest money."

I had planned to show Duane the place we were going to buy before I closed the deal because it would be half his. This was exactly what I had been looking for and I couldn't take the time. I didn't want to take a chance on it being sold before I came back with the earnest money.

When I got back to Lake City that night I told Grandma, Aunt Myrtle and Uncle Clyde what I had found and they thought it sounded like a good deal. The next day was Sunday, Clyde's day off, so we all drove out to see the chicken ranch I wanted to buy. It was in a district called Rose Hill, only two miles east of Kirkland. They all liked it for the price and thought the terms were good too. Grandma said I could borrow the 20 dollars needed for the earnest money and the down payment when the papers were ready for me to sign.

There was work that had to be done before our mother and Grace moved out from Wyoming and I would have to buy a cook stove which Uncle Clyde agreed to haul out from Seattle for me. I almost held my breath until the real estate office opened Monday morning so I could give Mr. Hozel the 20 dollars to close the deal. After signing the necessary papers I hitchhiked to Arlington to tell Duane and get the rest of my clothes. Roger's mother gave me a quilt for my bed and a few pots, pans and dishes. She agreed to loan me a brooder stove I would need to raise some baby chicks. Duane gave me money for groceries and other things I needed. I had some money coming from my jobs in Laramie which Buck would send. One of the first jobs I had to do was bale out the well and clean it and send a water sample to the health department to be tested. The water came in the well almost as fast as I could bale it out. When the test came back I knew we had a good well and I no longer had to carry water from a friendly neighbor.

Duane hitchhiked down to see our new place the first day off he had from his job. He liked it and he wanted to move in with me as soon as he could. He had to stay with his job until one of us found a job closer to our new home. It would take all the money we could scrape together to get started in chickens.

We decided to put a new shingle roof on the house. Duane bought the singles from a mill in Arlington and helped me put on a new roof. He also put up the money for the lumber and helped me on his days off to close in part of the back porch in order to have another bedroom.

We bought 200 baby chicks. I had to stay at the place getting the baby chicks started so I wasn't able to look for a job yet. I had plenty to do before our mother and Grace joined us, with caring for the chicks, remodeling the house and getting the vegetable garden ready and planted. Howard would be bringing them in his pickup, leaving Wyoming about May 1.

Chapter Twenty-three

A part of my childhood dream became a reality on my 21st birthday in 1939 when I signed the contract to buy a two-acre chicken ranch on Rose Hill two miles east of Kirkland. It would be our new home in the Washington I had heard so much about since early childhood. Aunt Myrtle and Uncle Clyde came over from Lake City several Sundays while I was living in the house by myself. Once they brought me a cake, another time a meat loaf. I guess Aunt Myrtle was afraid I wouldn't be eating right and she was looking out for me like a mother. One Sunday, Clyde helped me move a shed so I could relocate the outdoor toilet farther from the house. I think what Uncle Clyde and Aunt Myrtle gave me most was something I couldn't buy: encouragement. Although I had plenty to do, it was lonely living alone while waiting for Grace and our mother to get there from Wyoming.

It was a warm spring in Washington compared to Wyoming. When March arrived I had to start planting a vegetable garden. First the plot needed to be plowed. Not knowing anyone and without a car, I set out on foot to locate someone that did custom plowing. It was like exploring a new land in a foreign country. It gave me a good reason to look over the area and meet some of my new neighbors. A half mile or so north and east of our chicken ranch was a place called The Eastside Battery or Lottsville. It consisted of a little store where they sold a few groceries, gas and a garage that sold auto parts. This looked like a good place to inquire about finding someone to plow our garden. I went in to talk to the guy that ran the garage. A customer who was waiting to buy an auto part told me the owner was in back looking for a part for him. It was the weirdest auto parts store you could imagine. There were fan belts, gaskets and all kinds of auto parts you could think of hanging on the walls clear to the ceiling and the ceiling must have been fifteen feet high. Parts were also in piles and boxes on the floor.

I remarked to the customer, "I can't see how anyone would know what he had or how he could find anything if he did have it in stock."

"If you think this is jumbled, you should see the back room. If it's here Fred will find it. You don't need to worry about that. He can tell you before he looks if he has it and what it will cost you."

"Do you know anyone who I can hire to plow my garden?" I asked.

"Lots of them. Several on Newcastle."

"Newcastle?"

"Yea, you know the street east of here. I always get old man Recor myself. He lives by the Rose Hill School."

I knew where the school was but it was the other direction from our chicken ranch. I decided to walk over to Newcastle anyway since I had never been there before.

Most of the places were about the same as ours, some an acre or two, some five acres and some maybe ten. Facing the gravel street were small frame houses, some had chicken houses in the back. The apple trees that decorated the yards were not yet in bloom. The aroma of burning apple prunings and last year's raspberry canes filled the air. Birds were chirping while scratching for worms in a field of daffodils that were about to break into bloom. I could feel, smell, and hear spring everywhere.

I hired Mr. Recor to plow our garden and had it planted before Mother, Grace, Howard and Delbert Hopson arrived from Wyoming. Delbert Hopson was a classmate of Duane's and would stay with us until he found a job. It was a good thing I had borrowed a bed from Aunt Myrtle so we all had a place to sleep.

The baby chicks were doing fine but we had a lot more room in the chicken house. With money from the sale of our little house in Sundance I bought 200 more pullets. It took most of what was left of the 365 dollars our mother got for the Sundance house to pay back the 200 down payment I had borrowed from Grandma.

I was glad I was able to talk our mother out of using that money to pay off some of our dad's old debts. She didn't like to leave Wyoming owing people. I explained to her all the labor in that house was Duane's and mine. The lumber we used to build it with was part payment of what Milt owed Duane, Buck and me for wages. I believe in paying my debts but the grocery bill that was owed to the Franks and the Sundance Times was our dad's debt not mine. I knew we needed all we could scrape together to get established in Washington. Duane and I both had to find good-paying jobs before we could go on to college and finish our education.

We couldn't count on Howard for any help, he had to borrow money from Duane to get back to Sundance.

Duane quit his job in Arlington when we put the new roof on the house so we no longer had his wages for living expenses.

Grandma Perrigoue moved in with us and we were glad to have her but she did not help pay for the groceries. She made it clear to me, "It would be a sad day when she would pay a relative for room and board."

She liked to help in her own way and not be obligated to pay a set amount. She gave me 75 dollars to buy a Model A Ford so we could get around without hitchhiking. Duane's bicycle and our thumbs had been our only mode of transportation until then.

Finding jobs for Duane, Hopson and myself around Kirkland was our number one priority. The Model A Ford helped a lot on that score. I tried to get a job in the shipyard that was two miles south of Kirkland on Lake Washington. I ran into the answer that came up many times later, "We would like to hire you but you have to join the union first." When I talked to the union dispatcher in Seattle, he told me he had many union members out of work he had to put to work first. This was a problem I never heard of in Wyoming. It had never occurred to me that anyone couldn't hire me without first getting permission from a union.

Farm jobs were about the only ones that could be had without belonging to a union. Farmers were even supposed to hire union truck drivers if they hauled their products into Seattle. It made the newspapers when shots were fired at a farmer's truck when it crossed the mountain pass from eastern Washington without a union driver. Uncle Clyde belonged to the teamster's union and was required to hire teamster union swampers to unload his truck whether he needed them or not whenever he made deliveries on the waterfront. Uncle Elmer belonged to the longshoreman's union. When they needed more longshoremen than they had members in Seattle they would send to Portland rather than me getting a chance to get a few days of work. Uncle Wes had a floor covering business and always had to hire union help. Uncle Gus and Cousin Jack worked in the woods and belonged to still another union.

We found out about an employment office in Seattle that sold jobs, many were for farm help. The three of us Duane, Del Hopson and I were headed there looking for work when Duane was hit by a car that made an illegal left turn into a crosswalk. Duane wasn't hurt but the door handle of the car caught the pocket of his pants and almost tore them off him. The driver that hit Duane was very sorry and told us to get in the car with him and he would make it right and pay for any damages. He was trying to get us away from the scene before the police got there but a police car happened to be parked by the curb and saw it happen. We all went to the police station where the driver was booked.

I guess he was afraid of being sued so he asked us to have breakfast with him where he worked. It turned out he was in upper management at Fredrick and Nelson's, one of Seattle's biggest department stores. When we were having a friendly chat with him over coffee and rolls he asked if there was anything at all he could do for us. I knew the one thing we three wanted most was jobs. I told him we were headed for the employment office in hopes of finding work. We talked a little of what work experience we had. I didn't mention milking cows, driving a farm tractor, building a house or working in a sawmill. I knew a department store wouldn't have that kind of work. I mentioned I had worked in a restaurant while going to college.

He told us he should be able to find us something, maybe in the restaurant if we would accept jobs at first as bus boys. We told him we would consider anything he had to offer that we could do. He asked to be excused because he was already late and was holding up a management staff meeting. He would get in touch with us later after he had a chance to find out what openings the store might have. We exchanged names and it sounded as if we had gotten our first break at the expense of Duane almost losing his pants. Our new "friend" had one of the store employees give Duane some pants and we were on our way again looking for the employment office on Occidental Avenue.

We found the employment office in a part of Seattle that was called skid road. Never in my life had I even imagined there could be so many poor-looking characters all gathered in one area. When I wondered why they were all there, I couldn't help but think of the crickets with the "short legs" in Wyoming. This could have been called the bum center of the world as far as I was concerned. Men were just milling around, some old, others young, all dressed in ragged dirty clothes. One old man with an unkept beard was standing on a box giving a speech that was more like a sermon.

"The rich don't care if we starve," he said. "They say God will save us. That's what they want. They want us to all starve. After you're dead that's when you'll see God."

"This guy sounds crazy," I said to Duane.

"He's one of them commies," a man next to me said.

"What are all these people doing here?" I asked the stranger.

"What are you doing here?" Was his answer.

I knew he was telling me I was one of them whether I wanted to believe it or not. I was here looking for a job and I wouldn't let myself believe that kind of rubbish. I had one thing most of these people may not have had. I wanted to work and I still had confidence in myself.

The employment office was a rundown ramshackle building on the street level. The inside reeked with tobacco smoke and unbathed people. The atmosphere of hungry-looking people was frightening. Most of them stared with expressionless eyes that showed they were beaten men that had lost the will to fight life's battle. Job notices were scrawled on paper and stuck to the inside of the cracked unwashed front window so they could be read from the street side. Most were farm jobs, with the required fees posted along with the experience required and where the jobs were located.

Duane and Delbert Hopson found jobs that called for clean young men to work on the Hollywood farm not too far from our new home on Rose Hill. Clean meant bums need not apply. The pay included room and board so I decided to keep looking because I needed a job where I could stay home. Someone had to stay with our mother and grandmother to help take care of the chickens and garden.

It was a good thing we didn't wait around for the man that hit Duane, and ruined his pants, to give us jobs. After waiting several days for him to call, I phoned and was given the bum's rush. He referred me to his insurance company. I guess he had time to find out he was covered by insurance. Duane had to press him to get him to pay for a new suit of clothes. Since the pants that were ruined went with Duane's only suit, Duane insisted on a new one and not merely the cheap pair of pants he had been given the day he was hit in the crosswalk. Duane finally got the new suit but the promise of jobs must have been merely a ploy to get us to forget the whole incident.

I looked everywhere I could think of for work only to get the same answer. I had to belong to the union or have years of experience. When I was back at the employment office on skid road checking the jobs posted on the window, a man asked me to read the job notice to him. I knew he couldn't read. When I read part of the notice he asked about the last part.

"It says the fee is 10 dollars and must be paid in advance."

"If I had 10 dollars I wouldn't need the lousy job," he growled.

With Grandma living at our house I expected visits from uncles, aunts and cousins dropping by to see her almost every weekend. One Sunday when Uncle Hank and Aunt Flora were at our house, Uncle Hank told me he knew a man named Lambert just outside Redmond that might hire me. He ran a slaughter house and a farm where he fattened cattle.

"He's a good friend of mine," Uncle Hank said. "Tell him you're my nephew and I'm sure he'll give you a job."

I had been looking for a job so long without success I was beginning to feel like those men on skid road looked. I knew by now the only way to get a good job was to belong to a union or be someone's relative or know someone. I would have gladly joined a union but I needed some pull there too. Of all the uncles, aunts, and cousins I had in the Seattle area, not one had offered to help Duane or me find work. Uncle Hank had his own fertilizer business and he said he picked up dead animals at Lambert's Farm and slaughter house to be made into fertilizer.

Monday morning I was waiting for Mr. Lambert at his slaughter house when he showed up.

How to dress when looking for a job is always a tough question. Should I dress like I'm ready to go to work on a farm or should I dress a little better to look like a more presentable person. In order that I might not embarrass Uncle Hank I decided to dress up a little but not wear my only suit of clothes.

Mr. Lambert was a big man and talked with a foreign accent. When I told him I was Hank Robertson's nephew and needed a job his grumpy expression changed into a smile so broad he was almost laughing.

"The question is can you do farm work?" He asked.

I knew I was too well dressed to look like a farm hand but I assured him I had done a lot of farm work.

"Can you drive a team of horses?"

"You bet," I told him.

"Can you drive a tractor?"

"I've had a lot of experience at that."

"Did you ever off-bear from a small sawmill?"

"Yes, quite a bit," I said.

"Can you do carpenter work?"

"My younger brother and I built a house once."

By the looks in Mr. Lambert's eyes I could see he didn't believe me and his smile broke into a chuckle.

"You can do farm work, drive horses, drive tractors, off-bear from a sawmill, and you are also a carpenter and you can't be much older than 21."

"Twenty-one my last birthday."

When I thought about it for an instant, I couldn't expect him to believe me but it was all true. I had experience in all these jobs as I had told him.

"You can ask Uncle Hank." I pleaded.

"This Uncle Hank you got, Hank Robertson or whatever you told me his name was, I never heard of him."

I was embarrassed, not knowing what to say. I knew Uncle Hank liked to spread the bull a little but this was a cruel thing for him to do to me. Mr. Lambert's smirk became a friendly smile.

"You seem to want to work awful damn bad. That's the main thing I guess anyhow. You got me curious. I'm going to find out if you can do what you say you have done."

"I'm telling the truth," I assured him.

"I can use a farm hand in the beet field and maybe drive a tractor when we cut the grain. I'm going to need someone to off-bear at the mill and carpenters when we use the lumber to build a barn."

"I'm your man," I told him.

"Aren't you going to ask me what I pay?"

"Whatever it is I figure it'll be the same if I asked you or not. I need the job.

"I figured you did or you wouldn't have made up all that

stuff. Be here tomorrow morning ready to go to work. The pay is two bits an hour and we work ten-hour days from seven until five thirty and six days a week."

"I'll be here."

I knew he didn't believe me but so what, I thought, at last I have a job where I'll be home nights and help with the chickens and vegetable garden. Fifteen dollars a week was not as much as a union job would pay but it was only about three miles from home and it was more than I was making with no job at all. We could get by and I would keep looking for something that paid more. In a few months the 275 pullets would be laying and that would add to our income. My mother could feed the chickens, gather and clean the eggs while I would be at home to clean the pens and do the heavy work.

I never thought it would be so hard to find a good job around Seattle. At least Duane and me were both working. Duane was saving his money to start at the University of Washington and I expected to join him after we got a little better established. Buck had only one more year at the University of Wyoming. I was making enough to pay the bills. Our mother was happy to be back in Washington. My cousin Dottie had her own bedroom. Grandma and our mother were having a great time talking about the good old days, making up for the lost years. That was what I wanted most, wasn't it?

Chapter Twenty-four

My first assignment on Lambert's farm was weeding and thinning beets that were raised for stock feed. This was considered Mexican work back in Wyoming. I had heard people laugh and say Mexicans were better at it because they were built closer to the ground and didn't have to lean over so far. Being over six feet, three inches tall myself I could no longer see the humor in the remarks. Two of my fellow workers were of Mexican descent and we became good friends.

When the sawmill operated I got the job of off-bearing, as I had done at my brother's mill in Wyoming. Off-bearing is taking care of the lumber as it comes off the saw.

Lawrence, a farm hand, had the job of driving the team of horses. The lumber had to be hauled from the mill to where we would be building a barn. One day Lawrence didn't show up for work. I went to the barn, harnessed the team and hitched them to the wagon. When Mr. Lambert found me driving the horses he wanted to know what happened to Lawrence.

"I guess he's sick," I said. "At least he didn't show up for work."

"Who hitched up the horses?" He asked.

"I did."

Mr. Lambert looked the horses over as if he was observing them for the first time. I guess he was expecting to find the harnesses on backwards, upside down or something.

"Unhitch the team from the wagon," he said.

I did what he said.

"Hitch them up again."

As I followed his commands he watched my every move, I knew he doubted that I knew how to do it. I wanted to tell him if I had a dollar for every time I had hitched up a team of horses I surly wouldn't need his two-bit an hour job.

"Humph," he grunted. "You never told me you liked to drive horses."

"I never said I did, but it beats carrying this lumber on my back."

The old man gave me a funny grin and left. I always thought he liked me after that. Maybe he believed I had done the things I had told him when he hired me. Anyhow, when we started building the barn, I was assigned to work with the carpenter. This experience, plus what I gained when Duane and I built the little house in Sundance made me think maybe I should try working as a carpenter. Union Carpenters were paid over a dollar an hour. Lambert paid the Swede I was working with only fifty cents, but it was twice as much as I was making as his helper. I knew if I could get in the union I could do the work.

Duane and Del would come home Sundays, my day off, but I hardly got to see them. Grandma would usually want me to drive her to one of her two farms. She always gave me a dollar for gas. The first few times it seemed like that was the least I could do to repay her for giving me the money to buy the Model A Ford. Her farm that was near the town of Monroe had been mortgaged to build a new barn. The rent she got from it didn't do much more than make the mortgage payments. The other farm she owned only a half interest in, was in the Snoqualmie Valley near the little town of Duvall. Her share of the rent from this farm was her source of income. Aunt Myrtle told Grandma I would probably like a day off once in a while and for her not to ask me to drive her around every Sunday. We didn't go so often after that.

Our pullets were starting to lay which helped pay our living expenses. I missed not being able to read a daily paper so I splurged and had the newspaper boy deliver the Seattle Star weekdays, which cost three cents a copy and the Seattle Times delivered on Sundays, which was a little more. I looked forward to Sundays, the only day I could sleep late, that is when Grandma didn't want me to drive her to see one of her farms. The first Sunday in September my plans were to sleep late and enjoy the Sunday paper. I had been following the world news but I wasn't ready for the headlines that morning. Bold type covered half the front page.

"EUROPE AT WAR!"

Hitler had released his army on Poland. Great Britain and France both announced they were at war with Germany. Joe Stalin and Hitler had signed a non-aggression pack that I thought meant Russia and Germany were allies. I was of the opinion the United States would eventually have to stop Hitler.

Duane was able to save enough money to start the fall quar-

201

ter at the University of Washington. He found a job near campus working out some of his board along with a job on NYA. He worked on campus making $15 a month. Duane had always been a good student but things didn't go so well with him. I guess he got into an advanced math class without the basics. Neither Duane nor I had anyone we could turn to for advice on such matters. I suppose we relied on each other and didn't always come up with the right answers.

While Duane was struggling with college I was able to make the $15 per month payments on our chicken ranch and the other expenses of running a home. The news about the war in Europe was all bad and it looked as though my returning to college might have to wait longer than I had hoped. The days kept getting shorter and we couldn't see to work ten-hour days on the farm. As we gradually shortened our work days, I got less pay each week but the chickens were laying more each day and that helped.

I never realized before there was so much difference between what chicken ranchers got paid for their eggs and what the customer had to pay for them in the store. It amounted to about ten cents a dozen or about one third. By the time the chickens were in full lay, the feed costs were about eight dollars per week. Our 250 pullets layed on the average about 16 dozen eggs per day. Eggs sold for 22 cents a dozen. After paying for the feed, the chickens added about $16 per week to our income. This amounted to one dollar more than when I worked 60 hours for Lambert.

We had a great Thanksgiving our first year in Washington. Grandma cooked a turkey we had raised and she invited Uncle Gus and Uncle Will and their families over to our place for dinner. I couldn't but help think of the Pilgrims and their first Thanksgiving in their new land as I watched my happy 83-year-old grandmother scurry around basting the turkey and helping my mother prepare the dinner.

With the egg money coming in we could buy a few of the many things we needed to get started in our new home. About the time I thought things were starting to go my way I got the word Lambert would be laying off most of his farm hands. The only ones he would keep were those that were married. It wasn't really news because I could see it coming but it came right at Christmas. Anyhow we had a great Thanksgiving.

My mother and I agreed at Christmas that our family wouldn't exchange gifts because we needed so many things and I might not find another job right away. Mr. Miller, our next door neighbor, was on WPA because he couldn't find a job. I wasn't eligible for this kind of government help because I hadn't lived in Washington long enough and this help was available only for married people with a family. I've heard people say all that is really necessary for a family to be happy at Christmas is to be together. They should try it sometime without a tree, no exchanging of gifts and in a new land without a job.

My lifetime dream of moving my mother to Washington state wasn't turning out quite the way I had hoped. This was the first Christmas I had ever experienced without snow. Yes, I even missed the Wyoming winters. That first Christmas in Washington was the most stressful day I ever hoped to endure in my life. I knew times wouldn't get any better until I could get a union job. They were the only ones that paid enough so I could save for college. The constant rain was like a wet blanket smothering my spirits.

Before I got laid off at the farm, I would come home at night wet and tired after working outside all the daylight hours. My mother would complain about having to clean so many eggs. I really hadn't thought our move to Washington was a time for any one of us to retire. I knew she couldn't work on a job that took her out of our home with Grandma staying with us, but I never thought she would object to helping with the chickens.

It was my responsibility for what was happening to our family. Duane was not happy at the University of Washington. Del Hopson was still not able to get a good job as a milker as he had hoped. With the war threatening in Europe he was talking about joining the Navy. We didn't have enough laying hens to make a living. I had to find a job before we could increase the size of our flock.

I wasn't working so I tried again to get on at the shipyard located a few miles south of Kirkland. I talked to Fuzzy Fangler, a shipyard boss that ran the dry-dock.

"I could sure use a good strong man like you right now," he said. "But you'll first have to clear it with the Scalers Union."

At the union hall the business agent told me, "We have too many members out of work now, but you are welcome to stay in the hall and take your chances. You have to be here when the job comes in. If we run out of union members we send out non-members. The job may only be for a few hours, a day or so at the most. The members get first choice. Until you are a member you need only pay the union two-bits a shift."

I thanked him and watched the men who were waiting in the union hall. Some were playing poker using matches for chips, others were reading while still others were staring into space. It was a depressing-looking lot, about the same as the employment office on skid road. I watched unnoticed until a young man about my age noticed me reading his magazine over his shoulder.

"My name's Fred," he said. "Would you like the magazine when I'm finished?"

"I'm Link," I said. "Sorry,"

"You needn't be," he said with a friendly smile and held out his hand.

"Glad to know you Fred," I said as I shook his hand. "Do you belong to the union?"

"No. If I did I would have gone out on that last job."

"How long have you been waiting?"

"If you mean the last time I got any work it was one week ago. I was lucky, I got eight hours plus four hours overtime."

I was afraid to ask him how much he made but it couldn't have been as much as I had been making in a week working for Lambert. I could tell there wasn't much hope in getting hired at the shipyard near Kirkland. Fred handed me his magazine telling me he was finished with it. It will be something to read on the trolley and ferry back to Kirkland, I thought. The magazine was called Friday. I didn't have to read very far to find it was different than anything I had read before. It didn't have the usual ads. On my ride across the lake from Seattle to Kirkland I was sitting at a table on the ferry boat reading when a friendly man, his friends had called Scotty, asked me if I liked the commie magazine I was reading.

"It's different," I told him.

"And it tells the truth," Scotty said. "Can I have it when you're finished?"

"Sure I'm about through." I gladly handed it to him, because I was afraid to take it home after I realized I had been reading communist literature.

Through the help of Mrs. Belts, a neighbor, I got a job dismantling a mink farm. The mink got a disease so the owners had to move them to Idaho. They thought the damp Washington weather was the cause of their problem. This job paid two bits an hour the same as Lambert paid but because of the short winter days I could only make ten dollars a week. I worked outside and I think it rained every day the whole month of January. I hadn't noticed so much rain last year when I didn't have to work out in it all the time.

Some evenings after I got dried out I would join a few neighbors in the Rose Hill School gymnasium. It was a government-supported recreation program. My mother seemed to think I should stay home and help her clean the eggs. They had to be cleaned and crated before the wholesaler would buy them. We played volleyball most of the time and I met Ann, a neighbor girl, who was pleasant to talk to. She had finished college and had her first teaching job. We became good friends and I found her very appealing but I was in no financial position to ask her for a date. I couldn't afford a movie, go dancing, take her out to dinner or anything. It was embarrassing. I didn't want her to know I was so short on spending money or the way I felt about her.

With the cold damp rain we now had the added expense of buying wood and coal. I felt very depressed working out in the rain every day without the proper rain clothes.

While playing volleyball one night I met Ucke, a young man about my age. While the others were resting between games Ucke and I found a basketball and shot baskets. I was lucky that night, it seemed most of the shots I took went in.

"How would you like to play basketball with our team?" Ucke asked. "I play for the Griffith Dairy who sponsors us."

"I would like that," I told him.

"I'll ask Bill, our manager, next time I see him."

Ucke called at my house a few nights later and said they were short a few subs and if I could drive my car they would pay the gas, but he couldn't promise I would get to play. The team played in the King County League and if they got first place the team had a chance to get into the amateur play-offs that was back east some place.

Bill Bright, the team's manager and captain, was a friendly guy. This was a chance for me to associate with people my own age and interests as I hardly had a chance to meet anyone like this around Kirkland since I came here from Wyoming. We only had six players, counting me, and when one of our players was about to foul out, Bill asked me if I would like to play awhile. We were behind at the time and Bill didn't have to ask me twice.

When I got to play in that game I felt like I was among friends again. It was playing basketball that made high school so enjoyable for me. In college when I made the freshman squad, college took on a new meaning. I think maybe I felt inferior around other people most of the time, but not when I was playing basketball. Before that night was over, living in Washington took on a new meaning for me. I never before or since have played such a lucky game of basketball. It seemed no matter what shot I tried, a sky hook, one handed, two handed over my head, I even made a lay up with my left hand. We ended up winning the game and I had made several new friends. I got to play with the team the rest of the season. We lost the playoff for the league championship by one point after three overtimes.

The job at the mink farm only lasted through the month of February. I was glad winter was about over and looked forward to another Washington summer. One of the guys I had played basketball with told me there was an opening where he worked east of Redmond in a peat moss plant. The peat moss had to be scooped from the peat bog and dried in a big furnace before it was baled. It paid about fifty cents per hour and I wouldn't have to join the union until I got the job.

My friend told me the office that did the hiring opened at nine, an hour after the production workers had to report. I was there a little before nine and the office was already open but no one seemed to pay any attention to me. I could feel the weird smell of the peat bog in the air. I could see people in the back of the room but they were talking in low whispers so I couldn't understand what they were saying. It was spooky the way everyone acted. It's hard to explain but I knew something was wrong. I could feel my presence wasn't welcome. Someone finally asked me what I wanted.

"I heard there was a job opening," I said.

The look in that man's eyes was enough to tell me I had said the wrong thing. I had been turned down for jobs many times but nothing like this.

"Would you get the hell out of here!"

I left not knowing what I had done that deserved such a curt and final response. I had been bawled out before by some of the best, coaches, my older brothers, teachers and even an army drill sergeant who taught ROTC at college. Compared to this man's tone of voice they all seemed like Sunday school teachers. That night when I glanced through the paper I realized what had happened. There was a picture of my friend, the one who told me about the job. He had been electrocuted that morning when he put his foot on a wet motor to tie his shoe. I had asked for a job that morning only a few minutes after they had hauled my friend's body away. I felt sick and so ashamed of what I had done. I had heard of people applying for the job when they knew someone had been killed working in logging.

Duane quit at the University of Washington after the spring quarter and found a job working for a dairy. He didn't think he wanted to attend that university anymore, maybe he would try Washington State, after he had saved up enough money. Del Hopson joined the Navy. The only income we had to pay the bills in Kirkland was egg money. Anyhow we had plenty to eat. Last summer our garden had been great. Our mother had canned over 300 quarts of vegetables and fruit. And of course we had lots of eggs and chicken. The only thing that we lacked was fresh meat at every meal, which isn't all that healthy anyhow.

I thought if I could sell our eggs direct to the stores I could increase our income. After boxing them and stamping them with my identification number, at first I sold to both the Safeway and the Ebby stores in Kirkland. Art Case was the manager at Ebby's. I assured him my eggs were always fresh, less than a week old. Twice a week I would take out any that were not sold and replace them with fresh ones. I sold my older eggs to the wholesaler. It wasn't long before Art was buying all the fresh eggs I could supply. He used them for a leader and paid me the same as he sold them for, sometimes he paid me a penny or two more than his customer's paid him. This increased our income by about 50%.

The war in Europe was all bad. Germany and Russia had

gobbled up Poland and Russia had taken over three small countries on the Baltic (Latvia, Estonia and Lithuania) and part of Finland. I was afraid it was only a matter of time when we would be in the war too. Our grandmother thought the English should leave Hitler alone and there wouldn't be a big war. With her German ancestry there was no use trying to explain it to her otherwise.

Grandma gave me a check to buy some coal. I hesitated to take it, knowing how she felt about paying board and room from a relative. I had borrowed a pickup to haul the coal from a mine near Issaquah. I told her I wasn't sure how much it would cost but she insisted I take a blank check she had signed.

"You go on now. Take it," she said. "I loaned 500 dollars to Clyde when I was staying at their house. I never expected him to pay that back."

I bought and paid for the load of coal and tried to give her back the blank check she had sighed.

"You go on now. Keep it, in case something should happen."

Something did happen. It was late March when I came home from looking for a job and Grandma was sitting on the back steps and my mother was crying.

"Grandma has had a stroke or something." Mother said. "She can't get up."

I couldn't get her up by myself so I asked Mr. Hanson, a neighbor to help me carry her into the house and lay her on her bed.

Chapter Twenty-five

Grandma wasn't able to talk again after she had the stroke and never fully recovered. She died the first part of April 1940. She had been living with us less than a year. Her request to have her grandsons for pallbearers was made possible by Uncle Will's sons, Floris and Ralph; Uncle Gus's sons, Jack and Lyle plus Howard and me.

Howard had arrived in Kirkland from Wyoming after Grandma had the stroke but before she died. He bought a new Ford before leaving Wyoming and we pallbearers rode in it at Grandma's funeral. She was buried beside Granddad in Kent.

Howard left Wyoming with intentions of making Washington state his new home. He only stayed in Kirkland a few days before locating near Morton, Washington. Howard brought a friend with him who had an uncle who lived near there.

The morning Grandma died, several of our aunts and uncles came to our house. While we were having breakfast Grace started to cry. The stress of having someone die in our house made coping difficult for all of us.

Uncle Wes, Aunt Minn's husband, asked Grace, "What's the matter, are you afraid you'll have to go back to Wyoming?"

He seemed to be under the impression Grandma had been paying the bills for our living expenses. Nothing could have been further from the truth. I could smell whiskey on his breath and knew he was under the influence but what bothered me most was wondering how many of our other relatives thought the same.

Before Grandma died I showed Aunt Myrtle the signed blank check Grandma had given me. Aunt Myrtle had me draw out all the money and she used it to pay the medicine and doctor bills that were incurred when Grandma was sick. I was glad, especially for my mother's sake we had been able to move to Washington while Grandma was still living so she could live with us before she died, but she did not add to our financial well being. We all loved Grandma dearly and she was greatly missed, but her death would have nothing to do with our staying in Washington.

As the saying goes, life has to go on. We had a chicken ranch to run and I had to find a good-paying job before I could finish my college education.

Uncle Gus and Cousin Jack were doing some logging in Happy Valley, a few miles east of Redmond. They were yarding logs with a steam-powered donkey and they were to be paid according to the amount of logs they yarded and loaded on trucks that hauled the logs to market. Small logging operators such as these are called, gyppos. I think I found out why. Gus hired me to set chokers. Chokers fasten the logs to the mainline that the donkey moves logs from the woods to the landing. I stayed at their house and was to be paid after they got their money.

One day a big log got caught behind a stump. I had previously logged in Wyoming and knew I had to unfasten the log and run the choker around the other side of the stump and rehook it so the donkey could continue the log on its way to the landing. Uncle Gus was out in the woods with me handling the signal whistle that was on a long wire that led back to where Jack was operating the donkey. Because the donkey was not in sight of where Gus and I were working, Jack had to rely on the signals Gus gave to know whether we were ready for him to start the logs on their way to the landing.

When the log got caught behind the stump Gus gave the signal for Jack to stop pulling. Then he signaled for Jack to back up to put slack in the mainline so I could change the choker to the other side of the stump. I don't know if Gus gave the wrong signal, or what, but instead of putting slack in the mainline Jack tried to jerk it loose by pulling harder. The choker broke and I was out in the open with this cable, over an inch in diameter and a quarter of a mile long, coming straight for me with such force it would have cut my head off. I had no time to run, all I could do was drop down to the ground as the cable went sailing over my head. When it swung back like a pendulum I was laying in a little sunken place in the ground. It swung past me several times cutting away at the mound of dirt just over my head.

Gus and Jack argued about whose fault it would have been if I had been killed. I knew right then, union wages or not, if this was an example of logging in Washington I would have no part of it.

Duane was out of work and Uncle Wes wanted me to work for him so Duane replaced me setting chokers for Uncle Gus. As

I said earlier, it was correctly called gyppo logging, neither Duane nor I ever got paid anything but our board. I guess we should have been used to not being paid. It was like working for our brother Milt in Wyoming.

Uncle Wes hired me to work on a hot asphalt floor at the Rainier brewery in Seattle, and he paid union wages. Somehow he got the union's okay. Wes and I hit it off very well. At first I carried hot material. When the floor was setting up too fast for the finisher, Uncle Wes had me help the finisher. He complemented me by saying what a good worker I was and told me about other jobs he had coming up.

Uncle Wes said he was going to teach me the business and it looked as if there would be a great future for both of us. One day after work he showed me one of his completed jobs, so I would know the other kinds of flooring he installed. It was a restaurant that seemed way out by itself beside some railroad tracks. He remarked, who would put a restaurant in such a place. It has been expanded several times and became one of the better known restaurants in Seattle, Ivar's Captain's Table.

The job at the brewery lasted a little over a week and Uncle Wes gave me the impression he would hire me again when the other jobs were ready but he never asked me to work for him again. He used the excuse it was the union. I had a good talk with the union business agent and he told me my uncle could get me on as an apprentice but he would have to request it.

A few years later Uncle Wes took his own life. I found out my Aunt Minn was against him hiring a relative because the family would find out their personal problems. What she was really afraid of was that the family would know what an alcoholic her husband actually was. We all knew about his drinking which wrecked their marriage, ruined his business and led to his death. I have always felt it would have been different for both of us if I had continued to work for him. I believe he needed me and I know I needed him.

The money I had made working for Uncle Wes helped. Adding it to the money from selling eggs direct to a store, I was able to buy more young pullets that would increase our income even more when they were old enough to lay.

The weather was no longer dreary with constant rain. Our

211

Link ready for a flying lesson.

springs and summers in Washington are about the best you'll find anyplace. Everything is green and fresh with the smell of blossoms and the sound of song birds.

Duane had a better paying job milking cows and was saving to return to college. He would be going to Washington State instead of the University of Washington.

Grace was making enough to buy her clothes and spending money by picking berries and baby-sitting. She had one more year of high school.

Buck spent a few days with us in Kirkland before returning to Laramie. That June he graduated from the University of Wyoming, the first of the Kaisers to finish college. He was awarded the honor book, an award given to the outstanding graduating student of the Agriculture College. Each year the dean presented only one to his outstanding student. Buck had to decide between a job as day foreman at the Union Pacific Railroad freight house or working at the Colorado State College farm in Fort Collins, Colorado. He took the Fort Collins job even though it paid less because he would be working at what he had majored in at the University of Wyoming.

Howard was cutting pulpwood near Morton and made enough to trade in his almost new Ford for a brand new one.

Nazi Germany had overrun most of Europe and I was sure it

wouldn't be long before we would be at war. When I heard about a government program that would pay for my flying lessons, I signed up. If I successfully completed the curriculum I would get a private pilot's license. This was something I could do while still running the chicken ranch at home, working the garden and looking for a job. The flying lessons were at Boeing Field and ground school was held nights at the University of Washington. I had my first flight on July 4, 1940. It was the first time I had ever been in an airplane, a thrill of my life I might add.

I liked flying an airplane as much as I liked to play basketball, maybe even more. I always remember what Walt Tracy, my high school basketball coach, told me: "Whatever you do in life, do something you like. If you like it, you'll excel at it."

I never stopped looking for full-time work. The flight lessons usually lasted about an hour. I would spend the rest of the day in Seattle looking for a job. I think I contacted every place within miles of Boeing Field. When some people hear the statement, "Don't call me, I'll call you," they may think it's funny. It brings back different memories for me that are a long way from funny. The same question was always asked, "Do you belong to the union?" When I said no the next word I heard was, "Sorry."

After completing a flying lesson one day I stopped at the union hall to see Fred. With the war in Europe there was a lot more extra work at the shipyards. I could see there was a chance of getting a few day's work so I took my work clothes with me and waited in the union hall after finishing my flying lesson each day.

I got my first chance one day when they ran out of every one in the hall. There was even a vender selling hot dogs that went to work that day. I got to work overtime and made more in that one shift than I was paid for a week the summer before at the farm near Redmond. By the time I had successfully completed my flying lessons, I averaged a couple of days a week working as a shipyard laborer mostly at Todd's shipyard. I worked enough that the union business agent added my name to his list of names he called after all the union members had turned down a job.

One of the men that knew I had chickens and sold eggs asked me, "How come you're taking a job when you have a chicken ranch?"

"It's like this," I told him. "It was either me or the chickens.

213

One of us had to get a job so we both could eat. Since the chickens couldn't find work, I guess it's up to me."

My mother, Grace, the chickens and I were getting by when we got some unexpected and uninvited house guests.

Several of the Platners, a family from Sundance, showed up one night right after we had finished dinner. They had a pickup and a trailer loaded with all their earthly belongings. They planned to make their home somewhere in Washington. They asked about jobs and places to stay. When I found out they hadn't had dinner I thought the only decent thing to do was to invite them in. They had their own pots and pans and said they had their own food but would like to use our stove.

It was nice to talk to someone from Sundance and get caught up on all the gossip from back home. There were seven of them altogether and one was a small baby. We told them about some cabins they could rent in Juanita, about three miles away. Carl Platner (The Boss) thought they might have trouble finding the place in the dark and wanted to stay with us until morning. We didn't have beds for that many extra people so some of us bedded down on the floor in the feed room of the chicken house. One of them remarked how they used to make room for Milt when he showed up uninvited at their house in Wyoming. It sounded as if we were paying for one of Milt's debts.

I went to the union hall, as usual, to wait for a chance to work and when I came home the Platners were unpacking with no intentions of looking for another place to stay. I thought my mother had invited them and I guess she thought I had. When we had a chance to discuss it privately we discovered The Boss had invited himself.

If you've never had people just move in on you, you could never guess how it feels. They had been people we knew in Wyoming as neighbors and we had more or less gotten along together, but they were not what I would call good close friends of mine.

It was quite obvious we didn't have room for them when I was crowded out of my own bed. At first I thought they would have the decency to look for a place and leave. It shouldn't have been necessary to say anything. After they had been there a week or so, I remembered the time their house had burned down in Wyoming and they moved in with some neighbors and stayed until they had to be told to leave.

We had Thanksgiving dinner with Aunt Myrtie and Cousin Roger near Arlington, without the Platners. When we returned home late the Platners had already gone to bed and one of them told us to be quiet.

He whispered, "The Boss is drunk and we finally got him to sleep. If you wake him, he might be mean and beat up our mother."

I was glad he got drunk. That gave me the courage to ask them to leave without feeling like a heel. They didn't leave right away but they started looking for another place to live and finally moved out.

Duane had run out of money after only one semester at Washington State but soon found a job and started saving so he could go back. I was getting a few days of work in a Seattle shipyard, enough to pay the bills. The shipyard near Kirkland got a big government contract and was hiring quite a few new employees.

The union sent me out on one job in West Seattle that lasted over a month. I worked with a man that always went to Alaska each fishing season. The company he worked for let him pick some of his own men. He was the boss of a crew that repaired fish traps. He asked me if I would like to go along when the season started. He could fix it with the union so that was no problem. I told him the chance to get a steady job was the break I was waiting for and would be glad to work with him, but for one exception.

"I have been trying to get hired at the shipyard near Kirkland ever since I first came to Washington."

"Then I'll plan on you for my crew unless you get the other job. Right?"

"That's correct but I hope you understand why I prefer a job near home. I hope to save my money so someday I can attend the University of Washington."

"It's good you want to go back to college. I'll keep a place open for you just in case. It'll be a few weeks before we leave."

It was March of 1941 and time to order more pullets. I had been toying with the idea of filling the chicken house. It would handle about 1,000 layers. My mother told me I was always figuring out work for someone else. I knew she didn't like to clean

215

eggs and if I would be leaving for Alaska I wasn't sure she could handle any more chickens than we had. I had put running water in the chicken house and the feed store would deliver the feed and pick up the eggs. I knew if I sold eggs direct to the stores I could make about a dollar a day for each 100 layers. Since my mother wasn't happy with chickens and my feeling that a war was coming, I thought maybe it best to phase out the chickens a little.

I had completed making a box to ship the tools I would need on the Alaska job. It was Friday and I was expecting to be leaving the following Monday so I stopped by the union hall to tell a few friends good-bye.

The union dispatcher greeted me with, "I wondered where you were. I have an opening for you over by Kirkland."

"How long will the job last?" I asked.

"They have a big contract to build seaplane tenders. It will be for over a year and a lot longer if we get in a war. Who knows?"

"I'll take it." I said.

What a difference it made to have a steady job with a check every week. I didn't have to spend everything just to live. For the first time in my life I could take a girl on a date and didn't feel guilty about spending money I should use for something at home.

I had my private pilot's license and I intended to join the Army Air Force as soon as I knew my mother was able to get along without me. I could send her money to live on but I wanted to pay off the contract on our home before I left. I also wanted to work long enough to have a trade and belong to a union. When I returned to civilian life I wanted to have a job that paid enough so I could return to college.

Grace finished high school and moved to Everett. She got a job at Paine Field working on airplanes.

Howard got married and he and his wife lived in Kosmos, near where he worked in the woods.

They were starting to hire women for the jobs men usually had in the shipyards.

Duane quit the produce job he had in a grocery store in Seattle and got a job in the shipyard where I worked. That June, Hitler invaded Russia.

With Duane and me both staying at home and working at

good-paying union jobs, we made bigger payments on our chicken ranch. After we had our home paid for, we traded in the model A on a 1936 V-8 Ford. Our mother got part of her inheritance and bought her first refrigerator. Duane and I saw to it she didn't need to use her money for living expenses.

While working in the shipyard as a carpenter's helper, I learned what a carpenter had to know and do. The carpenters belonged to a different union than their helpers. When I asked the carpenter's boss to let me change from a helper to a carpenter, he told me he knew I could do the work but I had to get the okay from the union first. When I talked to the carpenter's union business agent, he said it was okay with him if they okayed it at the shipyard. I felt I was getting the run around until one day when the business agent was at the shipyard making his usual rounds. I saw him talking to the man who was in charge of the carpenters.

As the saying goes, the buck stopped right there. I got a raise in pay and most of all I joined a union with a trade. This would allow me to also work on houses or at any job that hired union carpenters. My pay was a dollar and twelve cents per hour and we were working most Saturdays at time and a half and some Sundays that was double time.

By late fall of 1941 it looked as though Hitler was going to overrun Russia. His armies were parked outside Stalingrad and within sight of Moscow. Howard and Buck had been drafted and I felt it was time for me to join the Army Air Force. I had been renting a small plane from time to time to keep my flying license current. The United States was supplying England and Russia with arms, giving all the aid we could, short of actually being in war ourselves.

Everyone knows what happened on December 7, 1941. It had a peculiar twist for me. Because we lost so many ships, many more had to be repaired and with new ship construction, all ship-yard workers who had a trade were frozen to their jobs. My plans to leave the shipyard job for the Air Force had to be postponed for a while.

Grace was still working on airplanes at Paine Field and staying in Everett. One night Duane confided in me something Grace had arranged. He told me our dad was living in Everett in the same apartment building with Grace. Grace had talked him into coming to Washington to get a job in the shipyard in Everett. Because he didn't have a birth certificate, and couldn't prove he was an American citizen, they wouldn't hire him. If we wanted to see our dad before he went back to Wyoming we better come up to Everett that very night. I was almost in shock. How do you greet a dad who abandoned his family of eight kids to fend for themselves when you were nine years old? Grace was four and Milt, the oldest, was 19 at that time. I was a little bit perturbed with Grace at first for not talking it over with me before she arranged everything. I guess I couldn't blame her, she hardly remembered seeing her dad at all.

"Don't you want to see him?" Duane asked.

I had to think about it for a minute. "Yes I do, but I think we better not tell our mother, at least not until we talk to Dad first."

Chapter Twenty-six

Duane and I finished our dinner and left for Everett without telling our mother where we were going. It could have been a shock, after all these years, for her to know our dad was in Everett, staying in the same apartment building with our sister Grace. Neither Duane nor I talked for the first few miles.

"Just what did Grace say?" I asked Duane as we turned left in Bothell onto the road that led toward Everett.

"She said our dad was up there with her and he couldn't get a job in the shipyards because he didn't have a birth certificate. He needs to prove he's an American citizen, you know, to work on government defense contracts."

"Yea I know, but what else did she say?"

"He's been up there a week or so trying to get a job in the shipyards. Because they wouldn't hire him he's going back to Wyoming."

"Grace must have told him where she lived."

"She wanted to see her dad so she wrote and asked him to come out to Washington. She thought he could find work in a defense plant of some kind or another."

"Are you sure Grace doesn't want us to bale her out, I mean help her keep her promise to Dad and find him a job?"

"Could be, but what difference does it make now?"

"You mean help him get a job in the shipyards?"

"We could you know. At least in the one where we work."

"But would he have the guts to accept our help? It's been about 15 years when he stopped sending home any money and a couple of years more since we last saw him. What would our mother think of him showing up after the way he left us when we were ragged-assed kids?"

"You don't want to help him?" Duane asked.

"I don't know. What do you remember about our dad?"

"I remember the time he called me a black-eyed wop."

"He couldn't call me that. The last time he saw me my hair was white. He called me whitey sometimes, but he can't call me that anymore because my hair has changed to light brown. The one thing I can't remember is him ever giving me a spanking."

"Not that you didn't deserve one, that was always our

mother's job."

"That is all in the past. What concerns me most is NOW. This is the first time our mother has had a decent house with hot and cold water and electricity since she married him. She now has her first washing machine, refrigerator, and bath tub. I wish Grace had talked to me first before she asked him to show up."

"We haven't anything to be ashamed of."

"I know but what about him?"

"Why don't we wait until we talk to him. "I'm sure we can get him a job where we work," Duane said. "You can use your influence with the union. I think I can get the personnel department to waive the birth certificate requirement, at first anyhow, if I tell them he's our dad."

"Yea I suppose we could. You know the people in personnel pretty well as evidenced by the way you've been needling management in your articles each month in the boilermaker's union paper. I should be able to ask the labor union for a favor. I was shop steward before I changed over to the carpenter's union."

"I really never knew for sure what came between our parents. Maybe there is something we could do to get them back together. Now that the struggle to keep from starving is no longer a problem."

Grace was expecting us and she had told Dad we would be coming up to see him. He was glad to see us. I was about nine years old and Duane was seven when we had last seen each other. It was like seeing him for the first time. He was about the same build as Duane, with my blue eyes and light brown hair. When he talked he pointed with his index and middle fingers spread the same way as our sister Helen. He chuckled sometimes when he talked, like his sister, our Aunt Myrtie. The way he rolled his eyes reminded me of our Cousin Roger. I guess Duane and I had both changed a lot more in 15 years than he had. We hardly had a chance to get reacquainted when it was time for Duane and me to leave. We had to work the next day and he was planning to take off for Wyoming in a day or so.

"Would you stay if we can get you a job in the shipyard near Kirkland?" I asked Dad.

"I need to prove I'm not a foreigner," he said with a chuckle. "And if I could do that, they tell me I still have to get the okay from the union before I can go to work,"

"Then you still want to stay in Washington?"

"Does your mother know I'm here?"

"Not yet."

"I would need a place to stay. I couldn't move in with your mother, not until I know how she feels."

"I've never heard her say anything bad about you."

"Fannie never says anything bad about anybody."

After spending the evening with Dad just talking, the past seemed like so long ago it never happened. Dad promised he would stick around a few days to see if we could help him find a job. We agreed to come back the next night and let him know how we did. He said he could go to work at once if we could fix it so he could.

Duane and I both played basketball for the Lake Washington Shipyard. Duane was the coach and manager of the team. Because the people at personnel knew both Duane and me, they told us if we said he was our dad that was good enough proof until he had time to get his birth certificate. The business agent for the labor union was glad to do me a favor and phoned his approval to the shipyard office. Next we had to find a place for him to stay. I inquired from others working in the yard and found a boarding house with room for one more. I made a phone call and made arrangements for Dad to stay there. All that was left to do was tell him and he could go to work the very next day. I still remember how hard it had been for me to find a decent job without anyone helping me when I first came to Kirkland.

Duane and I were very happy with ourselves when we informed our dad he could go to work in the shipyard near Kirkland the next morning. I looked for the expression on his face when we told him everything was taken care of, even a place for him to stay. Duane and I were both smiling from ear to ear.

Dad just cocked his head and looked at us for an instant before he said, "Well aren't we a couple of cockies."

I wasn't sure how to take his remark. I thought it was a strange way of thanking us for our effort. We helped him pack his few belongings into his Model A Ford and he moved to Kirkland that same night.

After a few days I broke the news gently to our mother and

she didn't seem upset. I asked if she would object to him moving in with us. She agreed it was okay if he slept on the couch in the front room.

The night our shipyard basketball team beat the Harlem Globe Trotters, Dad went to the game. He never said anything to me, but one of my friends told me after the game he could tell by the expression on our dad's face, while he watched us play, he was sure proud of his sons.

Milt was the only one of our family who still lived in Wyoming. When he knew he could get a job at the shipyards where Duane and I worked, he moved his family to Kirkland. We helped him find a house to rent and he had no trouble getting hired. Our dad got along fine at his work and with the help of some of our mother's friends to vouch for him, he was able to get his birth certificate.

As I stated, all shipyard workers with a trade were frozen to their jobs for several months after Pearl Harbor. There was a greater need for skilled workers in the shipyards than in the military service and they needed a little time to train our replacements. This gave me time to have second thoughts about what branch of the service I wanted to join. I liked to fly and had a private pilot's license. I had been thinking of joining the Army Air Force because I had heard the Navy had higher requirements. I had to decide if I thought I was good enough to become a Navy pilot or should I settle for the Air Force.

Although we weren't engaged, I was going steady with a girl named Dee Dee, short for Dorothy. Both branches of the service required student pilots to remain unmarried until they finished training and were made commissioned officers.

As soon as the shipyard let me, I put in my application to become a Navy pilot. I passed all the requirements, both physical and IQ tests, and was accepted into the naval cadet pilot's training program in November of 1942. I was told I wouldn't be called up until they had an opening in their training school, probably not until March of 1943.

When I told Dee Dee, my girlfriend, I had been accepted, she was very happy for me. I told her because it might be close to two years before we could think of being married, I couldn't expect her to wait for me. She said she would anyway which is what I had hoped she would say.

The next date I had with Dee Dee she had a change of mind. She told me that her mother said if I didn't want her to wait for me it probably was because I didn't love her. I tried to explain to her how I felt but her mother's advice seemed to be stronger than anything I could say. That was our last date.

With Dad staying at our house and Milt living in the area, our mother no longer needed me. I knew it would only be a matter of time before Duane joined the military service.

After I left to start my pilot's training, Grace got a job welding in the shipyard and moved back home. She became engaged to McAdoo Jones, the nicest guy you could ever expect to meet. He was from Texas, a Navy buddy of Del Hopson.

Howard's wife had died while he was in the Army, stationed in California. The last time I had seen Howard was when he came back to Morton for his wife's funeral. He had since been assigned to driving a reconnaissance jeep with headquarters company attached to General Patton's Army.

Buck was in the Army Air Force, stationed in Brady Texas, teaching instrument flying in a simulated instrument flight trainer.

My Navy pilot's training first took me to the University of Washington which consisted of mostly academics. In a crash course in mathematics we covered everything I had in grade school and high school plus trigonometry. We covered this math course in four weeks. Other subjects studied included physics, which was also a first for me. I also was introduced to navigation for the first time. We had a test each Friday on the work covered that week. Those who received failing grades for two weeks in a row were demoted to apprentice seaman and transferred to boot camp in San Diego. Those who successfully completed the pilot's training program would become Navy pilots with the rank of Ensign. Our military training included marching and close order drill that I had while attending the University of Wyoming.

We were told we were mentally and physically the top two percent of the young men in our country and over half of us would not make it all the way through training. To say I was apprehensive about my ability to keep up with the upper 50 percent of the top two percent, would be putting it mildly. I had never been known as a brain in my school work but becoming a Navy pilot

223

and commissioned officer was something I wanted, even more than finishing college.

After the first week I realized there was something about this training I had never experienced before in school. It's hard to describe the different feeling of not having to worry about paying for my room and board or work extra jobs as I had to do in college. In high school I had to think about paying the grocery bill, the rent, or whether or not we had enough wood for the winter. Even in grade school my success at trapping fur-bearing animals determined if I had warm clothes to wear. Now for the first time in my life all of these things were taken care of for me. All I had to do was study with the hope I could keep my grades up so I wouldn't be washed out. Anyone who was dropped from the program was referred to as being washed out. In the Navy grading system a 4.0 is 100 percent or a perfect score. Anything above 2.5 is passing. At the end of the my fourth week all my grades were 4.0 with the exception of one 3.9. I felt confident then that I could make it through the program so I slacked off a little. I enjoyed the challenge to be associated with a program that demanded the best of my peers and me. .

After successfully finishing the first stage of my training at the University of Washington, I was sent to Yakima where we were given our first flight training. The planes were similar to those I trained in when I got my private pilot's license at Boeing Field in Seattle. I had been flying a Taylorcraft there and our planes here in Yakima were Piper Cubs. Both are very forgiving and easy to fly. The Navy, of course, had a record of my previous flight training but my instructor never bothered to check that out and I didn't volunteer the information. On my first flight my instructor first stressed safety, then he showed me some simple maneuvers. After he explained what he was going to do, he next showed me.

"Now you try it," he would say.

Each time after I completed a maneuver, he would say, "Very good."

As we approached the field he explained the turn and what was required to make a good approach. As we crossed the end of the runway I could see my instructor's smiling face in the mirror. He sat in the front seat which was normal on a student's first flight. While smiling he methodically explained how to make a good landing, then blurted out as if saying, ha I got you, "Okay you land it."

I did. No one ever made a smoother landing. The plane was still in the roll out, losing speed after the landing, when my instructor, no longer smiling, unfastened his seat belt and turned around shaking his finger in my face.

"Okay. Okay," he said. "Tomorrow you bring me your flight log."

I was afraid I might have made my instructor hard to get along with. He tried to shake me up or get me rattled during our next flight, but when he didn't succeed we became the best of friends. He showed me things the airplane would do that I'm sure weren't in the training manual.

Duane came over to see me while I was stationed at Yakima and told me he would be leaving for military service himself and he wanted to talk to me before he left. It was good to see him. The war was getting nastier by the day, it was no telling when, or if ever for that matter, I would see Duane again.

I felt good knowing Grace was working at the shipyard and staying with our mother. Dad was there but still sleeping on the couch in the front room. Milt was living nearby also working at the shipyard.

In a letter from home, I found out Duane would be leaving for the Army Air Force to start pilot's training and both Milt and Dad were leaving Washington and going back to Wyoming to live.

When Milt worked for himself he hardly ever started to work by eight in the morning. He said if he got up each day and worked from eight until four thirty he could make as much money in Wyoming as he was making in Washington. I never did hear a reason given by our dad for his leaving. That left only Grace staying with our mother. McAdoo Jones, Grace's fiance was somewhere in or near Africa with the Navy.

On my way from Yakima to the Navy Preflight School in St. Mary's, California, I was able to stop a few days at home. I had my bank account changed to be a joint account with Duane. In case I didn't make it back, Duane could use the money to finish college. I realized how important it was to him to finish college.

At St. Mary's they stressed athletics with soccer, boxing, basketball, wrestling, swimming, football and more ground school but no airplanes. After St. Mary's my next training station was called E-Base at Livermore, California. It was here we flew the Navy biplanes known as the Yellow Peril. I loved that airplane.

I was able to get a weekend pass to see my sister Helen and brother-in-law, Fred Schock, for the first time since they were married. They lived in Lodi, California.

I enjoyed the Navy and flying more and more. I could write several books on my military experiences alone, some good and some bad. I mean bad experiences, maybe bad books too.

After three enjoyable months in Livermore I arrived at Corpus Christi, Texas in March 1944. My brother Buck had married a girl he met in Fort Collins and was stationed in Brady, Texas. He was still a link trainer instructor for the Army Air Force. We arranged to meet in San Antonio, where I first met his wife Charline.

All through flight training we were given check flights from time to time. Check flights were given by a pilot other than our own instructor. We had to pass check rides the same as tests in ground school, before we could advance to the next stage of our training.

I was near the final stage of my training when another student, a "friend" of mine, told my check pilot, "You're just wasting your time. Old Kaiser hasn't got a down since he's been in flight training."

A down was a failing grade in a check flight. When that happens you had to take another check ride with a different pilot. If you failed the second time you might be given extra training time. Depending on your past record, if you fail a check ride after you have been granted extra time, it usually meant the student was washed out. Many students were washed out at all stages of our training, some with only a month to go.

After that check flight I was no longer what we called a virgin. I got a down. The pilot that re-checked me asked me what caused me to get a down the first time. I told him what my "friend" had said to the check pilot. He told me some instructors don't believe it's safe for a student to get through the program without at least one down for fear they might get too cocky and kill themselves. I'm not sure I appreciated that theory at the time, but it

Link is designated a navy pilot and commissioned officer in 1944.

was assuring to know how safety was stressed in every way possible in preparation for hazardous military flying.

The news from Duane scared me. He wasn't given a chance to finish his pilot's training in the Army Air Force. Our losses in bombing Germany were so great they needed more aerial gunners, not pilots. Duane was reassigned to gunnery school and became a tail gunner in a B-17. His chances were far less than 50 percent of ever finishing the required 35 missions over Germany.

After the June 1944 invasion, Howard was with General Patton's headquarters company somewhere in Europe. I couldn't think of a more dangerous place to be. General Patton was sometimes called Old Blood and Guts. He had been known to say he would accomplish a certain objective if it took a truck load of dog tags. Some soldiers said it was their blood and his guts.

The only good news was that McAdoo Jones, Mac we called him, would be back in the States soon and he and Grace planned to be married.

I got my Navy gold wings and was commissioned an Ensign on September 27, 1944. I was granted a few days leave, enough time to be home for a few days and still see Duane in St. Petersburg, Florida before he shipped out for England. My next duty station would be at the Naval Air Station, Lake City, Florida where I would be flying P-Vs. They were twin engine patrol planes similar in size to the B-25 that General Doolittle used to bomb Tokyo.

It was good to get home if only for a few days. Our mother had a banner she hung in her front window. It had four silver stars. It meant she had four sons in the military service. The silver stars meant her sons were all alive. A gold star would mean a son had been killed in the service. She said after Grace and Mac were married she would need a new banner, one with five silver stars.

At one time in my life, the most important thing for me was to help my mother fulfill her dream and move back to live in Washington state. It also seemed important to me at one time that I return to college and finish my education. Earning my Navy wings and being commissioned a Navy officer somehow seemed more important to me than even a college degree. It was something I had earned. I had proved to myself I was capable of doing something so important, while I saw others fail. Many of my Navy friends were killed trying to accomplish what I had accomplished. Now my biggest concern was for the safety of Howard, Buck, Duane and Mac.

I felt sure I would make it through the war alive but it was unlikely that all five of us would. It haunted me thinking about my mother home alone, should she ever have to replace any of her silver stars with gold ones?

Chapter Twenty-seven

When I inquired, the officer on duty at the Air Force base where Duane was stationed near St. Petersburg, Florida, I was told Duane's squadron was restricted to base. He told me an airman in their squadron had stolen a parachute, since they didn't know who it was, all the enlisted men were refused weekend passes. When Duane's plane commander was informed Duane's visitor was his brother, a Navy officer, he offered to let me ride with them on their training flight that night. I knew this was against regulations and declined the offer so he gave Duane a weekend pass restricted or not. We went to a football game, played some pool and generally just talked, both knowing, it might be the last time we would see each other.

Shortly after I reported at my duty station, Lake City Naval Air Station in Florida, I got word from home that Mac was back from Africa and he and Grace were married. Mac would have shore duty for a few months on the east coast.

With Grace gone, our mother was living by herself in Kirkland. She had received the rest of her inheritance from Grandmother's farms, which wasn't very much after being divided among her three brothers and three sisters, not enough for her to live on for the rest of her life. I was able to get the Navy legal officer to declare my mother my dependent so she could receive an allotment from the Navy. The money was sent directly to her. It amounted to about $75 per month, not much but without having to pay rent she could get by without having to spend her inheritance for everyday living expenses.

The airplane I was flying, a twin-engine, land-based patrol plane, was a lot less forgiving than the training planes I had been flying. It carried a crew of five, two pilots, a radio-man, an ordinance man and a mechanic. The pilots were both Ensigns. Although I was designated PPC (Patrol Plane Commander) we took turns between flying the plane and navigating. Two fixed 50-caliber machine guns that fired forward were controlled by the pilot. The tail guns and the top turret guns were manned by two of the three enlisted men. Along with flying, our entire crew attended ground school.

After three months at Lake City, I was assigned to operational

Link kneeling on right with flight crew ready for submarine patrol off our east coast.

training at Beaufort, South Carolina. Along with more training, we flew submarine patrol off the east coast. I don't believe many Americans realized our east coast was under constant threat from German submarines. We lost many ships, mostly oil tankers and some Navy blimps until the blimps were replaced with patrol planes.

I kept in touch with my Cousin Roger West, with whom Duane and I stayed the first summer we came to Washington state. Roger was a radioman and gunner in a Navy dive bomber. I only knew he was somewhere in the Pacific flying off an aircraft carrier. One letter from him told me he had been seriously injured when his plane returned to its carrier and another crippled plane landed almost on top of him. He was hit by the landing hook and was now in the Navy hospital in Shoemaker, California. He had several bones broken and the nerve was damaged in his left shoulder. It was unlikely he would ever be able to gain the full use of his left arm. This would mean he would no longer be able to swing an axe in the woods or milk cows with both hands, about the only things he had done for a living before entering the Navy.

My duty was mild compared with what Roger, Mac, Howard and Duane were experiencing. I thought about the time when Duane was only seven and I was nine and he fell off the horse and cut his head open on the axe he was carrying. I remembered how scared I was, believing he was dead. I thought it was my fault and I had killed him. I remembered how I had prayed promising God if he let Duane live I would see that he was always good. Duane was now flying over Germany in B-17s as a tail gunner and he better be good. Could it be that he had been spared then only to die in this war?

When Duane and I were talking the last time I saw him in Florida, I reminded him if he ever had to use his parachute to be sure to save the red handle that was attached to the rip cord. I told him I would give him a bottle of whiskey for it. This was based on a superstition I had heard when I first learned to fly. If you concentrate on saving the red handle it would keep you from forgetting to pull it to open your parachute.

Because their mail was censored, neither Duane nor Howard could tell me much in their letters such as where they were stationed or what they were doing. What else was there to hear except knowing they were still alive. We had our own code when we wrote to each other to get through censorship. We would mention things that happened back in Wyoming. When Duane told me his squadron returned fat and sleek like Sheldorf's cattle on Beaver Creek, I knew he meant they had heavy loses because the cattle had eaten a poison weed that killed many of them. Once Duane told me he thought about going to see Howard but Howard had told him to stay the hell out of there. This meant Duane was bombing for Patton's third Army.

In this war some lived and others were killed doing the same thing. You had to believe the big guy was looking out for you. The news from Europe was all about the battle of the bulge. One night I woke up my roommate yelling, "Jump! Jump! For Christ sake Duane jump. Jump and pull the rip cord." In my dream I could see Duane as plain as though he were in the room, only he wasn't in a room. In my dream he was in an airplane and it had been hit and they were about to crash. I saw a great flash of light, but when I awoke the room was dark and my roommate grumbled about being awakened. I asked him if someone had turned the lights on and off?

"There have been no lights on," he said, "but if you can get this guy you called Duane to jump and pull the rip cord we both might get some sleep."

I didn't get any more sleep that night, because I was sure something had happened to Duane.

I was relieved when I got the next letter from him. He told me I owed him a bottle of whiskey but everything was okay now. He had been where Howard was for a while but it was always good to be back in Hawkin's bunkhouse again. The censor didn't understand his message or he would have cut it out. I understood everything Duane was conveying to me. My owing Duane a bottle of whiskey meant, Duane had bailed out and saved the parachute handle. Being where Howard was, told me he had landed in France. By saying he was back in Hawkin's bunkhouse, since Hawkin was the name of an English family in Wyoming, I knew he was back at his own base in England. The spooky part, the thing Duane's letter didn't answer, was that Duane's plane got hit and he bailed out over France the same night I had the dream as if I actually saw it happen.

I got a letter from Grace telling me Mac had to go to sea again. This time his ship was headed for the Pacific. She was in Indiana with our sister Eunice and was having trouble buying a railroad ticket back to Seattle because service personnel got first priority. I got orders for my copilot, our crew and myself to report to the Commander in Chief West Coast in San Diego for further assignment. This would mean Duane and Howard had about won the war in Europe and everything was getting set for the big push to invade Japan.

My travel orders included enough time to stop at home a few days before I reported for duty. I hadn't seen Eunice in a long time so I got a ride with another Ensign who lived in Chicago and he let me off at Eunice's home in Indiana. I had a good visit with her before Grace and I continued on home by train. Because I was in uniform I had no trouble buying tickets for both Grace and myself.

232

Back in Kirkland, Grace and I found our mother in good spirits but I knew she was glad to have Grace back home. It must have been hard for her to be all by herself with a war going on. She proudly showed us her new banner that hung in the front window. It now had five silver stars. It has a star for Mac she proudly announced. While home I rebuilt the pump in the well, it had been giving our mother a little trouble. The house had hot and cold water and a bath tub but no inside toilet. I hired a plumber to put one in. Before I left for San Diego the news came over the radio that President Roosevelt had died.

Roosevelt's death didn't change anything, we still had a war to win. It wasn't long after Roosevelt's death that it was reported Hitler had committed suicide. Whether he did or not didn't matter, what was important was that the war in Europe was about over. Duane and Howard should be headed back to the States soon and our mother could still proudly display her banner with all five silver stars. Many mothers were not as lucky. According to the news from Sundance, several of my high school friends had been killed.

After reporting to Commander in Chief West Coast I was sent to the Naval Air Station Moffit field in California. The United Nations charter was being drawn up in San Francisco at the time and we were on submarine patrol plus more training. It was quite obvious by our training we were being readied for the invasion of Japan.

Word from home was Eunice and her family had moved to Washington state and lived near Kirkland. My brother-in-law, Andy, had been doing some painting in Indiana and had no trouble getting a painting job in a shipyard. I guess to be a painter in the shipyards all he had to do was get up in the morning, put on a painter's cap and say, now I am a painter.

Duane returned to the States and, after spending a few days home, his new assignment was in Southern California. He was able to stop and see me at my base before reporting.

I was living on base in the BOQ, (bachelor officers quarters), with a roommate, another ensign. When I told him my brother was going to spend a day or so with me he found an empty room in the BOQ so Duane and I could be together. After Duane and I had dinner in the officer's mess we returned to my room to talk.

233

Duane was very tight mouthed until I brought out two glasses and a fifth of whiskey. I got a couple of bottles of Coke for chasers from the Coke machine in the lobby and we talked. Duane confirmed everything that I had figured out from his letter on his being shot down and bailing out over France. He told me how they made their way back to England. After a few drinks he told some real scary stories of his duties as a tail gunner over Germany in a B-17. Neither of us had noticed until we ran out of whiskey that we still had Coke left. We talked nonstop until it was time to go to breakfast.

Duane's experiences in Europe told me what I already knew. Planes and men were expendable in order to obtain an objective.

I was briefed on what to expect when we invaded Japan. According to the best intelligence information, based on past experiences when our forces had invaded Okinawa and Iwo Jima, we were told we would have nearly a half million causalities and we would probably kill between three and five million of the enemy.

"These are the sad facts gentlemen," our briefing officer said. "This is what we have to do to end this damn thing. Remember gentlemen, they started it but we are going to damn sure finish it if we have to kill the last Jap that stands in our way."

It's hard for anyone that didn't take part in the events of the time to realize how we felt when we got the news about a bomb that had been dropped on a city in Japan that practically destroyed the entire city. We didn't know much about atomic bombs or least I didn't. Anyone who read the papers or listened to the news on the radio or was briefed on the invasion of Japan knew that millions of lives had been saved by the atomic bomb. It's always sad that some people die so that others might live. That has always been the way of wars. Those thousands of people who were killed by the atomic bombs dropped on Hiroshima and Nagasaki actually gave their lives in order that millions more might live. It's hard for the unknown number of those who suffered as a result of those bombs to understand their sacrifices saved their country from possible total destruction. I often wonder how many silver stars would have been changed to gold if those two bombs hadn't given the leaders of Japan the excuse they needed to save face and end the war they started. The rest is history, Japan made it official on the battleship Missouri the first part of September 1945.

Chapter Twenty-eight

It was in the later part of October 1945 when I got my orders to report to The Naval Air Station in Seattle to be discharged.

I had most of my personal gear shipped home and caught the first bus heading north out of California. It seemed everyone had been putting off traveling until the war ended. The bus was packed. Several women were standing, so I gave one my seat and when the bus made a stop in Medford, Oregon I got off and hitchhiked the rest of the way home.

After being discharged from the Navy, it was good to be back in Kirkland even though I was without a job. This time it was different. I belonged to the carpenters' union and there was a need for many new houses. The GI bill would help pay for me to return to college. The shipyard near Kirkland was still operating and being a veteran I had the assurance of getting my job back if I wanted it. Like most returning servicemen I had to pick up where I left off.

I am home a few days when Duane comes in and pulls off his dog tags and throws them as hard as he can, like a wild horse getting rid of its saddle. Next, Mac's brother George shows up and stays at our house waiting for Mac's ship to pull into Seattle. It is good to have the house full of people all making plans as to what they will be doing now that we can get our lives back together.

When Buck gets out of the Air Force he goes to his wife's home town in Colorado. Being a college graduate he is offered a job as County Agriculture Agent. Charline's father insists Buck not take the County Agent job but manage one of his irrigated farms. They grow potatoes and raise sheep.

Duane can hardly wait to return to Washington State College (Now called Washington State University) with the GI bill paying part of the expenses.

Howard returns to working in the woods felling and bucking trees near Morton.

Milt is back in Wyoming running a sawmill.

Eunice stays in Kirkland with her family and Andy makes a living painting houses.

Helen is raising a family in Lodi, California where her husband Fred works in a cannery.

Mac and Grace decided Mac will stay in the Navy.

After everyone has gone their separate ways it leaves my mother and me in the Kirkland house by ourselves. For some reason I lost my desire to return to college, maybe it is because with overtime I can make more money following the carpenter trade than many college graduates are making. I plan to work for others only until I knew the building business better, then I will to go into business for myself.

I see more of Mac right after we all get back from the war than any of my brothers and sisters. He stays in the Navy and is stationed at Pier 91 in Seattle while I am following the carpenter trade building houses in the Kirkland area.

One day Mac and Grace come over to Kirkland where my mother lives with me on the chicken ranch.

"I can't figure this Kaiser family out," Mac said.

Mac was always kidding. "You're not supposed to," I said. "When you became part of this family you volunteered. Remember? So stop your bitching. I was drafted."

"That's just my point. Who drafted you?"

I could tell Mac wasn't kidding.

"As long as you're stuck taking care of your mother you can't get married or lead a normal life. Any girl you might want for a wife is going to think twice if your mother's welfare is all your responsibility.

"Our mother has to stay some place. She doesn't have a house of her own and she's too old to go it alone."

"I noticed five stars on her banner. The rest of them all went their own separate ways as if they didn't give a good rat's ass."

"What are you getting at?"

"Your mother will be eligible for a pension next year. Grace and I have talked it over. If you'll help, we're willing to put up the money to build her a house with the understanding that when she is too old to live by herself the house will belong to Grace and me."

"Brother you have made yourself a deal."

"You know the carpenter trade," Mac said. "If you'll show us how, I'll see that the rest of the family does their share."

Our mother's own house became a reality and when she got

236

her pension I no longer had to provide for her welfare.

Our mother lives comfortably in the little house we all helped build. I am working as a construction supervisor building apartments on Mercer Island when I meet Virginia, a Kirkland girl. Virginia and I are married and we make our home in Kirkland.

Many things changed after we all left Wyoming, but my mother never had to change any of her silver stars to gold.

One thing that didn't change is my love for the Kirkland area and my desire to make Washington state my home.

Buck and I no longer make Duane go back to the house so we can sneak off and go fishing without him.

Buck becomes a very successful farmer in Colorado. There is so much demand for his certified seed potatoes that he ships them by the semi-truck load as far away as California and Florida. The Columbia Sheep Grower's Association awards him a trophy as the breeder that did the most to advance the Columbia breed. He becomes known internationally as an expert on wool and has been in demand for years to judge wool and sheep at many of the big western livestock shows. He is elected more than once to serve as county commissioner in his home state of Colorado. Commissioner Kaiser and his wife Charline have a daughter and a son. Buck still likes to fish.

Duane receives his Bachelor of Science degree at Washington State University and his Masters degree at Oregon State University. He taught high school over twenty-five years before retiring to a full-time hobby. He and his wife owned and operate, The Green Branch Ranch, a u-cut Christmas tree farm near Fredrickson, Washington. It is a few miles south of Tacoma. Duane is elected more than once to serve in the Washington State House of Representatives. Representative Kaiser and his wife Kay have two daughters. Duane still likes to fish.

My wife, Virginia, and I were expecting our first child and had ordered the lumber to start our new Kirkland home when the Navy recalled me to active duty July 1950.

After returning from Korea I am stationed in Pensacola, Florida. I teach navigation in the classroom at the Navy School of Pre-Flight for two years. I return to Kirkland and run my own contracting business, building many homes in the Kirkland area.

When the postmaster in Kirkland retires, I take the written

Link on duty over Korea in a Navy Patrol Plane plotting a course back to their home base near Hiroshima, Japan.

Civil Service Exam and receive the highest score of the six who apply for the job. During the twenty years I serve as Kirkland's postmaster, Kirkland grows from a small town to a thriving little city. Virginia and I have two daughters and a son. I still like to fish.

The Three Sundance Kids, Commissioner Buck, Representative Duane and Postmaster Link, enjoy getting together almost every summer and fish for salmon in the Pacific Ocean. There's a good reason Buck and Link don't make Duane go back to the house any more and go fishing without him. Duane owns the boat.